INTERPRETATION
AND DIFFERENCE

MERIDIAN

Crossing Aesthetics

Werner Hamacher

Editor

Stanford
University
Press

Stanford
California
2006

INTERPRETATION
AND DIFFERENCE

The Strangeness of Care

Alan Bass

Stanford University Press
Stanford, California

©2006 by the Board of Trustees of the
Leland Stanford Junior University. All rights reserved.

Printed in the United States of America
on acid-free, archival-quality paper

Library of Congress Cataloging-in-Publication Data

Bass, Alan.
Interpretation and difference : the strangeness of care /
Alan Bass.
p.   cm.
Includes bibliographical references.
ISBN-10: 0-8047-5337-7 (cloth : alk. paper)
ISBN-10: 0-8047-5338-5 (pbk. : alk. paper)
ISBN-13: 978-0-8047-5337-1 (cloth : alk. paper)
ISBN-13: 978-0-8047-5338-8 (pbk. : alk. paper)
1. Interpretation (Philosophy) 2. Nietzsche, Friedrich
Wilhelm, 1844–1900. 3. Heidegger, Martin, 1889–1976. 4.
Derrida, Jacques. 5. Freud, Sigmund, 1856–1939. 6. Psycho-
analysis. 7. Psychoanalytic interpretation. I. Title.

B824.17.B37 2006
121'.68—dc22

2006017968

Contents

Introduction

This book is the companion to *Difference and Disavowal: The Trauma of Eros* (2000). *Difference and Disavowal* was written with an audience of psychoanalytic clinicians in mind, whereas this work is more specifically philosophical. But the two books are really one. In the preface to *Difference and Disavowal* I already began to explain that deconstructive thought sheds light on a problem at the limit of psychoanalysis as therapy—resistance to interpretation itself. This clinical argument about resistance to interpretation will introduce the philosophical issues.

How to understand patients who stay in analysis while resisting the interpretive process? These patients, who are surprisingly common, know that analysis is *really* about interpretation and yet seem not to know it. In two brief papers, Freud (1924a,b) began to examine the kind of perverse relation to the external world in which one simultaneously does and does not know something. A fantasy can be applied like a patch over the objectionable reality. But the very existence of such a defensive patch indicates that the reality is known. This is the beginning of the theory of ego splitting, of oscillation between reality and the fantasy replacement for it. In his paper on fetishism Freud called this process "disavowal"—the registration *and* repudiation of reality.

The understanding of fetishism as a compromise between registration and repudiation of reality was an important advance in rethinking the ego's relation to the external world. Freud had previously spoken of "reality testing" in fairly simple terms, but he now understood that the ego can split itself, can know and not know reality. However, the new understanding of fetishism also contains a major inconsistency. The theory is that the boy eventually knows that the woman (mother) does not have a penis, taking this as evidence of her castration. If as a man his castration anxiety is too intense, he can apply a patch in the form of an ideally erotized thing (the fetish), over what Freud insistently calls the "fact" or the "reality" of castration. The inconsistency is clear: while intense anxiety may often make castration feel like a reality, it is still a fantasy.

What, then, is the repudiated external reality in fetishism? The answer is in a clinical example. Freud described a fetishist who repudiated the *reality* of sexual difference, patching it with the *fantasy* of phallic monism. As a fantasy construction, phallic monism has two positions: castrated (absence) and noncastrated (presence). The fetishist oscillates between these two positions, which themselves are a substitute for registered and repudiated sexual difference. Fetishism turns out to be more complicated than Freud thought. It depends upon a primary disavowal of sexual difference, and a replacement of sexual difference with the coupled fantasies castrated–not-castrated.

This more consistent account of fetishism leads to an inevitable question. Why the primary disavowal of (sexual) difference? There are scattered references throughout Freud's work to the fear, strangeness, and hostility inherent to difference. This is the key to understanding resistance to interpretation. The possibility that one thing might mean another assumes difference. The defensive response to interpretation is fetishistic: it repudiates the registered difference of a relation of meanings, generally substituting for it two fantasies of threatening or relieving "realities," taken as uninterpretable objectivity ("concreteness"). This process often takes place in the transference, producing an impasse in the treatment. What the analyst thinks is most important to interpret is for the patient not interpretable at all.

In *Group Psychology and the Analysis of the Ego* (1921a) Freud envisaged a "general sensitiveness" always "directed to . . . [the] details of differentiation . . . the source of which is unknown" (102). This intuition of a generally defensive response to differentiation, which explains fetishism and resistance to interpretation, touches upon the most basic deconstructive idea. Nietzsche, Heidegger, and Derrida all explain how and why metaphysics cannot encompass the most radical implications of difference. In Heidegger's famous phrase, "difference is the unthought of metaphysics." Nietzsche, Heidegger, and Derrida all account for Freud's "unknown source" of the generally defensive response to differentiation.

The subtitle of *Difference and Disavowal, The Trauma of Eros*, refers to another aspect of defense against difference. In *Beyond the Pleasure Principle* (1920) Freud introduced Eros as a drive which brings "vital differences" into the psyche. To use the vocabulary of disavowal, Eros is the basic unconscious tendency to *register* difference. Simultaneously Eros binds, integrates with environment, with "reality." Crucially, it does not conform to Freud's usual model of the drive as inherently tending toward tension reduction. Rather, as Eros introduces "real" difference and binds, it raises tension levels. But raised tension levels are also the essence of pain and trauma. Part of the unknown source of the general sensitiveness to differentiation is the link of difference to tension, pain, and possible trauma. Nietzsche, Heidegger, and Derrida all explain how and why difference must be thought in relation to tension and pain.

In *Difference and Disavowal* I called the potential trauma of difference "internalization anxiety," in homage to Hans Loewald. Internalization, for Loewald, is the process of unconsciously taking in the *tension* of difference. As a drive, Eros is the possibility of this unconscious process and explains how interpretation works. Loewald says that every interpretation, no matter what its content, implies a differential between patient and analyst. The therapeutic action of psychoanalysis is modification of the unconscious via internalization of this differential. Taking Loewald one step further, the intense anxiety which motivates resistance to interpretation is the trauma of Eros—internalization anxiety. Nietzsche, Heidegger, and Derrida not only show why metaphysics cannot encompass difference as tension, pain, and trauma (something notably absent from Loewald's concept of internalization), but each also offers specific ways of thinking interpretation in relation to difference.

Nietzsche's attack on metaphysics famously led him to say that there are no facts, only interpretations. What does this mean? Before Freud, Nietzsche thought that metaphysics privileges consciousness in order to tranquilize itself against more disturbing unconscious processes. But such processes are not factual in the positivistic sense. Thus, they require a process of interpretation. Nonmetaphysical interpretation is actively differentiating—it opens up the unconscious realities that metaphysics avoids. Nietzsche calls this avoidance itself "reactive": metaphysics sees truth as identity in order to decrease tension and to avoid pain. Active, differentiating interpretation does not posit identities, does not decrease tension, and does not avoid pain. As nonmetaphysical, it has to operate without the usual categories of subject, object, causality, and opposition. How? Gilles Deleuze's early work on Nietzsche provides a helpful orientation here, especially because it also articulates a Nietzsche-Freud-Heidegger encounter around the question of difference.

In *Nietzsche and Philosophy* (1983) Deleuze emphasizes Nietzsche's much misunderstood notion of will to power. He makes it clear that will to power is not about any individual's attempt to exert domination over another. Rather, it is a way of understanding *all* phenomena in terms of conflicts between nonconscious differentials of force (6–7). Nietzsche's radicalization of interpretation, his sense that nonmetaphysical thinking has to proceed in terms of active, differentiating interpretation, is for Deleuze the way out of the two major metaphysical constraints on interpretation: positivism (the equation of the real with the factually objective) and dialectics (oppositional thinking). In *Difference and Repetition* (1994) Deleuze links Freud's Eros, the force which "introduces" "vital differences" into the psyche, to will to power: both describe unconscious "production of new differences" (109). Further, Deleuze thinks that both Eros and will to power are *relational* concepts. He says that will to power is "the differential element included in each force and by which *each is related to others*" (1983, 6; emphasis added). Freud's Eros, of course, is a force of binding, of relation. The idea that Eros and will to power are both forces of difference and relation leads to Deleuze's integration of Nietzsche, Freud, and Heidegger: will to power and Eros illustrate Heidegger's idea that difference must be "articulation and connection in itself" (1994, 117). The crux of a Nietzsche-Freud-Heidegger encounter is precisely that each comes to think articulation, difference, *as* connection. A major theme of this book is that the differentiating process of interpretation has to be thought as an articulating-connecting, tension-raising *relation*.

Its subtitle, *The Strangeness of Care*, links the trauma of Eros to several elements of Heidegger's thought. In his magnum opus, *Being and Time,* Heidegger seeks to destroy metaphysics by reviving the inevitably forgotten question of being (*Sein*) and by rethinking time. He calls his method phenomenological interpretation (hermeneutics), in the sense that it is simultaneously descriptive and analytic. Interpretation itself, for Heidegger, analyzes the *connection and separation* of being (time) and beings as usually conceived: the objectively present. Care, the way in which man can exist only as *related* to world, is the touchstone of this analysis. But just as Nietzsche rejects the tranquilizing aspect of any nonrelatedness

INTERPRETATION AND DIFFERENCE

of man and world, so for Heidegger care is strange (uncanny), and anxiety provoking. The uncanniness and *Angst* of care can be integrated with the trauma of Eros and internalization anxiety. In Heidegger's work after *Being and Time,* difference as the unthought of metaphysics and being (time) as relation are thought in relation to opening, the time and space of interpretation. These are essential resources for a nonmetaphysical conception of an interpretive therapy.

Jacques Derrida has described his own work as "an inconceivable union of Heidegger and Freud." It is organized around the question of difference as radically nonpresent. As nonpresent, but as "registered" (to use Freud's word), difference is "trace." For Derrida, Heidegger's notion of difference as the unthought of metaphysics has to encounter Freud's preoccupation with the unconscious as memory, with unconscious traces. Derrida radicalizes difference itself as *différance,* the nonpresent, spatiotemporal force that produces effects of difference. *Différance,* like difference for Nietzsche and Heidegger, is relational—but it is the relation to what is always other than presence, an idea crucial to the rethinking of interpretation and difference. It implies that the defensive concreteness of resistance to interpretation registers and repudiates the nonpresent trace of *différance.* This is why Derrida's work is so concerned with the memory (archive) of nonpresent, "virtual" reality. Derrida wants to think interpretation that modifies what it interprets (the aim of psychoanalysis), as spectral, suspended in the virtual realm between presence and absence. This virtual or spectral time and space is where Freud situates the "psychic apparatus." This is why Derrida, unlike Nietzsche or Heidegger, is always concerned with the technological implications of Freud's thought. Another major theme is that spectral interpretation is a function of this technology itself.

Derrida is also attentive to the paradox of difference as articulation-connection. Where Deleuze noted Eros as differential relation, Derrida focuses on a related conception in Freud: binding. Eros differentiates, raises tension levels, and *binds.* Derrida is fascinated by Freud's own description of binding as a tension that is both pleasure and pain, and that is even more primordial than the tension-reducing pleasure principle. For Derrida the intermediate pleasure-pain of binding opens the Freudian unconscious to a thinking of intermediate states sustained by tension—an idea I will treat in depth. Binding interpretation itself occurs in the intermediate, spectral space between pleasure and pain.

Derrida's spectral, binding interpretation extends Nietzsche's active and

Heidegger's descriptive interpretation. All can provide a rigorous theory of resistance to interpretation as disavowal of difference, the crossing, as Derrida puts it, of "a certain psychoanalysis with a certain deconstruction" (1995, 77). This crossing always has to rethink interpretation in relation to self-splitting. For Freud, disavowal describes an ego that splits itself, registering and repudiating reality. Nietzsche's theory of active interpretation is the counterforce to life against itself, the pain avoiding, reactive dedifferentiation intrinsic to the tension of difference. For the Heidegger of *Being and Time,* descriptive interpretation analyzes Dasein's inevitable flight from itself due to the strangeness and anxiety of being-in-the-world. For the later Heidegger, language itself contains the possibility of thinking difference against the oblivion that belongs to it. And Derrida has an elaborate theory of the autoimmune response provoked by spectral (intermediate, not-living, not dead, not absent, not present) reality. The very project of analysis comes out of this autoimmune response, which is why the possibility of analysis is always an encounter with the impossibility of analysis—the limit built into interpretation and difference. This is the limit that has always been intrinsic to psychoanalysis itself as an interpretive therapy, the limit that has always programmed resistance to analysis in analysis—disavowal of difference as the most general question about interpretation.

Most of this book was completed in the summer of 2004, before Jacques Derrida's death. I had hoped he would be able to read it, as my tribute to him. Instead, I dedicate it to his memory.

Chapter 1

Nietzsche: Active Interpretation

For psychoanalysts, the Nietzsche-Freud connection no longer seems as important as it once did. When Thomas Mann and Ludwig Binswanger published tributes to Freud in the 1930s—the date speaks for itself—both said that Freud had continued, expanded, or even completed Nietzsche's basic project (Assoun, 1980, 48–53). Mann thought that Nietzsche's auto-therapeutic genius had opened the way for Freud. Binswanger said that Freud had found a scientific way to put Nietzsche's ideas to work.

This topic was older than Mann or Binswanger knew. On February 1, 1900, two months after publishing *The Interpretation of Dreams*, Freud wrote to Fliess: "I have just acquired Nietzsche, in whom I hope to find words for much that remains mute in me" (1985, 398). Prophetically, the sentence concludes, "but have not opened him yet." In 1908 the Vienna Psychoanalytic Society held two meetings on Freud and Nietzsche, during which Freud said that he could never read more than a half page of Nietzsche at a time. (In his 1925 *Autobiographical Study* Freud would claim never to have read Nietzsche at all.) Nonetheless, in the first Vienna meeting Federn commented that "Nietzsche has come so close to our views that we can ask only, 'Where has he not come close?'" (Nunberg and Federn, 1962–1967, 1:359), and in the second Freud said that the "degree of introspection achieved by Nietzsche had never been achieved by anyone" (Nunberg and Federn, 1962–1967, 2:32). Nietzsche had seen the unconscious as the greater part of mind and had conceived it in relation to the body, drives, and affects; had understood repression; had analyzed guilt as internalized aggression. Psychoanalysts are perennially surprised by what Freud called "the resemblance of Nietzsche's intuitive insights to our laborious investigations" (Nunberg and Federn, 1962–1967, 2:32).

How did Nietzsche anticipate fundamental psychoanalytic concepts without clinical experience? Freud speculated that Nietzsche's own pathology gave him access to unconscious processes (Nunberg and Federn, 1962–1967, 1:30–31). But there is another possible answer to this question, an answer that psychoanalysts tend to overlook. Nietzsche's "insights" were the result of his critique of metaphysics. He could elaborate basic psychoanalytic ideas because, like Freud, he was trying to think beyond the philosophical equation of mind and consciousness.

Freud certainly knew that he shared the critique of consciousness with Nietzsche. There are discussions throughout his work of the way in which philosophy itself is the specific obstacle to a science of the unconscious. The decentering of consciousness common to Nietzsche and Freud made it mandatory for their thought *not* to be systematic—metaphysical systematicity itself reflecting the mistaken privilege of consciousness. All of Freud's remarks about why psychoanalysis cannot be founded on "clear and sharply defined basic concepts" (1915c, 117), cannot be a system (1925, 57), cannot be a *Weltanschauung* (1933), seem to echo Nietzsche almost word for word (Assoun, 1980). And although there is no conception of anything like formal psychotherapy in Nietzsche, he elaborated principles that remain essential to psychoanalytic practice. He understood that unconscious phenomena are not of the order of empirical facts, are not determined by a simple logic of cause and effect, and cannot be directly observed. Thus, they demand a practice of rigorous interpretation.

In *Freud and Philosophy: An Essay on Interpretation* (1970) Ricoeur famously conjoined Marx, Nietzsche, and Freud as the "masters of suspicion." For all three, consciousness is mystified. To dispel its illusions is to acquire a liberating knowledge available by no other means. Nietzsche began as a philologist who then extended the method of historical, linguistic interpretation over the whole of philosophy, eventually making interpretation a manifestation of will to power (25). Freud based his therapeutic practice on interpretation because of his understanding of symbolism in neurotic symptom formation. This led to his Nietzschean idea that morality and ideals are defensive distortions of the drives. For both, a genealogy of morals demonstrates that what we call the "good" is interpretable as a reaction against the "bad" of the body and the drives (35). Interpretation, then, cannot be divorced from the force of the drives: Ricoeur's central point is that for both Nietzsche and Freud *hermeneutics is always an energetics*. Once energy itself is intrinsic to interpretation the traditional opposition of *Natur-* and *Geisteswissenschaften* is questionable. Ricoeur, however, does not examine the role of *difference* in Nietzsche's energetics of interpretation. This is a critical omission: for Nietzsche, a theory of interpretation and difference is as intrinsic to the critique of metaphysics as is a theory of unconscious drives. A grasp of how this works is essential for a first understanding of the role of difference in Freud's energetic hermeneutics.

Difference in *The Genealogy of Morals*

In *The Genealogy of Morals,* Nietzsche says that "slave morality from the outset says No to what is 'outside,' what is 'different,' what is 'not itself'" (1967, 36). What is "slave morality"? A quick generalization would be: metaphysics itself. Metaphysics for Nietzsche begins with the Platonic notion of ideal forms situated in a supersensuous beyond. This philosophical doctrine is at the root of all devaluations of the sensuous. Its most important offspring is Christianity, dubbed by Nietzsche "Platonism for the people." Platonic Christian metaphysics, slave morality, is opposed to what Nietzsche calls the "noble" affirmation of distance, difference, and the sensuous. In fact, Nietzsche undertakes the "genealogy of morals" in order to demonstrate how the noble affirmation of difference became evil itself for the slave. As soon as a supersensuous beyond is posited, true value, and even the value of truth, are rooted in the beyond. The slave's "no" to difference becomes metaphysical morality. And once slave morality itself becomes an unquestioned set of assumptions, one needs a "transvaluation of all values" in order to think outside metaphysics, in order to affirm difference.

When ultimate value, whether in Platonic or Christian terms, is situated in the nonmaterial beyond, life itself becomes the negative fall away from the good. Hence, the inherent nihilism of slave morality, its condemnation of the body and sexuality, "the anti-sensualist metaphysics of desire for nothingness" (32). Anyone familiar with Freud's basic thinking about religion as a neurosis of civilization will see immediate parallels with Nietzsche here. What is less familiar about Nietzsche is his understanding of where the "no" to life comes from at all.

For Nietzsche the "no" comes from a conflict within life itself. The antisensualist metaphysics of slave morality, the devaluation of difference, the privileging of the beyond, all correspond to something within life that turns life against itself (117). What is this? Nietzsche starts from the observation that the "ascetic ideal" of the metaphysician-priest has thrived for millennia. If so, there "must be a necessity of the first order that again and again promotes the growth and prosperity of this *life-inimical* species—it must indeed be in the *interest of life itself* that such a self-contradictory type does not die out" (117). The life whose interest is served by the ascetic ideal is what Nietzsche calls "degenerating life" (120). Degenerating life is the life which can no longer sustain the "injury, assault, and destruction" (76) intrinsic to difference itself. In other words, for Nietzsche the "yes" to difference is also a "yes" to pain, the pain without which life cannot extend itself.

The degenerating life which refuses the pain of difference continues to preserve itself through the "artifice" of the ascetic ideal (120). The existence of the metaphysician-priest "indicates a partial physiological obstruction and exhaustion against which the deepest instincts of life, which have remained intact, continually struggle with new expedients and devices . . . [the ascetic ideal] is among the greatest conserving and yes-creating forces of life" (120–21). How does the nihilism of the ascetic ideal preserve life? How does its "no" to difference become a kind of "yes" to life?

Nietzsche's answer is that the ascetic ideal redirects the dangerous resentment felt by the slaves, the dedifferentiated herd, against the nobles, the differentiated individuals. The metaphysician-priest tells the herd that its suffering is due to sin, the fall into the sensuous. Thus, slave resentment is directed away from the noble, and turned back against the slave himself (127–28). In other words, any tendency within life to dedifferentiate mandates that life protect itself from itself. In its pure form, nihilistic metaphysics could eventually destroy life. But once this destructiveness is turned back against the slave, through guilt and bad consciousness, the dedifferentiating herd instinct is to an extent curbed, if never entirely eliminated.

Freud and Nietzsche: Parallels and Divergences

It is tempting to translate Nietzsche's slave morality into the Freudian superego—the opposition to sexuality and internalized destructiveness of guilt. The temptation increases when one recalls some of Freud's own "speculations" about life and death in general. Freud came to see the superego's internalized destructiveness as a manifestation of the antilife force of the death drive (1923, 53). In fact, Freud also called the death drive the "Nirvana principle," corresponding exactly to Nietzsche's "desire . . . for nothingness," the avoidance of pain as the ultimate good of Platonic-Christian morality. For both, there is a contradictory tendency within life to destroy itself. Thus, Freud sounds quite Nietzschean when he speaks of Eros, life itself, as a "disturber of the peace," which the death drive struggles against (46–47). These comparisons, however, do not take into account some fundamental differences between Freud and Nietzsche on preservation of the individual versus the preservation of life; pleasure and pain; the nature of truth; science and religion.

For Nietzsche, an individual's wish to preserve himself is the opposite of the preservation of life. In *The Gay Science* he said that the "wish to preserve oneself is the symptom of a condition of distress, of a limitation of the really fundamental instinct of life which aims at the expansion of power and wishing for that, frequently risks and even sacrifices self-preservation" (1974, 291). The individual preserves himself by avoiding pain, by equating pleasure with the satisfaction of basic needs. For slave morality, the absence of suffering is the supreme good (1967, 129). Again, God becomes nothingness, an invitation to sleep, the embodiment of tension reduction and need satisfaction (129). Those who do not wish to preserve themselves are those not seduced by the Nirvana-like calm of need satisfaction, the antisensualist ideal of the metaphysician-priest. Nietzsche understands pleasure—including sexual pleasure—as an enhancement of power irreducibly linked to pain, the differentiating increase of tension.

On the whole, Freud tends to see the tension reduction of need satisfaction as the essence of pleasure. Tension reduction becomes the regulatory force of the pleasure principle.[1] Freud's entire understanding of wish and defense, dreams and neurosis, assumes an automatic unconscious tendency to get rid of tension, which itself is a consequence of the physiological need to assuage hunger. Sexuality for Freud is always understood on a "hunger" model. He defines *libido* as the equivalent of hunger in the sexual sphere: it is a physiological need that creates a tension which demands relief.

Here there is a sharp contrast between Nietzsche and Freud. For Nietzsche the power of the unconscious is its power to enhance life by raising tension, opening itself to pain. For Freud the power of the

Pleasure Principle that the death drive actually seemed to serve the pleasure principle (1920, 63) inevitably would bring Freud back into the most
questionable aspects of Schopenhauer's pessimism—i.e. nihilism.

Nietzsche and Freud on Repetition

These differences between Freud and Nietzsche are essential to understanding their opposed views of repetition. For Nietzsche eternal return
is essential to the thinking of will to power. The two concepts appear
together in his late thought. In Nietzsche's last published writings, eternal
return is the manifestation of circular time. Everything that will occur has
occurred. For metaphysical, Platonic-Christian man, the circular nature
of time is a burden which increases his submissive, nihilistic attitude to
life. For the overman, beyond good and evil in their metaphysical sense,
circular time is a liberation. Eternal return compels him to adopt the slo-
gan of *amor fati*, love of destiny, including all that is painful within it.
Overman wills eternal return joyfully.

In *The Will to Power* (which is actually a posthumous compilation of
Nietzsche's unpublished notes from 1882 to 1888), there is a much more
sophisticated account of eternal return. (It took quite some time for
adequate versions of these notes to appear. The Nietzsche, ordered but
not opened, by Freud, would not have contained a volume called *The
Will to Power*.) The notes make much clearer and more compelling why
Nietzsche thought will to power and eternal return together in their relation to difference.

Eternal return makes "everything break open" (1968, §1057). Nietzsche
means "everything" literally. Just as will to power looks at *all* phenomena
in terms of differentials of force, eternal return is a thinking of time as
repetition that applies to everything. Nietzsche often speaks of all phenomena, of everything, as "world." Will to power and eternal return are
meant to be ways of thinking about "world" outside the structures of
consciousness. This means that "man" and "world" cannot be seen as two
separate things. In *The Gay Science* Nietzsche had already written that
any pose of "man against the world" is a world negating principle, a way
of measuring world on the scales of human consciousness and inevitably
finding it wanting. Thus, says Nietzsche, "We laugh as soon as we encounter the juxtaposition of 'man and world,' separated by the sublime
presumption of the little word 'and'" (1974, 286). If will to power con-

cerns the intrinsic relatedness of all differentials of force, eternal return is the temporality of this relatedness.

This temporality of will to power depends upon an analysis of the finite and the infinite. The only way to think force and difference nontheologically, Nietzsche says, is to think it as finite. Infinite difference would be the difference between the world and a God outside it. And only an infinite God is capable of infinite novelty. Once there is no infinitely different God capable of infinite novelty, repetition and finitude are conditions of each other. But there is an infinity of past time, because time itself is not an object that could have begun in some place, at some time—hence, *eternal* return. And precisely because there is an infinity of past time in which anything possible has already occurred, if there were any possibility of a nondifferentiated state of rest or equilibrium, it already would have to have been reached. Since such a state manifestly never has been reached, the meeting of infinite time and finite difference has to imply repetition. This too is a rigorous consequence of thinking nontheologically. Only a conception of God as universal consciousness can justify any assumption that the world *intends* to avoid repetition. Beyond the metaphysics of consciousness, there is no timelessness. Time is the repetition of finite differentials of force (1968, 1057–62).

The temporality of difference gives additional purchase on difference as a relational concept. In another note Nietzsche writes, "Nothing is self sufficient, neither in ourselves nor in things," and proceeds to speak about time as the condition of non–self-sufficiency (1968, §1032). This is akin to the idea that there is no such thing as man "and" world, and takes it further. Just as infinite difference would imply a God *outside* world, only such a God could be infinitely self-sufficient. Finite difference implies the openness of all phenomena to each other. In other words, *finite difference, time as repetition, and non–self-sufficiency all belong to a thinking of "relationality" as unconscious process. Process* is a key word here. Difference as repetition, such that there can never be a permanent state of rest or equilibrium, means that everything is in a state of flux and tension. This process is what Nietzsche calls "becoming." Permanence, equilibrium, identity, infinite and universal consciousness, he calls "Being"—the preoccupation of metaphysics.

Nietzsche says that the "high point" of his "meditation" is the realization that eternal return is the closest approximation of a world of becoming to Being (1968, §617). He is making a statement that he knows could appear metaphysical, because it is a statement about everything. But he wants to do so nonmetaphysically. This is why Deleuze takes Nietzsche to mean that eternal return itself is the way of being of that which becomes, of the flux and tension of differentials of force (1983, 48). To understand Nietzsche, Deleuze says, one has to distinguish between "eternal return of the same" and "eternal return of the identical." Nietzsche's "same" is difference itself. The identical would be a state of equality, of equilibrium, of nondifferent identity—precisely what Nietzsche does not mean. Thus, says Deleuze, a self-identical object does not return. Return itself constitutes everything as temporal, as being in a state of differential becoming. And as an intrinsic characteristic of will to power, eternal return must be thought of as synthesis (48). It is the temporality of the inter-relatedness of all differentials of force (49). This is another way of thinking what Nietzsche means when he says that nothing in ourselves or in things is self-sufficient. Repetition as difference *is* life as simultaneous articulation and connection.

"Eternal return of the same" is a phrase indelibly associated with Nietzsche. Freud uses it on several occasions. But according to the understanding of eternal return from *The Will to Power,* he uses it in exactly the wrong way. In two roughly contemporary works, "The Uncanny" (1919) and *Beyond the Pleasure Principle* (1920), Freud speaks of the repetition compulsion as "the eternal return of the same," in other words, as the automatic repetition of the identical. However, the published discussions of eternal return easily lend themselves to this distortion. Freud uses the phrase as a kind of Nietzschean cliché.

Nonetheless, psychoanalysis was from the beginning based on a principle of return—return of the repressed. For Freud, return is by definition a pathological process. When the repressed forces its return, there is an inevitable attempt to force it back out of consciousness again. The result is neurosis. And the repressed itself returns because of the repetitive pressure of the drives, which never cease to oppose repression.

Repetition quickly becomes the index of the most recalcitrant therapeutic problems. In 1915 Freud introduced the "repetition compulsion." The repetitive way in which the repressed returns only to be re-repressed is the source of transference and resistance, and indeed of transference *as* resistance. Freud's assessment of this phenomenon is double-edged. On one hand, transference as resistance is the essence of psychoanalytic treatment, the very possibility of effective psychotherapy. On the other, it produces the need for indefinite working through, an essential limitation on the effectiveness and durability of clinical results.

When Freud returns to the repetition compulsion in *Beyond the Pleasure Principle* he intensifies this ambivalent assessment of repetition. His problem is how to explain the repetition of painful experience, for example in the repetition of severe trauma in dreams, or in the automatic repetition of radically unpleasurable patterns in some people's lives. Both forms of repetition seem to defy the pleasure principle as a principle of avoidance of pain. And if transference as repetition becomes an automatic, or even "demonic," repetition of pain, psychoanalytic treatment can become impossible (1920, 18). Do these perplexing clinical realities mandate a revision of basic theory?

Freud's answer is multifaceted. First, in rethinking repetition in relation to trauma, he does revise basic theory. He distinguishes between the traumatic anxiety of being overwhelmed by unanticipated pain and the signal anxiety of being frightened by anticipated danger. He alleges that the repetition of painful experiences in dreams and life is an attempt to *develop* the signal anxiety which would have mitigated the impact of trauma. Second, in again thinking about the drives as tension states which compel return to a previous, less excited state, Freud radicalizes the tendency to repetition. He specifically links the repetition compulsion to the death drive as the very essence of the drive.

Many psychoanalysts simply dismiss this idea. However, the most rigorous readers have always understood that as soon as Freud postulated a basic unconscious tendency toward tension reduction, there had to be something like a death drive in his thinking. In this sense, it is quite consistent for Freud to link the repetition compulsion to the death drive. When he discusses what he calls the resistance of the id or the unconscious in *Inhibition, Symptom and Anxiety* (1926), the emphasis again is on how difficult it is to influence repetitive patterns of drive discharge. Repetition for Freud is the dedifferentiating, antilife manifestation of the most destructive elements of the unconscious.

But as Deleuze said, this apparently leaves Eros, the differentiating, tension increasing force opposed to death, without a concept of repetition. In the posthumously published *Outline of Psychoanalysis* Freud finally broached this problem. He says that the idea of the death drive fits in very well with the idea of drive as a *return* to a previous state, but that in "the case of Eros . . . we cannot apply this formula" (1940a, 149). In other words, life, tension increase, and differentiation are the way out of fatal repetition. But as a force of differentiation Eros is not for Freud a force of affirmative repetition, even if the drives themselves are bound to repetition.

On the question of repetition we seem to find a complete divorce between Freud and Nietzsche. But this leaves a very large question unanswered. Why is psychoanalytic treatment founded on a principle of repetition? The move away from a possible single encounter with a hypnotist to repeated therapeutic sessions over weeks, months, and years became the hallmark of psychoanalysis. Is this a result of a fatal power of unconscious repetition, weakly and uncertainly opposed by working through, by repetitive interpretation of transference and resistance? If so, would Freudian analysis be haunted by a fear of the repetition compulsion? Or can the repetitive nature of psychoanalysis as a therapy of interpretation be thought in terms of the intrinsic link of repetition and difference?

Difference, Self-Preservation, and the Psychic Apparatus

Nietzsche and Freud must be read as scrupulously as possible. This means grasping their general principles in all their complexity, and then proceeding to a more subtle examination. The question of psychoanalysis as a practice of repetition can only be answered in terms of the more subtle approach.

Let us assume that psychoanalysis, like any form of psychotherapy, is undertaken with the conscious intent to enhance self-preservation. If self-preservation were no more than the narcotized search for need satisfaction, then psychoanalysis could indeed be one more version of religion, of slave morality. In fact, a case can be made that much contemporary psychotherapy, including psychoanalysis, operates in just this way. But self-preservation is not the simple question it appears to be for Freud. Once self-preservation is viewed in relation to the theory of the psychic *apparatus,* a very different picture emerges.

From the very beginning of his psychoanalytic work, Freud elaborated a theory of self-preservation in terms of unconscious memory. He did so for two large reasons. The first is that the unconscious for him is the meeting of what traditionally had been the separate realms of body and mind. The second is that he wanted to understand how neurotic symptoms could be the product of memories not available to consciousness. For Freud it is always a question of body and storage, physical need and memory trace.

These twin requirements are first thought together in the unpublished *Project* of 1895 and became the theoretical foundation of *The Interpretation of Dreams.* Freud thinks that when a hungry baby is fed, it forms a trace of what he calls the "experience of satisfaction." The hungry baby is not a conscious being and does not consciously intend to remember being fed. Rather, this is a process of automatic, nonintentional memory—unconscious memory. How to account for nonintentional formation of memory traces? Freud construes unconscious memory in terms of *Bahnungen,* the opening of pathways (termed *facilitations* in the *Standard Edition*). Such opening of pathways takes place because of the meeting of a difference of forces: the force of unconscious resistance to an opening versus the force of what it encounters. This is why the question of unconscious memory is also from the beginning a question of trauma. Trauma is tension, force— which is why Freud says that "pain leaves behind specially abundant facilitations [*Bahnungen*]" (1895, 321). (In *The Genealogy of Morals,* Nietzsche [1967] too derives memory from pain.) Note that the unconscious must have the capacity to register increased tension, or there would be no unconscious memory, particularly of trauma. That is the point: there are unconscious registrations of trauma not available to consciousness. But the point is equally that there is an unconscious primary process which tends to decrease tension, through wish fulfillment and defense.

In these terms, Freud's hungry baby is a paradoxical creature. If a memory of being fed is registered unconsciously, a pathway has been opened, and there has been some increase of tension due to the encounter of a differential of forces. However, in terms of need satisfaction, the tension of hunger has been assuaged. The consequence of this paradox is pivotal for Freud's entire theory of mind. In a hypothetical "next" experience of hunger, several things happen at once. Hunger is a tension which the baby wants to get rid of as quickly as possible. A pathway has been opened in which the image of the object which relieved tension the "last" time ("breast") is "stored." There is then an automatic unconscious tendency to relieve tension via the route already opened. Mental energy travels down the pathway of the registration of the experience of satisfaction. When this happens, the "stored" image of the tension relieving object is recathected—that is, revived with hallucinatory intensity. To hallucinate, that is, to *see,* such an image is to expect to have tension relieved by it. The primal wish combines the drive to get rid of the tension of hunger with the hallucination of the "breast." This process is the origin of dreams. Dreams are a form of hallucinatory wish fulfillment.

Freud's dream theory mostly concentrates on the subsequent way in which latent wishes are defensively distorted to form the manifest dream. But the very possibility of latent dream content, of wishes as the hallucinatory revival of memories, is based on the paradox of the hungry baby. *The unconscious memory of tension relief depends on the tension raising, differential opening of a pathway.* To think of self-preservation in terms of the psychic apparatus cannot mean to think of it *only* in terms of tension relief.

Freud did not explicitly develop this implication of his fundamental principles. Nevertheless, they make the idea of wish fulfillment more "Nietzschean." As a hallucination, a wish is a conscious experience. One *perceives* a hallucination, just as one perceives a dream. The hallucinatory or oneiric awakening of consciousness certainly does equate perception with tension relief, with the avoidance of pain. But a complex unconscious process precedes this awakening of consciousness. There has been an encounter of a differential of forces; registration has occurred. The registration itself is two-pronged: the opening of a pathway and the storage of an image. When the image is revived intensely enough to become a hallucination, i.e. to awaken consciousness, the fact that it is actually a memory is eliminated. In other words, the *conscious* association of perception with tension relief is a function of the *unconscious* elimination of a prior, tension-raising opening of a differential pathway. For Nietzsche, differentiating raising of tension levels not controlled by consciousness is the essence of life. Freud's linkage of unconscious memory to physiological need depends upon the same possibility.

In an early work, *Human, All Too Human,* Nietzsche explained why dreams are the origin of metaphysics (1995, Part 1, #5). He said that primitive men misunderstood dreams, and took them as coming from a second real world. This misunderstanding produced belief in both a distinction between body and soul, and in the spirits and gods who reside in the second real world. Nietzsche also said that the clarity of representation in dreams led to unconditional belief in their reality. This is why hallucinations were quite common in primitive man (§12–13). Nietzsche understood that the apparent perceptual reality of dreams has to be related to a primal hallucinatory consciousness. Thus, he says that dreams are a regression to archaic forms of thought. Freud cites this sentence approvingly in *The Interpretation of Dreams* (1900, 549).

Nietzsche's linkage of dreams and hallucination to the origin of metaphysics can be integrated with Freud's conception of hallucinatory wish fulfillment. The primal hallucination of the breast attempts to create a "perceptual identity" between previous tension relief and current hunger. Subsequently, dreams depend upon perceptual identity for their tension relieving effect. In other words, perceptual identity eliminates a difference in time—if I *see* the tension relieving object *now*, it creates the same equilibrium now as it did then. In Nietzsche's terms, the dream creates the intertwined privileging of tension relief and identity, which are the bases of the metaphysics of consciousness. The dream, one can say, is itself an instance of the registration *and* repudiation of difference, in that it depends upon, but eliminates, the reality of an unconscious differentiating process. As a hallucinatory awakening of consciousness dependent upon perception, identity, and tension relief, the dream is not only the origin of the belief in a second real world. It is the model for a consciousness that says "no" to difference. Freud gives a psychodynamic account of the process Nietzsche attributes to degenerating life. But Freud does not make this account central to his conception of unconscious processes.

Sexuality, Autoerotism, and Self-Preservation

The paradox of the hungry baby is but one of a series of difficult inferences derived from the linkage of self-preservation and unconscious registration. In his initial and middle periods Freud generally thinks of an *opposition* between sexuality and self-preservation. He sees the human baby's prolonged helplessness as the breeding ground for neurosis. The child represses the drives out of dependent love for the parents who ensure survival. In this familiar version, self-preservation is an affair of consciousness, and sexuality is the core of the repressed unconscious. Further, this repressed sexuality is mostly autoerotic, as a direct consequence of the theory of wish fulfillment. The ontogenesis of autoerotism itself, however, like the ontogenesis of the wish, has a more complex relation to self-preservation.

The primal hallucination of the breast is an attempt to relieve tension *oneself*. Infantile sexuality begins at the hypothetical moment when a baby uses its thumb to recapture the erotic stimulation of the breast in the mouth, without seeking to relieve the tension of hunger. Universal thumb sucking becomes the model for the autoerotic origin of sexuality. If one calls the mother or the breast an "object," infantile *sexuality* begins with the separation of aim (oral stimulation) and object (mother, breast). This theory is the basis for many of Freud's most important innovations. It explains why "the disposition to perversion" is as universal as thumb sucking—precisely because "perversion" itself is a manifestation of infantile sexuality. The Freudian revolution tells us that no matter what our conscious picture of "biological," reproductive sexuality, unconsciously we are all perverse, because we have all been babies. At its origin, sexuality is not intrinsically connected to an object or to reproduction.

But there is a major problem embedded within this essential idea. Once repressed infantile sexuality itself becomes the focus of the theory, autoerotic separation of aim and object makes it look as if there is an intrinsic *separation* between unconscious and world. In less familiar passages, Freud says that in terms of self-preservation there is an intrinsic *connection* between unconscious and world (1905, 222). The baby's initial experiences of feeding and erotic stimulation are one and the same. Only with thumb sucking do self-preservation and sexuality begin to go their separate ways. The important implication is that before any opposition of sexuality and self-preservation, before the separation of aim and object, there is an original state of connection between them. The opposition of unconscious and world is not originary.

When Freud speaks of the original connection to an object, he does not say that the *unconscious* registration of the experience of satisfaction already expressed the same idea. In fact, there was no place in the initial theory of the neuroses at which this idea seemed to have any weight. The goal was to understand how adult symptoms were distorted versions of the return of repressed infantile sexuality. In the same way, dream interpretation was a question of undoing manifest distortion to arrive at latent dream *content*. The prior opening of memory pathways was a necessary theoretical inference, nothing more. As an *unconscious* process, however, the paradox of the hungry baby should lead to some major questions. For example, when Freud speaks of connection to an "object" in the original state, he does not question his use of the word "object." He is making a naturalistic observation: the baby is connected to the mother, to what later psychoanalysts also call a primary "object." An "object" as something distinct from oneself implies a "subject." In terms of unconscious process, however, the baby is not a subject and the mother is not an object.

How to conceive an unconscious process without the usual categories of subject and object? Freud's theory is that a process of memory formation occurs while the baby is fed. Dedifferentiating need satisfaction meets differentiating opening of a pathway. This is a version of *self-preservation in which unconscious and world are linked in terms of differentials of force.* It is implicit to Freud's project of thinking the unconscious in terms of *both* physiological need *and* memory. It is a version of self-preservation which Nietzsche could not think. But Freud did not realize that he had elaborated a theory of self-preservation that was more than a question of tension reduction. Nor did he realize that he had developed a theory of *articulation (differentiating memory) as connection (intrinsic tie of unconscious to world) not conceivable in subject-object terms.* This theory also accounts for the transformation of difference (articulation and connection) into an opposition of unconscious and world. The original libidinal–self-preservative drive becomes an opposition of self-preservation and (autoerotic, infantile) sexuality, the separation of aim and object. Dream theory offers a similar account of the transformation of memory into hallucination, of differential trace into perceptual identity.

Binding, Unconscious Thought, Primary Narcissism, Difference

In scattered places, at passing moments, Freud extends these ideas. These extensions tend to occur whenever he discusses "binding." Binding itself is the raising of tension levels, "unbinding" the discharge of tension. On the question of "binding," there is again a sharp contrast between the familiar and the unfamiliar Freud. The more familiar Freud is the one who sees binding of energy as the possibility of ego formation. The ego is defined as that part of the psychic apparatus modified by its contact with reality. Binding and access to external reality become synonymous, as do the unconscious, the pleasure principle, tension discharge, unbinding, and lack of contact with reality.

The introduction of the reality principle in 1911 mostly follows this logic. Since everything starts from the unconscious, the reality principle must be a modification of the pleasure principle. When the hungry baby "learns" that hallucination does not assuage hunger, it cries in order to bring the real breast to itself. This implies an inhibition of automatic hallucination. Self-preservation is pitted against libido as delayed versus immediate discharge, binding versus unbinding. But even here Freud is compelled to offer other formulations.

He is interested in the origins of objective thought. A hallucination does not assuage hunger. Delay of immediate discharge is essential if the objectivity of the "real, external world," where relief from hunger is to be found, is to be part of the psychic apparatus. Binding *is* this delay. But it is not yet objective thought itself, which depends upon two things: first, the "conversion" of unbound into bound energy, and second, the linkage of such bound formations to words. As unconscious, binding occurs before language acquisition in the usual sense—i.e. the preconscious or conscious use of words. It also brings about what Freud calls a higher "cathectic" level in the entire psychic apparatus (1911, 221), i.e. it increases tension. Thus, before objective thought there is what Freud calls "originally unconscious thought." What is this? The somewhat surprising answer is that it is the binding of "relations between impressions of objects" (221). "Impressions of objects" are *Objekteindrucke*, meaning "impressions" in the sense of registrations. The unconscious origin of thought is in tension raising registrations of the external world not linked to words.

This is another ramification of the unconscious registration of the experience of satisfaction. Freud himself says that the idea of a psychic apparatus *exclusively* governed by the pleasure principle does not take into account the actual care of the infant by the mother. Rather, he thinks, from the infant's point of view, it *appears* as if there is no such care, as if the tension of hunger is omnipotently assuaged by wish fulfillment. Since there would not even be a wish had there not been unconscious registration of the experience of satisfaction, Freud is certainly consistent when he postulates nonverbal "impressions" of the object. As always, he does not explicitly discuss this train of thought. Nonetheless, he does add binding to the possibility of unconscious registration. This is a more refined version of the paradox of the hungry baby. Binding and registration are "as unconscious" as unbinding and wish fulfillment. They explain why there is an unconscious origin of "thought."

A few years later Freud came to speak about primary narcissism. He called it "the libidinal component of the instinct of self-preservation," for which there is no representation of an external world and no coherent organization of an ego (1914, 75). As the ego develops, and with it a boundary between self and object, investment of libido in the ego becomes possible. This is secondary narcissism, the more familiar narcissism of self-love (75). Typically, Freud does not link primary narcissism to all his other descriptions of a libidinal-self-preservative drive and of differentiating unconscious memory traces. Like them, primary narcissism allows one to think of an unconscious process in which there is registration of something *other* than oneself which also *is* oneself—articulation *as* connection. This is what Freud had already called "originally unconscious thought." But this conception of primary narcissism is counter to the usual one of an untenably self-enclosed, "autistic" infant. Because primary narcissism is in fact a description of an original, unconscious relatedness of unconscious and world, in Nietzsche's terms it is another way of thinking about why "nothing is self-sufficient." It is another opening to a theory of self-preservation as an unconscious, differentiating process.

The introduction of Eros in *Beyond the Pleasure Principle* (1920) is actually a culmination of these developments. Freud takes up the point that the theory of neurosis was based on an inherent opposition between libido and self-preservation. However, he says, the study of narcissism compelled postulation of a libidinal force of self-preservation, although he does not specifically say that this is primary narcissism. But he does conclude that "the original opposition between the ego-instincts and the sexual instincts proved to be inadequate" (32). Typically, Freud makes this statement as if it were a new discovery. He seems repeatedly compelled to forget and to reinvent this trend of his thought. Nor was he in any way attuned to the philosophical importance of thinking self-preservation in terms of difference—which always implies a rigorous emergence from the metaphysics of subject and object, from all the presumptions of opposition between mind and world.

Binding, Periodicity, Need

The large discrepancy between the implicit theory of self-preservation and the more explicit version of Freud is critical in relation to time. In "The Unconscious" (1915b), Freud summarized an entire train of thought when he called the unconscious timeless. In *The Interpretation of Dreams* he had already said that there is no past or future in dreams, only the present of perceptual identity. Analogously, the theory of repression states that the past is maintained intact in the unconscious, that the unconscious is

not modified by the passage of time. Here again there seems to be a radical difference between Freud and Nietzsche. Nietzsche is opposed to any
timelessness of unconscious processes: eternal return is the temporality of
will to power. For Nietzsche, in fact, there is a link between timelessness
and neurosis. He often speaks of the neurotic as someone who cannot
forget, whose slave-like resentment makes him preserve the past, chew-
ing over it as a kind of self-induced indigestion (1967, 38). Contrary to
Freud, for Nietzsche repression is the *positive* power of forgetting. It is the
opening to a present and future not dominated by the antilife force of
resentment (1967, 39). Nietzsche is consistently the advocate of an "active
forgetting" which enhances life, as opposed to the bad consciousness and
tormented memory of the ascetic ideal. Repression for him is the possibility of time *as* difference.

   But there is an unintegrated thinking of unconscious temporality in
Freud. It has three major strands: a series of references to periodicity; a
paragraph on unconscious time in *Beyond the Pleasure Principle*; and the
theory of deferred effect.[2] Periodicity is directly related to the question of
self-preservation. Hunger is a periodic process, with an inherent rhythm
of arousal, distress, and relief. The pleasure principle has the same rhythm
of energy buildup, tension, and release. Hypotheses about unconscious
periods and rhythms stretch across Freud's work. He speaks of periodic
cathexes and decathexes, states of excitement and states of rest. The periodicity of excitation and rest itself mediates the relations of psyche and
world. On several occasions Freud ventures the idea that periodic "inner-
vations" are originally what makes the psyche send out "feelers" to sample
the external world. He variously attributes this process to the ego and to
the unconscious itself. The attribution of this sampling function to the
unconscious would support a link between the "natural" rhythm of need
arousal and the opening of memory pathways. The registration of the
experience of satisfaction, or originally unconscious thought, has the periodicity of hunger. In the "Note on the Mystic Writing Pad" (1925c) Freud
integrates his references to the periodic extension and retraction of "feelers." The unconscious, he says, periodically "samples" the external world
through consciousness. When consciousness is periodically invested with
psychic energy, it is "lit up"; when the feelers are withdrawn, consciousness is "shut down." This *periodic* sampling of the external world by the
unconscious, says Freud, is "the origin of our sense of time" (1925c, 231).

   Something similar had already been broached in *Beyond the Pleasure*

Principle (1920). Freud had discussed periodic sampling as a function of changing levels of excitation within a given *period* of time. On the book's last two pages, he undertakes a complex analysis of the relations between binding and periodicity. Despite the title and the more familiar reception of *Beyond* . . . , the death drive is not the beyond of the pleasure principle. As the essence of tension reduction and unbinding, Freud says, the death drive seems to serve the pleasure principle (1920, 63). The problem is really the "before" of the pleasure principle, what Freud calls the tendency to binding. Again counter to the familiar version of his theories, binding is an unconscious principle of raising tension. Freud takes up the idea that if there were no possibility of unconscious raising of tension, there would be no need for tension discharge. Since unconscious processes generally seem to be regulated by the pleasure principle, "binding" is a "tendency" that precedes it. Here, Freud notices that as the "before" of the pleasure principle, binding itself cannot be understood as *either* pleasure *or* pain (62–63). It contains elements of both. This is understandable in terms of the paradox of the hungry baby: binding is libidinal, self-preservative, tension raising, synthetic, differentiating. Because it is libidinal it is pleasurable, even if not in the sense of tension discharge. For just this reason it also contains the possibility of pain, but neither can it be called painful in the conventional sense. Its tie to self-preservation links binding to the periodicity of both rise and fall of levels of excitation and to the sampling of the outer world. This periodic temporality of binding is "rhythmic," Freud says. Rhythm is a repetition of differential intervals. Differential opening of pathways depends upon differential time.

Binding, of course, is another name for Eros and libidinal self-preservation. In this sense, when Deleuze said that Freud does not link the differentiating force of Eros to a force of repetition he was not entirely correct. The potential link is in the analysis of binding as periodicity. Deleuze's own analysis of difference is "intervallic": difference as that which lies between two repetitions, and repetition as "the differenciator of difference" (1994, 76). The intervallic nature of difference, in fact, leads Deleuze to an analysis of "need." Soon after describing repetition as the "differenciator of difference," Deleuze writes: "The *repetition of need*, and of everything which depends upon it, expresses the time which belongs to the synthesis of time, the intratemporal character of that synthesis. Repetition is essentially inscribed in need, since need rests upon an instance which essentially involves repetition" (77). This is a Nietzschean conception of need—in the sense that "nothing is self sufficient"—because it conceives need in relation to time as difference and repetition. And when Deleuze says that repetition of need expresses the intratemporal character of time, he is saying that need is a way of thinking about time temporally. Freud seems to have stumbled across something like this in his analysis of binding and periodicity as the *before* of the pleasure principle. This opens the question of *pain* and time.

In *The Will to Power*, when Nietzsche rethinks pleasure and pain, like Freud at the end of *Beyond . . . ,* he speaks in terms of rhythm.[3] But unlike Freud, for Nietzsche pleasure is a differential increase in power, and not tension discharge. Therefore, it cannot be divorced from pain. This is why Nietzsche says that pleasure is a "kind of pain" (1968, §490). If will to power is the unconscious interrelation of differentials of force, and if the repetition of difference is its temporality, then will to power has to be conceived as a rhythm of "pleasurepain." Thus, Nietzsche calls pleasure "a rhythm of small painful stimuli" (§687)—"small" because, like Freud, Nietzsche also sees pain as the essence of trauma or shock (§699). Too much is overwhelming; too little is dedifferentiating. In this context, however, Nietzsche, as always, is insistent that in terms of unconscious processes there is no self-preservation. Differentiating pleasurepain, increase of power, he says, cannot be understood in terms of hunger. Hunger is about replacement of what has been lost, and tends toward unification. In this sense it is like metaphysics, which "senselessly" derives the conditioned from the unconditioned (§574). In other words, metaphysics promotes unification over difference, sees unity as the original good lost in the fall into the body and its hunger. One recalls the dream as the origin of metaphysics.

Freud's hungry baby both does and does not conform to Nietzsche's understanding of hunger. Hallucinatory wish fulfillment is most definitely a concept of reunification, of making good a lack. The perceived presence of the tension relieving object in the primal hallucination is an attempt to rectify its absence. Thus, perceptual *identity* is essential to tension reduction. This is why Freud's conception of sexuality on the hunger model is always a theory of the absent or lost object, and in Nietzsche's terms nihilistic. But, as Freud consistently demonstrates, and just as consistently forgets, there is an unconscious force of binding "before" the wish, before one can speak of an absent or present "object," before "objectivity" itself ("originally unconscious thought"). As such, binding is a "rhythm of small painful stimuli." "Need" is double-edged in this theory because binding concerns hunger in relation to both unconscious differentiation *and* unconscious dedifferentiation. Further, because need is the possibility of unconscious differentiation, it must be thought in relation to the idea of an apparatus capable of unconscious *registration*. Primal registrations themselves are a question of need, difference, and repetition.

The setting or frame of analysis itself is often thought to draw upon the unconscious dynamics of the baby-mother relation. If one compares the analytic patient to the hungry baby, inevitably one compares the analyst to the feeding mother. But there is a paradox of the mother as much as there is a paradox of the baby. In her conventional role as guarantor of self-preservation, the mother is always seen as the provider of relief from distress. Some psychoanalytic theorists go further, and reasonably insist that the mother has her own sexuality, that feeding is as erotically stimulating for her as for the baby. In his work on seduction, Laplanche says that the unconscious communication of the mother's sexuality during feeding "implants" an arousal the baby cannot metabolize. Such arousal is an "enigmatic signifier" and is the origin of unconscious sexuality (1999). Alternately, thinkers like Winnicott (1951) and Loewald (1980) see the mother as a source of gratification and eventual frustration. The gratification promotes the internalization of a "good" object, and the frustration just enough aggression to make separation possible and tolerable. But theories of the clinical situation as a replication of mothering tend not to take the psychic *apparatus* into account. Because feeding is libidinal–self-preservative, it takes place in a context of primary narcissism, of articulation as connection without a subject-object structure. This is the unconscious origin of thought as differential and binding. The mother herself *is* the differential that opens a pathway, is the tension raising trace or impressive force of unconscious registration. Like the paradoxical hungry baby, the paradoxical mother consciously relieves tension while unconsciously raising it. The meeting of unconscious memory with repetitive need is this process. The repetitive nature of psychoanalytic therapy itself can be conceived in terms of repetitive, differentiating need, of self-preservation rethought as will to power and eternal return.

Unconscious Time

All these considerations must be brought to bear on Freud's unique discussion of unconscious time in *Beyond*. . . . The discussion is significantly situated in the context of protection against trauma. Freud has for the first time said that protection against stimuli is as important as reception of them—too much stimulation is trauma itself. Thus, he postulates the existence of a stimulus barrier. When this protective barrier is broken through by too much stimulation, the trauma is automatically repeated until the disruption can be repaired. This explains the repetition of trauma in order to develop anticipatory signal anxiety. But Freud also specifies that the stimulus barrier only protects against stimuli coming from the outside. There can be no stimulus barrier against internal stimulation, most prominently from the drives themselves.

And what if there were an unconscious, internal *time* which also acted in the manner of an overly stimulating drive? How would one protect oneself against it? This is precisely the possibility that Freud envisages, in his only critique of his own doctrine of the timelessness of the unconscious. He writes:

> We have learnt that unconscious mental processes are in themselves "timeless." This means in the first place that they are not ordered temporally, that time does not change them in any way and that the idea of time cannot be applied to them. These are negative characteristics which can only be clearly understood if a comparison is made with *conscious* [author's emphasis] mental processes. On the other hand, our abstract idea of time seems to be wholly derived from the method of working of the system *Pcpt.-Cs.* and to correspond to a perception on its own part of that method of working. *This mode of functioning may perhaps constitute another way of providing a shield against stimuli.* (1920, 28; emphasis added)

To paraphrase: Freud is explicit that to understand the unconscious as timeless is too simplistic. This only says that if there is an unconscious, its temporality cannot be that of consciousness. More subtly, what we take for granted as time itself belongs to the overestimation of consciousness *as* perception. This equation of time with conscious perceptual time may itself be a protective barrier against an unconscious time. Like the drives, unconscious time would (apparently)[4] come from within. If it were disruptive, there would be no stimulus barrier against it. However, the conflation of conscious time with time itself would be a way of attempting such a protective maneuver. The clear implication is that there is an unconscious time which potentially raises tension levels. The psyche needs conscious time as the tension reducing equivalent of an impossible stimulus barrier against unconscious time. The timelessness of the unconscious, the idea that time does not modify unconscious wishes, itself would be conditioned by the possibility of tension raising time. This is the time of periodic, differentiating opening of pathways, the prior condition of the wish. There would be no timelessness of the unconscious without this possibility.

Significantly, in this context Freud for once is willing to question Kant. He introduced the discussion of possible unconscious time by saying: "As a result of certain psychoanalytic discoveries, we are today in a position to embark on a discussion of the Kantian theorem that time and space are 'necessary forms of thought'" (1920, 28). What discoveries does Freud mean? He does not say. At the very least, he seems to mean that the assumptions about time and space intrinsic to perceptual consciousness are defensive. Kantian time and space as a priori categories of mind are up for grabs. Note that Freud includes space here. Is this any more than a conventional reference to an overly familiar idea of Kant's? Can one extend Freud to be envisaging the possibility of an "unconscious space" which is as potentially disruptive as unconscious time? In other words, would this be a way of thinking psyche and world in terms of a Kantian a priori synthesis, but in unconscious terms? Before the opposition of pleasure and pain? As a Nietzschean displacement of Kant?[5]

Kantian time and space are infinite and permanently present. Unconscious time and space would have to be finite and rhythmic, much as Nietzsche had already thought, and as Freud begins to think here. This is the time-space of the openness of psyche and world to each other in terms of differentiating force, radical non–self-sufficiency. Binding is a way of thinking need as difference and repetition. It is the time-space of pleasurepain, of self-preservation as something other than tension reduction. In fact, it is self-preservation thought outside consciousness altogether, and most particularly outside perception. The nonperceptual structure of originally unconscious thought and primary narcissism would be its necessary complements. But originally unconscious thought and primary narcissism have to be conceived in relation to trauma. They *call for* perceptual time and space as a protective barrier. The paradoxes of the hungry baby and the feeding mother embody this structure: in terms of an unconscious apparatus tension reduction and tension increase must be thought as differentially bound together.

Deferred Effect, Unconscious Time,
and Therapeutic Need

Does unconscious time as periodicity and potential trauma have any-thing to do with deferred effect? Freud's entire theory of the unconscious depends upon differential pathways. In his more naturalistic mode, he started with the clinical observation that a real trauma might not affect an individual until a considerable time after the fact. It can act by delay. Eventually, delay explained why adult psychopathology can have its roots in the past. Freud linked neurosis to infantile sexuality in terms of the delay in maturation he thought was unique to human sexuality—the latency period. Whether one is thinking of actual traumatic seductions or of the vicissitudes of infantile sexuality, including the Oedipus complex, the fact that the child does not have the sexuality of the adult means that the traumatic impact of early sexual experience may not be felt until much later. Delay, deferred effect, joins the theory of trauma to the theory of sexuality.

This understanding of deferred effect is akin to the exclusively physiological understanding of hunger. It derives from rigorous thought about clinical and physiological realities, integrating the theory of trauma with the theory of sexuality in terms of unconscious memory. However, this understanding does not take into account the following: if unconscious registration of difference always raises tension levels, it too is always potentially traumatic, and can be handled by deferred effect. When Freud says that conscious time may be the equivalent of a stimulus barrier against unconscious time, one can interpret that conscious time is the deferred effect of unconscious time. When conscious perceptual time is projectively equated with time itself, consciousness is attempting to keep itself undisturbed by unconscious time. In fact, the arousal of consciousness in hallucinatory wish fulfillment is based on this possibility. It is the deferred effect of the differential opening of a pathway. It depends upon an unconscious process of registration and repudiation of unconscious time-space. As a rigorously unconscious and tension raising process, differentiation will never be grasped in a conscious, perceptual *now*.

Here we return to the question of psychoanalysis undertaken with the conscious intent of self-preservation, as a felt *need* for therapeutic intervention. Conscious self-preservative intent can indeed be understood on a hunger model. It bespeaks a tension state from which one seeks relief.

But psychoanalytic therapy is not a question of feeding—literally or figuratively. If it conceives therapeutic need only in terms of satisfaction, it misses the complex, unconscious dynamics of self-preservation. Is there an "object" relation between patient and analyst based on need? In terms of consciousness, of course. But in terms of the unconscious dynamics of self-preservation, the encounter between patient and analyst, like the relation between baby and mother, must be conceived in terms of unconscious differentials of force. Therapeutic need, radical non–self-sufficiency, is a condition of difference and repetition, binding and pleasure-pain. For psychoanalysis, need must be thought in terms of disruptive unconscious time

This is where the rethinking of psychopathology in terms of primary disavowal, registration, and repudiation of difference, is critical. Freudian theory remains a theory of unconscious conflict. Much current developmental thinking has given rise to a theory of deficits, of lacks in psychic structure. Nietzsche allows us to see that the privileging of lack is always a privileging of consciousness, unification, and tension reduction. Certainly, patients appear in analysts' offices who seem to suffer from the deficits described in so much of the clinical literature.[6] However, the theory of the unconscious demands that the analyst ask whether the appearance of a lack is the result of the repudiation of difference. Wherever there is a conviction of absence, there is also a counterconviction of a presence that will compensate for it. This can be an imperative push toward dedifferentiating unification with a tension relieving *object*, in the strict sense of the word. In psychoanalytic terms, reunification with an object is the essence of hallucinatory dream consciousness. In other words, unification with the present object that remediates absence is fantasy.

A conception of therapeutic need not based on fantasy driven remediation of absence demands a revised conception of therapeutic action. How would interpretation work in terms of need as difference and repetition? Freud's use of interpretation as a therapeutic measure was developed in concert with the repression theory, but he did not think through the questions of truth and science in relation to interpretation. Science for Freud was both objective and the antidote to metaphysics. Repression provided a nonmetaphysical view of mind *and* an objective picture of mind's unconscious contents. Apparently objective interpretation provided the first scientific, nonmetaphysical rationale for psychotherapy. Anything like Nietzsche's challenge to the scientific *faith* in truth in relation to a theory of the unconscious did not occur to Freud.

And yet for Nietzsche interpretation is the only way of thinking un-conscious differentials of force. Once fetishism becomes the model of psychopathology, and once fetishism itself is understood as unconscious registration and repudiation of difference, then interpretation itself must be rethought in more Nietzschean, differential, terms. It is very much to Loewald's credit that he based his understanding of therapeutic ac-tion on the internalization of the differential implicit to every interpreta-tion. His conception of the differential, however, is rather tame. It is the difference between the analyst's accurate capturing of the level to which the patient has regressed and a higher level of development to which the analyst wants to bring the patient (1980, 240–41). Metapsychologically, Loewald takes the crucial step of understanding the internalization of the differential in terms of primary narcissism and Eros (1980, 235). However, he does not grasp registration and repudiation of difference as a basic unconscious process, or understand Eros and binding in terms of plea-surepain, the opening of unconscious pathways, and the potential trauma of unconscious time.

An interpretation that potentially modifies unconscious processes oc-curs in unconscious time-space, because the patient's *need* for a differen-tiating process is itself unconscious. This is the lesson of fetishism: reg-istration and repudiation of difference can occur unconsciously, and be replaced by fantasy in consciousness. The possibility of unconscious regis-tration of difference was always intrinsic to Freud's theory,[7] but he did not see that the question of repudiation of reality demanded a return to the question of difference. Without such a return there is no understanding of therapeutic need in relation to the psychic *apparatus*. If the apparatus is capable of unconscious registration and repudiation of differentiating process, need is a question of periodic articulation as connection. It oc-curs before—and here we would have to add, during and after—the plea-sure principle. Before, during, and after the opposition of self-preserva-tion and libido, pleasure and pain. Therapeutic need always implies an unconscious, potentially disruptive differential of force. The interpretive stance of psychoanalytic therapy embodies this differential.

The most difficult implication of the idea of the potentially traumatic aspect of interpretation is that the more effective the interpretation, the more the patient's response will be in terms of deferred effect. The un-anticipated way in which some patients will not understand, not hear, become confused, immediately forget, or even fall asleep in response to something the analyst says is an indication of unconscious registration *and* repudiation. The apparently *immediate* domination of consciousness by tension reduction can only occur if the "now" of forgetting and sleepiness is a deferral of raised tension. There can be an attempt to create something like a stimulus barrier against interpretation itself, and usually against those interpretations which most effectively meet therapeutic *need*. This is a rigorous result of the paradoxes of the hungry baby and the feeding mother: the differentiating registration of the experience of satisfaction becomes dedifferentiating wish fulfillment as defense, or even stimulus barrier.

The repetitive nature of psychoanalytic therapy itself is a function of the unconscious dynamics of need. Psychoanalysis is a practice designed to effect the periodic encounter of differentials of force. The theory of the psychic apparatus itself demands that psychoanalytic treatment be repetitive, periodic, rhythmic in order to be differential. The repetitive nature of psychoanalysis is not only due to the force of a repetition compulsion weakly opposed by working through. It is also due to the repetitive way in which need is differentiating. The repetition compulsion as the dedifferentiating force of the death drive is intertwined with the repetitive, differentiating force of need, of Eros, of binding.[8]

Nietzschean Self-Preservation and Interpretation

Is it Nietzsche's lack of a theory of the psychic apparatus that makes him understand differentiation and dedifferentiation in terms of a "life" which "degenerates" and has to "protect itself"? Does this explain why Nietzsche eventually offers a theory of self-preservation in terms of difference, despite Zarathustra's love for those who do not preserve themselves? In his last published work, *Ecce Homo*, Nietzsche develops an empirical application of the "noble" affirmation of distance. He speaks of the "instinct of self-preservation" (!) which is expressed "in the choice of nutrition, of place and climate, of recreation" (1967, 252). How are such self preservative choices made? As a function of "taste," which "commands us not only to say No when Yes would be 'selfless,' but also to say *No as rarely as possible*. To detach oneself, to separate oneself from anything that would make it necessary to keep saying No . . . is the art of self-preservation—of selfishness" (253–54).

Nietzsche finally cannot avoid the relation of *self-preservation to differ-*

ence, but can only think of it in terms of *conscious* choices. He is aware that he seems to be contradicting himself. Self-preservative "taste" leads him to endorse a Christian principle he had ferociously dismantled in the past: "love thy neighbor"—not that Nietzsche proposes "neighbor love" as the path to salvation. Rather, it paradoxically assists self-preservative selfishness: "forgetting oneself, *misunderstanding* oneself, making one-self smaller, narrower, mediocre, become reason itself. Morally speaking: neighbor love, living for others, and other things can be a protective mea-sure for preserving the hardest self-concern. This is the exception where, against my wont and conviction, I side with the 'selfless' drives, here they work in the service of self-love, of self-discipline" (254).

One might be amused that the thinker who opposed self-preservation and neighbor love is finally forced to develop a rationale for them. Freud could say that here Nietzsche finally does bow before *Ananke,* necessity: the unavoidable need to preserve oneself in relation to others. Certainly Nietzsche wishes to do so as an affirmation of difference. But even if Freud might have a kind of last laugh here, he most likely would continue to forget that the theory of the psychic *apparatus* had always included a Nietzschean description of self-preservation as "will to power and eternal return"—the unconscious repetition of differentials of force.

This is the key to the psychodynamics of interpretation. One of the reasons why Nietzsche says that there are no facts, only interpretations, is that he saw positivism as the obstacle to understanding unconscious differentials of force. Science remains metaphysics to the extent that it seeks to understand phenomena in terms of equalities and identities. A nonmetaphysical science of the unconscious would have to use interpreta-tion as a force of differentiation itself. This is what Nietzsche calls "active" thought, versus the "reactive" tendency to replicate equalities and identi-ties. "Active" interpretation does not discover facts or objective truths. An-other way of describing Nietzsche's view of interpretation is that it opens the differentiating unconscious realities inevitably repudiated because of their pain. To rethink psychopathology in terms of an unconscious regis-tration and repudiation of difference is to understand why the differential implicit to every interpretation is also its active function. The patients who most automatically resist the process of interpretation teach us about this unconscious function of interpretation. They also teach us why the meeting of therapeutic need, effective interpretation as self preservative, can be so powerfully repudiated.

For Nietzsche, metaphysics projectively replaces difference with opposition (1968, §552). Opposition itself presumes negation and lack. Self-preservation conceived on a conventional hunger model is for Nietzsche a logic of negation and opposition, in which pleasure is the opposite of pain. His rethinking of pleasure *as* pain is intrinsic to his critique of conventional hunger models of unconscious processes. Thus his eventual rejection of the opposition of life and death. Life, he tells us in *The Gay Science,* is a special form of death (1974, 168). Life and death are intertwined because of the nature of difference. Difference connects, but difference articulates. Every articulation is also a breaking down, a decay (1968, §655): difference as life is difference as death. Whether Freud knows it or not, it is this Nietzschean logic of difference that makes him deconstruct some of his own fundamental oppositions, for example the opposition of libido and self-preservation, the opposition of unconscious and world, the opposition of time and timelessness. The very idea of a psychic *apparatus* implies that on the level of the unconscious life and death cannot be simply opposed: the most life sustaining, self preservative need has to be thought in relation to the automatic functioning of a "machine" which registers, repudiates, differentiates, dedifferentiates, raises its own tension levels and reduces them. Repetition as difference cannot simply be *opposed* to a dedifferentiating repetition compulsion.

In his analysis of fetishism, Freud entangled himself in an equation of sexual difference with "the reality of castration," because he could not move beyond a logic of sexual *opposition.* When the fetish becomes an *object* that makes good a subject's conviction of essential lack, the differentiating force of sexuality is contained. The fetishist functions within a closed, internally consistent system based on the apparent objectivity of absence. He illustrates Nietzsche's idea that reactive metaphysics turns active difference into opposition. Once fetishism itself becomes the model for all compromise formations, Freud's thought potentially becomes even more Nietzschean: all substitutions of fantasy for reality create closed systems of oppositions in order to repudiate unconscious registration of difference.

The unconscious openness to differentials of force creates tension states with their own rhythms and periodicities. But this rhythmicity and periodicity do not determine exactly when registration of difference will occur. This is also why there are necessarily unanticipated moments of registration *and* repudiation of interpretation in analysis. For Nietzsche, will to power and eternal return are affirmations of chance. Strict determinism, for him, is a positivistic, inherently theological, reactive notion. There is another sharp difference between Freud and Nietzsche, then, on the question of determinism. For Freud, the tension reduction of the pleasure principle guaranteed an unconscious determinism. Without unconscious determinism there is no scientificity of psychoanalysis and no objectivity of interpretation. Freud's largest conception of interpretation, the reversal of repression by making the unconscious conscious, is also a way of restoring the lost history of what *causes* psychopathology. Repression can be reversed by interpretation because repression itself is energically a function of the pleasure principle (tension reduction). Repression works energically by separating preconscious word presentation from unconscious thing presentation (1915b). Unconscious determinism is the possibility of causal, verbal interpretation. Certainly Freud early on introduced the idea of "overdetermination" of neurotic symptoms in order to counter the naive belief that a symptom could be resolved by the interpretation of a *single* memory. But his conception of overdetermination did not contradict his basic convictions about causality, determinism, and tension reduction.

Nietzsche would say that a deterministic unconscious is a metaphysically closed system. He calls "interpretation by causality a deception" (1968, §551). The truth of interpretation is not in finding something objectively there, "not a becoming conscious of something that is in itself firm and determined." Rather, interpretation "gives a name to a process . . . introducing truth, as a *processus in infinitum*, an active determining" (§552).

Clinically, the repudiation of the differential implicit to interpretation is a quasi-traumatized unconscious response to the analyst's processive "activity." It cannot be reversed if the analyst conceives interpretation only in terms of becoming conscious of something "firm and determined": a differentiating process is not objective, perceivable, or deterministic. Repudiation of it is not a detachment of word presentation from thing presentation. Rather, it operates on the level of originally unconscious thought, before the use of words—which is not to say that it cannot be named. It is not causal in the usual deterministic sense—which is not to say that it is without effect. In the area of registration and repudiation of difference, then, interpretation indeed "gives a name to a process," but without relying on causal connections. The words used to name the process become an act of differentiation. History itself means something other than it usually does: where there is no objective content to be made conscious, there is no possibility of restoring a history of repressed causes.

It is difficult for psychoanalysts, beginning with Freud, to think outside of conventional conceptions of causality and history. Yet there is compelling evidence of the failure of causal, historical interpretation in all the clinical situations of fetishistic compromise formations. And if fetishism itself becomes the model of compromise formation, the registration and repudiation of difference mandates rethinking interpretation. This has to mean rethinking interpretation outside conventional causality and history.

All the notions grouped under the rubric of binding actually imply an open, nondeterministic unconscious. The transformation of difference into identity through wish fulfillment is the "origin" of unconscious transformation of an intrinsically open to an apparently closed system. The function of (active) interpretation is to reopen such closed systems in the act of giving a name to this process. This is the nonmetaphysical rationale for an interpretive psychotherapy.

Is Freud's persistent forgetting of the entire train of thought that made him think binding as unconscious differentiation itself a form of registration and repudiation of difference? A need to construct a deterministic unconscious, when his own thinking depended upon nondeterministic processes, processes which do not fail to reappear at intervals in his thinking? A repeated registration and repudiation of a logic of difference which would have to transform the basic understanding of interpretation and the therapeutic *setting* themselves? For interpretation reconceived in terms of unconscious time implies unconscious space. The *space* of analysis is unconsciously a place of differentiation if it is a place of interpretation. It is what Nietzsche called "world." In this sense, despite the empirical privacy of the analytic setting, the unconscious dynamics of need place it very much in the world.

In terms of the repression model, the unconscious is an internal container in which thing presentations pushed out of consciousness can be stored. It is not "in" the world, but "buried" in the mind. However, the space of unconscious differentiation as a space of interpretation "in the world" cannot be thought as an internal container. It is rather a surface receptive to "impressions of relations between objects." This surface is not static. It is a process of integrating-differentiating-binding, inherently temporal in its periods and rhythms, conceivable only as pleasurepain.

Chapter 2

Heidegger: Descriptive Interpretation

Interpretation and Being-in-the-World:
Freud and Heidegger

The differential of force intrinsic to psychoanalytic space by virtue of its interpretive stance places it in the world, in the Nietzschean sense. All of Heidegger's early magnum opus, *Being and Time,* is about what he calls being-in-the-world, a being-in-the-world that produces a rethinking of time and interpretation. His later work is dominated by the question of difference as the unthought of metaphysics. For these reasons alone, Heidegger is essential to a psychoanalysis whose theory and practice must understand the constraints of metaphysics.

But Heidegger's Nazi affiliation and ontological orientation tend to make him antipathetic to psychoanalysts. There have been some notable exceptions. Ludwig Binswanger, who wrote the tribute to Freud comparing him to Nietzsche, was a correspondent of Freud's and Heidegger's. Medard Boss, a Swiss psychiatrist, developed a school of existential psychoanalysis. He also organized the Zollikon Seminars, in which Heidegger addressed an audience of mental health professionals for many years. Lacan at various points refers to Heidegger and translated his essay *Logos.* Hans Loewald tells us in the introduction to his collected papers that he studied with Heidegger before he left Germany, and remained "forever grateful" for what he learned, despite Heidegger's "most hurtful betrayal" during the Nazi period (1980, xiii).

Heidegger reads the entire history of philosophy—including the modern science that emerged out of metaphysics in the seventeenth cen-

tury—as a *forgetting*, a forgetting of the question of being. This is a philosophical, not a psychological, forgetting. Heidegger contends that not to
understand this forgetting is to remain within metaphysics, despite claims
to go beyond it. Freud's creation of an allegedly nonmetaphysical discipline that was both scientific and interpretive did not specifically take
into account the forgotten relations between metaphysics, science, and interpretation. From Heidegger's point of view, even Nietzsche's demystifi-
cation of science, which demonstrated its genealogical roots in Platonism
and produced a rigorous practice of interpretation, finally did not engage
the forgetting of being. Heidegger's account of the forgetting of being in
modern science and philosophy leads to a rethinking of interpretation
itself as the condition of thought.

In *Kant and the Problem of Metaphysics* Heidegger describes his overall
approach: "what is essential in all philosophical discourse is not found
in the specific propositions of which it is composed but in that which,
although unstated as such, is made evident through these propositions"
(1962, 206). To analyze discourse in terms of what is unstated, but nonetheless evident within it, is to treat discourse "symptomatically." Does
not the very possibility of a symptomatic reading—the understanding
of history as a form of forgetting—call for a detailed juxtaposition of
Heidegger and Freud? Freud's thinking itself is a strange amalgam of Kantian ideas about science and Nietzschean ideas about the unconscious.
Heidegger sees Kant as having "recoiled" before an understanding of time
that brought him to the "abyss of metaphysics," and sees Nietzsche as having failed to think through the question of time altogether. Given Freud's
Kantian and Nietzschean inheritances, does he repeat their conceptions
of time? Is there another conception of time that insists symptomatically
in this repetition?

The critical point made by Deleuze—that Nietzsche, Freud, and Heidegger are all thinkers of difference as articulation and connection—is
nowhere examined by Heidegger himself. (He most likely would have
contested Deleuze's point, just as Deleuze contested Heidegger's reading
of Nietzsche.) However, Deleuze's argument can serve as a guiding thread
for an encounter between psychoanalysis and fundamental ontology.
Does Freud's continuous postulation and forgetting of a force of binding
as difference and repetition have to do with an unknown insistence of the
question of being in his work?

This question can be answered in relation to the *place* of interpretation in Freud's and Heidegger's practices. "Place" here is meant both in the usual figurative sense, but also in a more literal one. To articulate the forgotten and the unstated in symptoms and discourse is to interpret them. From a Nietzschean perspective, interpretation is necessary to understand *world* as the relatedness of unconscious differentials of force. In the juxtaposition of Freud and Nietzsche, therapeutic need for interpretation became a question of difference, repetition, unconscious time and unconscious space, the need to open what has become defensively closed. The question now becomes: is being in Heidegger's sense unknowingly, but insistently, implicit to the place of analysis, the therapeutic setting created by Freud as a place of interpretation? Does it have an intrinsic relation to being-in-the-world?

This question was already raised in relation to psychoanalysis as a practice of repetition and periodicity—inherently temporal concepts. Another way to consider it is to note that psychoanalytic practice is not only interpretive, but *timed*. Why is the psychoanalytic setting, the session itself, at fixed times for a fixed duration? Why not do otherwise? Freud gives no theoretical account of the relations between fixed, timed appointments and the space of interpretation. When Heidegger says at a critical juncture that "measurement of time is constitutive of being-in-the-world" (1996, 306), he opens possibilities of thinking interpretation, time, and space together.

Dasein, Interpretation, and Time

To explain this possibility is to come up against *Being and Time*. Its project is to investigate Da-sein, the human mode of existing, in order to revive what appeared to be a dead issue in philosophy—the meaning of being itself. The link between the meaning of being and Da-sein is that in however rudimentary a way, Da-sein always has an understanding that it *is*, that it exists. The title and opening pages of the book make it clear that Heidegger proposes to rethink what "is" means in relation to time, through an unpacking of Da-sein's understanding that it exists: "we need an *original explication of time as the horizon of the understanding of being, in terms of temporality as the being of Da-sein which understands being*" (1996, 15). From the very outset it is a question of understanding—interpretation—and time. And from the very outset it is a question of time in two ways—time as the possibility of history and the limitations of time as conventionally understood.

Heidegger calls time as the possibility of history "historicity." His aim is not to think of the events that occur in history, but to think that as a mode of existence, Da-sein is always historical, always exists in the present in relation to past and future. This complicates the conventional understanding of time, for which the past and the future are not in the present, are *not now*. For Heidegger, metaphysics always thinks being as things that are there *now*, as beings. Metaphysics cannot possibly understand the meaning of being in general because it cannot free itself from preoccupation with actually present beings: "what remains concealed in an exceptional sense, or shows itself only in a distorted way, is not this or that being but rather . . . the being of being" (31). In *Being and Time* Heidegger characterizes our own era as the one in which beings are conceived as the objectively present. We can confuse being with beings, with the objectively present, because objective presence itself depends upon a millennial assumption about time: time is a succession of now points. As a symptom, this traditional assumption conceals, but carries along with it, other ways of thinking time. The implication is that the concealment can be "destructured" in order to see its limitations and to free the thinking of time implicit in the concealment (20). This other thinking of time can explain the historicity of Da-sein.

Is it not Freud's innovation to say something analogous about neurotic symptoms? A symptom is not simply what it is; it is historical. Whether in the initial trauma theory or in the theory of infantile sexuality, Freud's is always a theory of how a symptom that appears to emerge at a given moment comes into being through the operation of a past that is remembered without consciousness, and that operates by deferred effect. The conjoint theories of sexuality, repression, and unconscious memory have an intrinsic relation to historicity as differential time. This does not mean that Heidegger and Freud are saying the same thing about historicity. From Heidegger's point of view, Freud's linkage of past and present would still unquestioningly presuppose an objectively present past operating in an objective present, and Freud probably would not disagree. For Freud, past and present are linked by associative connection and by the imbalance of force between repression and the repressed. Freud does not ask—as Heidegger does—whether the relation of past and present *itself* has to be thought temporally. But because time and history are critical to psychoanalysis, in Heidegger's sense they could symptomatically conceal other ways of thinking about time. These other ways of thinking time are hinted at in terms of periodicity, disruptive unconscious time, and the expansion of deferred effect to explain the relation of conscious to unconscious time.

Interpretation is the method to undo historical concealments. Just as Heidegger and Freud are not saying the same thing about time and historicity, they do not use interpretation in the same way. Certainly both are concerned with meaning: what is the meaning of being? what is the meaning of a symptom? But to interpret the historically concealed meaning of a symptom is not to interpret the historically concealed nature of time. However much Freud complicates the theory of cause and effect with the theory of deferred action, however much he insists that symptoms are overdetermined, his aim is still to interpret *causality* in order to reverse the repressions that produce symptoms. As in Nietzsche's nondeterministic conception of interpretation, Heidegger's method of interpretation is not causal. It is descriptive, or phenomenological. He says that "ontology is possible only as phenomenology" (31). This means several things at once. Phenomena are not simply what is objectively present. Being itself is a phenomenon, but as phenomenon it is concealed. In fact, it is concealed in the mode of objective presence. Therefore, to bring being out of concealment cannot mean to make it present. Causal interpretation by definition makes causes, however various their natures, present. Heidegger insists that to interpret the historical concealment of being as time is to *describe* time as the *possibility* of history. Interpretation of possibility is not interpretation of cause. "[T]he methodological meaning of phenomenological description is *interpretation*." Phenomenological *description* is itself an "analysis of the existentiality of existence" (33). In this context, Heidegger famously remarks that the possible is "higher" than the actual (34). In the realm of the possible, description *is* interpretation and analysis.

Care, Concern, Interpretation, and Time

Heidegger's most fundamental phenomenological-descriptive interpretation of Da-sein is that it only exists as being-in-the-world. Da-sein cannot be thought of as an ego or a subject which is "next to" something else called "world" (1996, 43, 51). Just as Da-sein is not a pregiven subject, world is not a pregiven object (56). Rather, the "in" of being-in-the-world expresses "existential spatiality" (53). (After a long detour, existential spatiality will become existential temporality.) At this stage of his analysis, Heidegger for the first time characterizes being-in-the-world as "care." Care is not any kind of production, manipulation, or objectification, but "simply lingering with" (57), "dwelling together with" (58). The emphasis is on the idea that "lingering" or "dwelling" take time. As taking time, care is the possibility of encountering "something as something," the precondition for any perception of what is objectively present. Paradoxically, being-*in*-the world as care immediately places Da-sein *outside* itself, as always together with things.

Whether Freud knew it or not, he created a therapeutic setting based on "lingering with," "dwelling together with." Even though hypnotic treatment could conceivably take place in a single session, one has only to read Breuer's account of the first patient to use hypnosis as a "talking cure" (Anna O., whom he treated from 1880 to 1882), to see him "lingering" with her. The first condition of analysis is that analyst and patient spend a good deal of time with each other—"weeks, months, or even a year or longer," as Freud put it in 1912. Can we begin to understand this taking time in relation to being-in-the-world as care? To think about this question one must always remember that for Heidegger care and being-in-the-world cannot be conceived in subject-object terms. In line with his method of phenomenological interpretation, Heidegger is describing something very simple: every encounter of "something as something" takes time, a time intrinsic to the space of being-*in*-the world. In Heidegger's conception, one would have to reverse the usual perspective and say that therapeutic care is itself made *possible* by being-in-the-world as care. If so, there would have to be an ontological aspect to the therapeutic setting. But this immediately would mean that to understand the setting, neither patient nor analyst can be taken as subject or object.

We already encountered something like this in Nietzsche's mockery of the "and" in the expression "man and world": both must be understood in terms of differentials of force and can only be conceived as related. Subject and object are metaphysical illusions synonymous with the privilege of consciousness.[9] Freud, entirely without intending to, lodged a principle of care as relation without a subject-object structure within his thinking, in such concepts as unconscious registration of the experience of satisfaction, primary narcissism, and Eros. These concepts are structurally related to his passing conception of the mother's actual care of the infant as the unconscious origin of thought—*Objekteindrucke*, the differentiating registration of a *relation* to what can only be called a nonobjectified "object." For both Nietzsche and Freud, raised tension levels are intrinsic to differentiating processes not organized in subject-object terms. Time is thought as periodicity, repetition, rhythm. Can such conceptions be thought in relation to "care" in Heidegger's sense?

To answer this question, it is necessary also to understand Heidegger's concept of "concern." When he moves from care as being-in-the-world to concern as being-with-others, he examines another question essential to the therapeutic setting: the possibility that one person can understand another. In existential terms, just as Da-sein can only exist "in" a world, so it can only exist "with" others. Concern is to being-with-others what care is to being-in-the-world; being-with-others is constitutive for being-in-the-world (113–14). Heidegger discerns two possibilities of concern. One possibility takes the other's "care" away from him, *leaps in* for him. "In this concern, the other can become one who is dependent and dominated even if this domination is a tacit one and remains hidden from him" (114). By contrast, there is concern which does not leap in for the other, but leaps ahead of him, "not in order to take 'care' away from him, but first to give it back to him as such. This concern which essentially pertains to authentic care, that is, the existence of the other, and not to a *what* which it takes care of, helps the other to become transparent to himself *in* his care and *free* for it." This form of concern is "guided by considerateness and tolerance" (115). To it belongs the very possibility of understanding oneself *and* another, precisely because Da-sein *is* as being-with. Just as care makes the encounter of "something as something" possible before objectivity, so concern makes understanding the other possible without objectifying the other as a "what": "This understanding, like all understanding, is not a knowledge derived from cognition, but a primordially existential kind of being which first makes knowledge and cognition possible. Knowing oneself is grounded in primordially understanding being-with" (116).

As a form of psychotherapy, psychoanalysis has always seen itself as the form of concern that "does not leap in for the other." To help the patient become transparent to himself and to be free for his own care, to guard against tacit, hidden domination through interpretation of the transference, are explicit components of Freud's therapeutic setting. For Freud, these components of the setting are a combination of therapeutic ethics

and psychodynamic understanding. Heidegger's existential point that being-with-others and authentic concern themselves make therapy possible
most likely would be taken by Freud as an abstraction.

Yet this would leave Freud singularly uncomprehending in those situations in which understanding and concern themselves become the focus
of the patient's resistances. Clinically, these are the phenomena so con-
spicuous in the treatment of concrete, desymbolizing patients, patients
who almost universally can *only* see their relation to the therapeutic setting in terms of dependency and domination. Such patients have "fetishistic" transferences, because they view the analyst as an object who makes
good an objective lack within themselves, a fetish compensating for the
"reality of castration"; or because they view the analyst as embodying that
very lack. Either way, therapy is viewed as a form of dependency and
domination from which understanding and concern, which aim to free
the other for his or her own care, are conspicuously absent. The clinical literature on such patients is full of accounts of endless, stalemated
analyses, in which the patient feels hopelessly dependent and the analyst
hopelessly despairing. In Heidegger's terminology the patient would be
insisting that inauthentic concern simply *is* concern.

Existential Moods and the Flight from Concern

Heidegger has a complex analysis of how and why authentic concern
and understanding themselves can be turned away from. It is grounded
in what he calls the "everyday" existence of Da-sein as a "they-self." Our
preontological but existentially given way of "being-with-others" is as being like everyone else. In this everyday sense, being-in-the-world becomes
"absorption in the world," preoccupation with the objective presence of
the things in it (1996, 121). These inauthentic forms of being-in-the-world
and being-with-others are not unfortunate accidents, but "primordial"
phenomena. Why are such forms of inauthenticity primordial, why are
they intrinsic to being-in-the-world? Because of the relation between
turning away from authenticity and "mood."

Heidegger's analysis of mood is related to the existential analysis of being-in-the-world. Being-in-the-world is not an "interchange" between a
subject and an object. Nor is Da-sein this "between" itself. Either conception "*splits* the phenomenon beforehand, and there is no prospect of
ever putting it back together from the fragments" (124). In terms of the

inherent relatedness of Da-sein and world prior to any splitting, the literal meaning of Da-sein—being *there*—requires special attention: what is the "there" as being-in-the-world? Heidegger says that Da-sein's "there" is its "in," its existential spatiality. Being-*there* as being-*in* means that Da-sein "bears in its ownmost being the character of *not being closed*" (125; emphasis added). Heidegger calls Da-sein's openness "the clearing." Like "lingering with" or "dwelling with," the "clearing" is a precondition for any objective presence or absence, because it is the *possibility* of disclosure. And like authentic understanding, disclosure is not cognizable in the usual sense. The "they-self" of preoccupation with what is objectively present is "attuned" to the world such that disclosure and the clearing remain unthought. Such attunement is "mood."

What Heidegger calls "being in a mood," such that Da-sein unquestioningly exists in its everyday sense, has a complex structure. The ontic, everyday mode of existence *is* the way in which Da-sein evades clearing and disclosure as the *possibilities* of objective presence. Ontologically, however, this means that "in that to which such a mood pays no attention Da-sein is unveiled in its being delivered over to the there. In the evasion itself the there *is* something disclosed . . . *Attunement discloses Da-sein in its thrownness, initially and for the most part in the mode of an evasive turning away*" (127–28). In other words, everyday attunement or mood are symptomatic of the necessary forgetting of being. Just as such forgetting is metaphysical, and not psychological, so is mood. As attunement, mood is not something psychical, is not an inner condition which then reaches out and affects things. Rather, as an evasion of the ontological sense of being-*in*-the-world, mood is made possible by being-in-the-world. Da-sein's "openness to world" is primordially evaded in everyday preoccupation with the objectively present. The "splitting" that makes a subject-object structure appear irreducible is a component of the evasion of openness.

A psychoanalyst will have a great deal of trouble thinking of mood as something that does not come from within the psyche. Simultaneously, a psychoanalyst has no trouble at all conceiving an evasion that reveals what it evades. From a psychoanalytic point of view the two can be integrated by considering processes that occur within primary narcissism, *before* a subject-object structure, and yet always related to an "object." Because the term *object* is so unsuitable here, Heidegger's term, *world,* is preferable. If care and concern ontologically belong to being-in-the-world, then the patients who so strenuously resist this component of the setting manifest the evasion of openness. This is why they resist understanding and inter-pretation—not so much because of the content of the analyst's interpre-tations (the analyst's usual assumption), but because of entrenchment in objective presence, in everydayness.

What has traditionally made such patients so baffling for analysts is that they do not seem able to understand transference symbolically. Such patients' discourse is characterized by the certainty that whatever they feel in relation to the analyst is simply objectively true. They *know*, they are "attuned." *Difference and Disavowal* (2000) begins with the example of a patient who said that she *knew* that her analyst was angry at her for being late to her session. Since her knowledge was objective, there was no reason to question its significance. Such patients are preoccupied with objective presence in order to split off being-in the analytic setting as "world," as care and concern. This occurs in response to the openness of being-in-the-world (the setting). It is an attempted flight from a possibility that one cannot evade, precisely because one *is* this possibility, a possibility that also structures the setting.

The psychoanalyst would have many questions here. The first might be a clinical one. How would one interpret such defensive flight? What are its dynamics? Heidegger puts the analyst in the very difficult position of having to wonder whether evasion of openness is intrapsychic at all. One would have to make the difficult adjustment of thinking about processes occurring within primary narcissism, such that mood might not simply be an internal state. Further, one also would have to adjust to thinking about the patient's evasive "mood" in relation to the "existential structure" of the setting. "Transference" here might not be a repetition of an object relation to the analyst, a repetition of a piece of the patient's history as usually understood. This would take the analyst into uncharted territory.

There have been psychoanalytic accounts of defensive flight from con-cern. This topic was broached by Karl Abraham in 1924. He was the first to wonder how the infant emerges from domination by sadistic fantasies in which "part objects"—he coined the term—are incorporated and ex-pelled at will. How does it become possible to preserve the object in-ternally, to have some care for it? Abraham answered with a new theory of patterns of object relations which accompany the phases of infantile sexuality. He contended that once the infant could bite, oral incorporative love was inevitably destructive. He then divided the anal phase in two. In the first, expulsive anal phase, part objects are still expelled at will (in fantasy). In the second, retentive anal phase, there is a wish to hold on to the object in order to dominate and control it. This is the first step toward internal preservation of the object, the first mitigation of destructiveness on the way to object love.

Abraham's thinking opened the way for Melanie Klein. She considered the same problem, but came up with a different answer. Klein thought that within the oral phase objects are split into "good" and "bad," gratifying and frustrating, and are expelled at will. Because of the dominance of projection and splitting in this phase, she called it the paranoid-schizoid position. As rudimentary awareness dawns that incorporated and projected good and bad part objects might be the same "whole" object, there is anxiety over contamination of the good object by the bad, producing fear of loss of the good object. Klein calls this early fear of loss of the good object depressive anxiety. (She calls it "depressive" because Freud understood depression in terms of object loss.) For Klein, toleration of depressive anxiety is essential to the overcoming of splitting. Good and bad part objects are integrated in the "depressive position." In the paranoid-schizoid position, "reckless" aggression against the object is equal to self-destruction. Depressive position integration makes concern for the object and for oneself possible. Like Abraham, Klein (1946) gives a developmental account of the movement from unfettered destructiveness to concern. Her innovation is to see both positions as psychic structures that we unconsciously move between throughout life.

Winnicott rebaptized Klein's depressive position the "stage of concern"—although not in reference to Heidegger. His conception is that while the infant has sadistic, "ruthless" drive and fantasy experiences, the mother is always taking care of it. The mother's caretaking is an invisible "surround," the environment of primary narcissism. Winnicott thinks that the depressive position is not a question of integration of the good part object with the bad, but of sadistic drives and fantasies with the caretaking environment. When previously split instinct and caretaking are integrated, what Winnicott calls an "internal environment," in which concern for the object is concern for oneself, becomes possible. Winnicott makes the often overlooked point that if drives remain split from environment, that is, if depressive position integration provokes too much anxiety, interpretation of history is impossible in the clinical setting. For there to be history, there has to be the possibility of a process which occurs over time—historicity. Winnicott (1951) says that this temporal possibility develops out of the rhythm of environmental care—the infant is hungry, fed, and digests.

Heidegger says that care—taking time—is essential in order to encounter "something as something." Winnicott says that depressive position integration of environmental care as the "time factor" makes it possible to "do something about something" (1954, 263). In his work on transitional phenomena, Winnicott specifically links the environmental time factor to a conception of space. Transitional phenomena (as in the too-well-known examples of the security blanket or the teddy bear), are early forms of depressive position integration. Because this integration is derived from environment as primary narcissism, transitional phenomena maintain its organization, which is neither subjective nor objective (1951, 231). This is why the transitional "object" has to be thought as phenomenon: it exists in a time-space in which what *later* will be called subject and object are still simultaneously connected, but articulated. This is the temporal space of historicity. If depressive anxiety is too great, then this temporal space is closed, and historicity is precluded. There is no space of past related to, but not identical with, the present. If the analyst then interprets according to the assumption that the transference repeats the patient's history, the analyst ignores that the patient is evading the temporal space of historicity. Or in Winnicott's terms, the analyst is interpreting as if transitional space can be assumed, where in fact it is a question of establishing it. Equally the analyst may presume that the patient has come to analysis in order to "do something about something," while the patient is evading just that possibility, in order to evade care and concern.

Winnicott's conceptions of primary narcissism, concern, time, and space cannot simply be assimilated to Heidegger's. His conception of the time factor in relation to empirical need—the infant is hungry, is fed, and digests—would doubtless be seen by Heidegger in terms of objective presence. And Winnicott's account of why depressive anxiety might prevent integration simplistically states that environmental "provision" has been problematic. A mother has not adequately taken care of her baby, producing traumatic "impingement." It is not that such developmental thinking is incorrect. Clinical experience often, but not always, confirms it. It is more that it fails to take complex psychodynamics into account. In Freud's conception, the meeting of empirical need, the experience of satisfaction, is *also* a question of its unconscious registration. Because the unconscious is an "apparatus" capable of memory, it is always "differentiable," open. And it is open in terms of primary narcissism: its "differentiability" is not originally organized in subject-object terms. This differentiability is the *possibility* of modification of the unconscious, and is therefore a precondition of interpretation. Further, this structural possibility is always a question of raised tension levels and must be thought in relation to anxiety. Can such structural anxiety be conceived as "depressive anxiety"—anxiety over integration that evades care and concern? Is there an existential aspect of depressive anxiety?

Anxiety and Interpretation

Heidegger does have important things to say about anxiety in relation to interpretation and being-in-the-world. He reminds us that existential understanding is always about possibility. Possibility and being-in-the-world are conjoined as disclosure, the clearing. Interpretation itself is a development of such understanding, not as "acknowledgment of what has been understood," but as holding open the space of possibility (139). This space is the space for the encounter of "something as something," with the emphasis now on the "as" (140). (Heidegger might say that Winnicott's conception of transitional space does not think the "as" of something *as* something.) Interpretation in this sense does not demonstrate the meaning of what is objectively present. Rather, the "as-structure" of interpretation is the clarification of what is "always already" relevant, because of Da-sein's openness to world. "Always already" is the expression used by Heidegger to describe existential structures, structures irreducibly *there*.

Because interpretation is such a structure, Heidegger knows that he might be on very thin ice here. Scientific proof must never presume what it is to find, and yet he is proposing a theory of interpretation operating within a kind of a priori understanding. Is this a vicious circle? In conventional terms, yes. This is why historical interpretation is usually "banned *a priori* from the realm of exact knowledge" (1996, 143). Here we have the entire problem of *psycho*-analysis as an interpretive discipline with pretensions to scientific status. Since *existential* analysis treats the question forgotten by both the interpretive and scientific disciplines, Heidegger says that what appears to be a vicious circle is actually the result of understanding interpretation *only* in relation to grasping what is objectively present. In this traditional conception, the necessary circularity of interpretation, the "hermeneutical circle," is precisely what separates interpretation from objective science. In terms of analysis of being, however, the task is "to get into the 'circle' in the right way" (143). If there is a scientificity of existential analysis, it is a question of rigorous phenomenological *description*. Such description delineates the existential possibilities presumed, but forgotten, by both the interpretive and scientific disciplines. In principle, then, it is even more rigorous than the exact sciences (143). (Heidegger will continue to develop this theme throughout his life. He always asserts that the exact sciences are not sufficiently rigorous to understand their most basic presuppositions.) Far from being a vicious circle, the "as-structure" of understanding is intrinsic to meaning itself (143). In other words, "meaning" is no more irreducible than is objectivity: its precondition is the possibility of the "as-structure." Interpretation itself must be thought in relation to this structure.

Because interpretation is a form of discourse, its "as-structure" must be related to the structure of discourse itself. Heidegger refers to Aristotle's understanding of *logos* (discourse) as *synthesis* and *diairesis*: "when something is understood with regard to something else, it is taken together with it, so that this confrontation that *understands, interprets,* and articulates, at the same time takes apart what has been put together." The "as-structure" of interpretation and discourse means that "binding and separating can be further formalized to mean a 'relating'" (149). Existentially, then, interpretation is a relating that simultaneously differentiates and integrates. Here we find the relational structure, articulation as connection, that Deleuze thinks is common to Nietzsche's will to power, Freud's Eros, and Heidegger's being. Nietzsche and Heidegger explicitly think interpretation as a form of relation not conceivable by metaphysics, whether in terms of unconscious differentials of force or in terms of the as-structure. Freud himself did not entertain such a conception of interpretation. In either Nietzsche's or Heidegger's sense, he mistakenly assumed that interpretation could conform to the structure of objective, conscious knowledge.

Loewald did conceive interpretation as a form of relation. For him the "therapeutic action of psychoanalysis" depends upon internalization of the differential phenomenologically implicit to every interpretation. Internalization can take place because of the openness of the unconscious, an openness which Loewald explicitly links to primary narcissism and Eros. He categorically states that internalization can only be conceived as an interactive process, a form of relating that is *not* identification with an object (1980, 241). Interpretation, then, does not simply convey objective knowledge that reverses repressions.

This articulating-connecting form of relating is for Loewald empirically derived from the differential intrinsic to maternal care, making the theme of differentiation central to the structure of care. Winnicott only tangentially thinks difference in relation to care, but he does include depressive *anxiety* in his account of why analytic interpretation might misfire. Loewald has no theory at all of anxieties related to interpretation as articulation-connection, to internalization as the unconscious, phenomenological *possibility* of interpretation. Heidegger's understanding of interpretation in terms of discourse, the "as-structure," articulation-connection, itself produces the theory of existential anxiety.

This anxiety is a structural component of Da-sein's everyday existence, "thrownness" as the "they-self." As an ontological structure, thrownness has no moral connotation, and is not something that might be overcome in some advanced state of culture. Thrownness characterizes the they-self, preoccupied with the objectively present, "entangled" with it, "tranquilized" by it (Heidegger, 1996, 164). Without forgetting essential differences of level, we must recall here Nietzsche's herd mentality, which says no to difference in order to narcotize itself against pain. Nietzsche's conception is explicitly valuative: he undertakes a "transvaluation of all values" in order to affirm the "noble" difference conventionally seen as "evil" by the herd's ascetic ideal. Heidegger claims not to be engaged in valuative thinking. Rather, the tranquilized they-self is structured by the evasion which reveals what it evades. But if it *is* an evasion, then Da-sein's absorption in the they reveals "something like a *flight* of Da-sein from itself" (172). Again, without forgetting differences of level, we can recall that for Nietzsche the ascetic ideal is a manifestation of "life" against itself. Nietzsche's "life" and Heidegger's "Da-sein" are structured so that they must flee *themselves*, "defend against" themselves. Psychoanalytically such defense against oneself is conceived as "splitting." Can one say that "life" and "Da-sein" split themselves in their flights from themselves?

Flight is related to fear. Heidegger says that fear is conventionally understood in relation to something dangerous that is approaching. When Da-sein turns away from itself it must be shrinking back from something threatening, "yet this being has the same kind of being as the one which shrinks back from it—it is Da-sein itself" (174). Thus, what Da-sein shrinks back from cannot be grasped as *something* frightening. Heidegger calls the fear that makes Da-sein flee itself *Angst*. Because *Angst* is not about an innerworldly being, the threat is completely indefinite. It emerges from no definite region—it is already there and yet nowhere. One has *Angst* about being-in-the-world. *Angst* is the mood or attunement that discloses the world as such (175). And because being-*in*-the-world is disclosure or openness, in Da-sein's flight from itself its "authenticity of being a self is closed off and repressed" (173). Heidegger provides an account of a structural anxiety that produces defense against openness. When Da-sein "represses" being-in-the-world, it is tranquilized by objective presence. Heidegger would insist that this "repression" is philosophical, but it seems very close to the psychical. One might even say that it produces the psychical as subjectivity enclosed in itself in the everyday, thrown sense.

The patients who are preoccupied by objective knowledge in the analytic setting are themselves in flight from the analytic setting as being-in-the-world, from unconscious differentiability or openness. Their defensive closedness can be conceived as a form of splitting *themselves* equivalent to a flight from interpretation as a differentiating relation. The major psychoanalytic theories of splitting are also always about *self*-splitting. Klein said that the "ego cannot split the object without splitting *itself*" (1946, 181). In his late writings Freud placed increasing emphasis on a different form of "self-splitting"—the "splitting of the ego." He ultimately came to see splitting of the ego as intrinsic to the very "process of defense" (1940b). All defense is directed against something psychically registered, but anxiety provoking. Defense intrinsically splits the ego, because something registered as psychically real is repudiated. Self-splitting is the registration and repudiation of reality—disavowal.

When Freud explained fetishism in terms of splitting and disavowal he entangled himself in the idea that the fetishist disavows the "reality of castration." In Heidegger's sense, one can say that Freud's theory treats the absence of something once objectively present (castration in the largest sense), as an everyday fear of something approaching. Freud in fact says almost exactly this in *Inhibition, Symptom, and Anxiety* (1926) when he links anxiety as the fear of an approaching danger to separation anxiety; castration itself is then an approaching threat of loss. Certainly, the fetishist does seem to treat castration as an objective threat. Why else would he need the presence of an object in order to make himself potent? But the threat of objective absence always remediable by objective presence tranquilizes the fetishist against the reality of sexual difference, which is what is primordially registered and repudiated. Can the anxieties which produce repudiation of difference be related to the *Angst* of being-in-the-world? Can sexual difference be understood as a relation that articulates and connects?

When Heidegger says that the meaning of being is the meaning of the difference between being and beings (1996, 33), he opens the possibility that questions of "empirical difference" cannot simply be understood in terms of objective presence or absence. He writes: "to be missing means not being objectively present. A lack, as the not being objectively present of what ought to be is a determination of being of objective presence. In this sense, nothing can be lacking in existence, not because it is complete, but because its character of being is distinguished from any kind of objective presence" (261). Being, difference, is not a being, but it is not absent—or present. Existentially, difference is a question of an articulating and connecting relation, the "as-structure." Existential interpretation, not entrapped by the conventional opposition of the scientific and historical disciplines, is itself a form of "binding and separating [that] can be further formalized to mean a 'relating'" (149). Any splitting operation directed against the reality of difference would be related to something like *Angst*, the fear that comes from everywhere and nowhere, because it is not grounded in presence or absence. *Angst* is fear of being-*in* as being-*open*, fear of the "as-structure." Any repudiation of the "reality of difference" would have to produce a fetishistic or concrete transference against the possibility of interpretation itself.

Heidegger's brief references to fetishism and signs already understood something like "concreteness." A fetish as sign may coincide with what it indicates, meaning that "the sign has not yet become free from that for which it is a sign" (76). The fetish-sign does not have the "spatiality" of being-in-the-world (77, 102). When transference in particular becomes a fetish-sign, the spatiality of interpretation is closed off and repressed, to use Heidegger's expression, or registered and repudiated, to use Freud's. As a response to the *Angst* of the possibility of interpretation—being-in as being-open—the fetishistic transference is the result of a self-splitting. It is an evasion of a possibility that one *is*, a defensive flight into objective presence. This is where the question of being is uncircumventable for psychoanalytic theory and practice.

Winnicott (1951) understood transitional *space* as the possibility of interpretation built into the analytic setting. He offered an empirical theory of why depressive anxiety might collapse transitional space (environmental failure). Loewald understood that the differential implicit to interpretation produces a nonobjective form of relating that he calls internalization, but he does not link internalization to anxiety. *Difference and Disavowal* (2000) proposed a clinical account of "internalization anxiety," a specific and intense fear that emerges when the analyst effectively interprets fetishistic or concrete defenses against the *possibility* of interpretation. Such interpretation addresses the "self-splitting" intrinsic to registration and repudiation of being-*in* the setting. Because the differentiating process of interpretation comes from everywhere and nowhere in analytic space, defense against "internalization," in Loewald's sense, is related to anxieties which are not about absence, about loss as an approaching danger. Like *Angst*, internalization anxiety is more general, more threatening than objective anxiety.

Everything that Heidegger has said about interpretation explains why effective intervention in the realm of self-splitting and internalization anxiety has to be phenomenological-descriptive. Such descriptive interpretation addresses the invisible, phenomenological, *process* of defense directed against an equally invisible phenomenological possibility of historicity. Therefore it is not causal in the usual psychoanalytic sense. A typically entrenched, long-term analytic stalemate dominated by concreteness can be transformed if the analyst moves from objective interpretation grounded in the patient's history to *description of the splitting processes against the differential relating intrinsic to the analytic setting*. This is akin to Nietzsche's conception of noncausal interpretation which "gives a name to a process." The surprising result can be the liberation of nearly traumatic "internalization anxiety."

Patients will sometimes use a "symbolic-existential" vocabulary for the first time when such anxiety is liberated. Examples include the patient who "knew" that her analyst was angry at her for being late. In this analysis there were many years of stalemate characterized by concreteness on the patient's part, and insistence on objective, historical, causal interpretation on the analyst's part. Over time, the analyst shifted to description of the dedifferentiating interaction between him and the patient. Unexpectedly, the patient one day said: "This feels like trees flying through the air. I want you to be more like me and *stop being different*." Another patient emphatically insisted that any interpretation repeated an objective trauma from her past. For many years the analyst had either said the same thing or had been reduced to countertransferential withdrawal, because interpretation of history did not modify the patient's concreteness. When the analyst began to interpret why she and the patient could not be "on the same page" about what they were doing together—that is, when the analyst interpreted the splitting that had prevented analytic relating—the patient unexpectedly responded, "If you and I were ever on the same page, my world would fall apart."

In another long-term, stalemated analysis dominated by the patient's objective literalness, the analyst had often interpreted that the patient viewed him as being like her father. The patient agreed, because she said that the analyst was indeed like her father. When the analyst began to describe the patient's relief at "knowing" that he was like her father, so that she could automatically split off any differential relation between them, the patient responded, "When you say that I feel like my brain is fibrillating." The patient was having a sudden, traumatic "heart attack" of the thinking process. Modification of the splitting that had allowed her to evade being-*in* the analytic setting as being-*open* raised tension levels in a way that felt almost physiological.

Freud's revolution was to think the unconscious as body-mind in terms of sexuality. We have here the more ontological possibility of thinking body-mind—a "fibrillating brain"—in terms of articulation-connection as a form of relating. In essence, this is what Freud called "originally unconscious thought," the differentiating registration of a relation. Such registrations must be thought as body-mind because they simultaneously concern the physiological experience of satisfaction and unconscious registration of it.

Uncanniness and Interpretation

Heidegger's analysis of *Angst* brings him to the theme he most famously shares with Freud—uncanniness, *Unheimlichkeit*. Because *Angst* comes from everywhere and nowhere, it gives one an uncanny feeling in the literal sense of *Unheimlichkeit*—not-being-at-home. The pervasive feeling of not being at home in one's everyday world collapses its familiarity. Heidegger specifies that when Da-sein is brought back from its everyday they-self it is "individuated," but individuated as being-in-the-world. To paraphrase: Da-sein is not an individual subject, but individuates in terms of articulation as connection. To individuate as being-in and being-open brings Da-sein into "the existential 'mode' of *not-being-at-home*" (176). The flight toward the tranquilized familiarity of being-in-the-world as objective presence is a flight from uncanniness. But since Da-sein evades—or splits—itself in this flight, "uncanniness constantly pursues Da-sein" (177). The everyday sense of uncanniness—the "weirdness" in which familiar things somehow become unfamiliar—"'phases out' . . . existentially and ontologically primordial not-being-at-home" (177). Not-being-at-home is primordial, because as always already being-*in*-the-world, Da-sein is always already *outside* itself. Always already outside itself, Da-sein is intrinsically "ahead of itself, 'beyond itself'" (178), that is, never comfortably "at home" with itself. The tranquilized they-self understands "uncanniness" only as an exceptional "weirdness," in order to flee Da-sein's being ahead of itself. Again, one hears the echo of Nietzsche's herd and its "no" to difference.

In his essay on the uncanny Freud cites a long dictionary entry in which at-homeness, *Heimlichkeit*, comes to coincide with not-at-homeness, *Unheimlichkeit*. The route to this coincidence of opposites is through the image of the "home" as an interior space in which things can be hidden. The unfamiliar can emerge at the heart of the familiar. Freud compares the unfamiliar at the heart of the familiar to the unconscious "hidden" by repression from the everyday, conscious sense of oneself. He too alleges a primal uncanniness. But his essay contains much more. Freud looks at uncanniness in terms of the "weirdness" of doubling phenomena, of machines that appear to be alive, of automatic repetition, and of the blurring of the boundary between the imaginary and the real.

Doubling is particularly important here because Freud understands its uncanniness in relation to primary narcissism. He refers to the earliest stages of development in which the ego has not yet separated the world from itself, but in which there is still "something" other than itself (1919, 236). (This is another example of Freud's continual, and continually forgotten, postulation of unconscious articulation-connection not organized in subject-object terms.) The encounter with what is other than oneself that is oneself—the "differentiating double"—is primordially uncanny. It leaves one vertiginously undecided in relation to the most basic question: is it me? is it not me? One can say the same about the unconscious itself. Since it is not part of what one consciously considers to be oneself, and yet emerges from "within oneself," it has to provoke the feeling that it is me and not-me.

All the uncanny phenomena examined by Freud share the "*x* is not-*x*" structure, which he had already found in his dictionary entry (the *Heimlich* is the *Unheimlich*). Freud is implying a homology between language and unconscious processes. This is not surprising in light of his earlier essay "'On the Antithetical Meaning of Primal Words'" (1910). There he also alleged that the history of language repeats the history of the transition from the unconscious to consciousness (161). The further back one goes, the more one finds words with double meanings, reflecting the coincidence of opposites characteristic of the unconscious. But here the double meaning of *Unheimlichkeit* also means that double meanings themselves have an *Unheimlich* effect. As in the encounter with the differentiating double, they leave one structurally undecided about whether they mean *x* or not-*x*. The unconscious and literary fiction themselves, in their shared capacity to produce uncanniness, can leave one equally undecided about whether something is "dead" or "alive," "real" or "not real." This suspension can be repeated automatically by mechanical devices which seem to be alive. This reference to automatic repetition produces Freud's mention of the "eternal recurrence of the same," characterized in Chapter 1 as a "Nietzschean cliché." Does the use of "eternal recurrence" to describe uncanniness add a Heideggerean dimension that might be less clichéd?

Heidegger had mentioned doubling phenomena rather dismissively in his account of understanding as concern. In order to stress the existential character of understanding, he had contrasted it to "the problematic of understanding 'the psychical life of others'" (116). Just as mood is not existentially intrapsychic, but a structure of being-in-the-world, so existential understanding of others is not a bridge from one's own subjectivity to another's subjectivity. Heidegger says that the bridge from subject to subject is "unhappily" called "empathy" (117). The ontological problem with empathy is that as a relation of subject to subject, it makes being-with-others "a projection of one's own being toward oneself 'into an other.' The other is the double of the self" (117). In such projective doubling, being-*with* as being-*open* is not even a question.

Is Heidegger implying something about psychoanalysis? Are the analyst's interpretations a form of projective doubling? The dismissal of psychoanalytic interpretation as projection is almost as old as psychoanalysis itself. We know from one of Freud's letters that Fliess had contemptuously called him a "mind reader" who was merely projecting his own thoughts into others (1985, 447). Much later, Freud became interested in the criticism, and answered it in terms of the unconscious "grain of truth" in every projection (1922b). However, the criticism becomes more barbed when it is made by a patient in analysis. For example, the patient who "knew" that her analyst was angry at her for being late dismissed any attempt to interpret her anger as his projection. In another example, a patient said to her analyst: "I know you're a jerk, just like me—and don't tell me that's transference." In his published account of this case, the analyst commented that interpretations of projection were useless (Frosch, 1995, 441). Why would one remain in an interpretive psychotherapy if one thinks that interpretation is merely the analyst's projection?

Kleinian theory accounts for such clinical binds with a special version of projection—projective identification. The patient has hypothetically split off a bad or hated part of him- or herself, and has projected it *into* the analyst. The analyst is then identified with this aspect of the patient, and becomes the patient's persecutory double. Bion extends Klein's thinking with his idea that the analyst is being used to "contain" an "unmetabolizable" aspect of the patient (1967, 44ff). This unmetabolizable part must not be prematurely forced back on the patient. Clinically, however, neither *interpretation* of projective identification (Klein) nor *containment* of projective identification (Bion) can modify the patient's defensive evasion of the interpretive function of the setting itself.

Conscious dismissal of interpretation as projective doubling is grounded in the unconscious registration and repudiation of the openness or difference implicit to interpretation. The patient then maintains an everyday objectivity which *only* understands interpretation as subjective, and hence questionable. Heidegger's contention that "empathic doubling" belongs to everyday evasion of being-with as being-open is entirely to the point. But is everyday, empathic doubling an evasion of uncanny existential doubling—a possibility not considered by Heidegger? When a patient is entrenched in defense against the possibility of interpretation, is not only *Angst*-like internalization anxiety being split off, but also the essential uncanniness of the setting itself?

The setting is existentially uncanny because therapeutic need is both self-preservative and differentiating. Freud says that primary narcissism is uncanny because within it the world is my double, but my differentiating double. I am and am not it. All processes that occur within primary narcissism have this quality. The tension raising registration of the experience of satisfaction *is* the opening to the "differentiating double." In fact, the double is the minimal condition of differentiation as simultaneous connection and articulation: it is and is not me. To increase the difficulty, the double is also the possibility of identificatory dedifferentiation: it is me, you are me, world is me. This is the structure of Heidegger's empathic doubling or Klein's projective identification. But Heidegger says that in the flight from uncanniness, empathic doubling itself is a flight from differential relating. In a sense not described by Heidegger, all differential relating would involve the most uncanny of doubling phenomena: the inescapable tie to what is (not) me as the possibility of interpretation. When a concrete patient says "I know you're a jerk just like me—and don't tell me that's transference," the patient is making the analyst her dedifferentiated double. But the patient is doing so in order to preclude the possibility of transference interpretation, in which her double both is and is not her. This is particularly clear in the case in which the analyst began to describe the patient's defenses against interpretation, to which the patient responded: "I want you to be more like me, and stop being different." The patient is potentially in the space in which the analyst's interpretive difference *is* her own difference, the space in which the possibility of interpretation opens her to what is and is not her. Because all defense is grounded in splitting, effective interpretation always concerns that which feels as if it is "me and not me." To resist interpretation per se is to flee the uncanny individuation of being-in the analytic setting, the opening to differential relating. One can then objectively dismiss interpretation as subjective projection.

The opening to a differential relation *is* the unconscious as an apparatus "in the world"—primary narcissism. For the analyst to interpret what is unconscious, he or she must be in the position of the differentiating double, the paradoxical mother of primary narcissism, who is and is not the baby. This is why the analytic setting must never simply be understood in relation to empirical mothering. Winnicott (1954), for example, cannot see that the time factor of empirical mothering (the rhythmic periodicity of hunger, feeding, satisfaction), produces the automatic repetition of tension raising registration of the differentiating double: the environment mother of primary narcissism. Loewald (1980) cannot see that for exactly the same reasons, internalization would have to be resisted, because as the condition of therapeutic change it could hardly be less reassuring—it is tied to *Angst* and *Unheimlichkeit*.

When Freud came to see splitting as the *process* of defense, he simultaneously came to see fetishism as the model for all compromise formations; both are based on the possibility of registration *and* repudiation of reality. But if fetishism itself is about the "reality of difference," then reality itself must be thought in relation to the *Angst* and uncanniness of difference. Heidegger says that the they-self preoccupied with objective presence (and absence) evades the uncanniness of being-in-the-world. Da-sein is *individuated*—i.e. differentiated—in being-*in* as being-*open*. As Heidegger consistently says, this means that Da-sein is outside itself. Thus, he writes: "What is more alien to the they self than the self individualized to itself in uncanniness?" (1996, 255). The uncanny, individualized self here cannot mean anything like the narcotizingly familiar self of subjectivity, which empathically doubles itself to understand others. Rather, this is a "self" as differential relation, open to interpretation as differential relation. In either existential or psychoanalytic terms, this is the "self" of primary narcissism, the "self" that exists as its double, the not-me, the "world," to which need and the psychic apparatus open it.

Resistance to interpretation is most powerfully a resistance to transference interpretation. ("I know you're a jerk just like me—and don't tell me that's transference.") Freud's enormous innovation at the outset of his thinking was to see that neurosis produces transference for the same reasons that neurosis is grounded in the past: the relation to the analyst will include repetition of the patient's repressed history. Interpretation of transference becomes the key clinical-theoretical concept. But Freud had no conception of how anything like historicity, or the nonobjective reality of difference, could be the possibility of history and object relations. Thus, he famously said that when the transference cannot be interpreted historically, analytic therapy is impossible. He could not understand that the possibility of both transference *and* interpretation is grounded in historicity, in the primordial uncanniness of the "self" as differential relation.

Psychoanalysts often assume a reassuringly fictive quality when dealing with transference, what they call its "as-if" quality. Patient and analyst are presumed to share this assumption, which is actually quite complex. For example: I, the analyst, can say to you, the patient, that you feel toward me as you did toward your father, because we both know that I am not your father. We know this because we know the difference between an internal feeling and an external object, between past and present, between the fictive and the real. As concerns the latter in particular, we both know that fiction itself can produce a feeling of reality, but is not real—and hence neither is transference. When the patient does not share these assumptions the analyst can give up, as Freud did, or persevere in the usual way, while presuming that the patient can somehow be brought around to the obvious, objective truth of the analyst's presuppositions. Neither approach understands that fictive reality effects, uncanny doubling, repetition, and suspension between opposites are all built into any possible thinking about differentiability. The double is doubly uncanny: its suspension between me and not-me suspensively opens and closes the space of difference.

This is the reality registered and repudiated by the patients who objectively see the analyst as their double. When the patient says, "I know you're a jerk just like me—and don't tell me that's transference," the patient is saying that an apparently objective doubling of "the reality of castration"—patient and analyst are *really lacking* intelligence—is preferable to "existential" doubling—the "me"–"not me" differentiating process linked to intelligence. Like the patient whose brain was fibrillating, this patient too was splitting off the openness of "originally unconscious thought." This empathic, dedifferentiating doubling registers *and* repudiates the differential doubling of the possibility of interpretation. In his account, the "jerk" analyst did say that there was something about the possibility of interpretation that was linked to "overwhelming affect" (Frosch, 1995, 443). From both Freud's and Heidegger's points of view, one can understand such affect in terms of the link between primordial uncanniness, anxiety, and primary narcissism as being-in-the-world. In primary narcissism, as in being-in-the-world, affect or mood is relational, but—as always—not in subject-object terms.

Heidegger predictably says that the conflation of objective presence with reality itself evades being-in-the-world. Less predictably, he then says: *"The objective presence together of the physical and the psychical is ontically and ontologically completely different from the phenomenon of being-in-the-world"* (190; original emphasis). A psychoanalysis that understands the unconscious as the objective being-together of the physical and the psychic—on the whole, Freud's major presupposition—will not be able to account for the unconscious possibility of the analytic setting as being-in-the-world. Further, it will not be able to understand the setting as care: "being (not beings) is dependent upon the understanding of being, that is, *reality (not the real) is dependent upon care*" (196; emphasis added).

Wherever it is a question of understanding the setting in terms of empirical maternal care, as for Loewald and Winnicott, there is registration and repudiation of care itself as differential relating. This is why Loewald's and Winnicott's analyses of the setting are so important, but also why they must be read symptomatically. In terms of the psychic apparatus, maternal care itself has to have a tension raising, uncanny quality, because it is always the registration of difference within the organization of primary narcissism. *Real* gratification of need through maternal care *is* the *reality* of differential relating as existential care.

Truth and Interpretation

If reality is dependent upon differential relating, if interpretation is grounded in a differentiable unconscious, can one dispense with the question of the truth of interpretation? If the possibility of interpretation has nothing to do with objectivity, then the entire question of whether interpretation is or is not objective would be misguided. Nietzsche already considered this question in relation to unconscious processes, and understood the truth of interpretation not as the discovery of something objective, but as infinite process. As active, interpretation opens up unconscious differentials of force, new areas of reality. As existential analysis, interpretation is phenomenological description. In relation to the registration and repudiation of differentiating processes, interpretation would seem to be a combination of both, because it is descriptive and tension raising. "Would seem to be," because we have as yet no integration of interpretation as active force and interpretation as phenomenological description. The link is in Heidegger's existential conception of truth.

In line with his symptomatic approach, Heidegger cannot simply dismiss the traditional understanding of truth. It belongs to the "forgetting of being." It is no accident that the metaphysical conception of being in terms of beings always thinks being in relation to truth. In one of his annotations, Heidegger writes that this is "the real place to begin the leap into Da-sein" (1996, 197). The unquestioned traditional concept of truth inherited from Aristotle is that truth is agreement. In our era, this means agreement of a *subject's* representation with the *object* represented. The inclusion of the subject here is the great Cartesian innovation. Particularly as reelaborated by Kant, this innovation simultaneously established the modern metaphysics of conscious subjectivity, which Freud contested, and the modern conception of science, which Freud on the whole accepted. Heidegger reinterprets this conception in relation to being-in-the-world as disclosure, and rethinks the meaning of truth. He says that a true statement is one that discovers beings in a literal sense: it lets beings be seen. Heidegger here employs another gesture that will remain constant in his work—the return to the Greek sense of truth as *aletheia*. He understands *aletheia* as "un-forgetting," "unconcealment," from the privative *a-* and *lethe*. Truth as unconcealment cannot mean agreement between a subject's representation and the object represented, since it is about the truth of being, not beings. When Da-sein takes time to take care of beings, it can "discover" them, because disclosedness is the basic character of Da-sein as being-in-the-world. This is another example of the (vicious) circle of interpretation, and again it is a question of getting into the circle in the right way.

Heidegger by now has a complete existential conception of the being of Da-sein as care. It is a complex structure of being-ahead-of-itself (being-in as being-outside, Da-sein as possibility); of always already being-in-the-world (being-in as the opening of historicity); and as always being-together-with things and others. In terms of this complete conception, Da-sein is as disclosedness, as unconcealment, as *aletheia*. Hence the correct entry into the circle: "Da-sein *is 'in the truth'*" (203), in the existential sense of truth as unconcealment. However, Da-sein also always *is* in the everyday sense of absorption in objective presence, where truth as agreement holds sway. Since this truth forgets the truth of being as unconcealment, "*Da-sein is in 'untruth' in accordance with its constitution of being*. . . . The full existential and ontological meaning of the statement 'Da-sein is in the truth' also says equiprimordially that 'Da-sein is in untruth'" (204).

"Untruth" here means "concealment": the traditional conception of truth conceals truth itself (as unconcealment). The *a-* of *aletheia*, or the un- of unconcealment, implies that to bring beings into truth, truth itself must be freed from its traditional understanding. "Beings are torn from concealment" as a kind of robbery (204). Later, Heidegger says that because of Dasein's "*own tendency to cover things over* . . . the existential analytic constantly has the character of *doing violence*" (288). Here then, phenomenological-descriptive interpretation is unthinkable without force. Or rather it *is* force as the counterforce to Da-sein's evasion of itself. Evading itself, Da-sein splits itself from truth as bringing into the open, as unconcealment. A truthfulness of existential analysis, a "science of being as such," cannot be grounded in the understanding of truth as *agreement*. Such agreement is the dedifferentiating positing of an identity, which conceals its own violence *as* concealment. Only in these terms can one analyze what belongs "to the concept of a science of *being as such*" (211).

The force of truth as unconcealment is the tension of differential relating. For Freud, as for Nietzsche, difference is always a difference of force. This is another reason why Deleuze can link will to power with Eros: both are conceptions of difference as relation in terms of pain or raised tension. Nietzsche opposed any view of science that thought in terms of identities, equivalences. This is the reactive—Cartesian or Kantian—"science" whose faith in truth is part of the narcotizing ascetic ideal. When Freud thought about the truth of interpretation, he generally fell back upon the conception of truth as identity-producing agreement. Psychoanalysis ever since has been divided along the lines of the two traditional interpretations of interpretation: it is either scientific and objective, or not scientific and subjective. However, Freud's theory does contain the possibility of thinking interpretation in terms of the differentiability of the unconscious, which would have to link interpretation to both primary narcissism and raised tension.

When Loewald (1980) links internalization of a differential to primary narcissism and Eros, he is quite attentive to the idea that Eros itself is a tension raising principle. Loewald, however, only thinks of raised tension levels in relation to ego development, "binding" in the usual sense of secondary process. He does not look at the obvious: raised tension, particularly in relation to differentiation, is also for Freud the definition of pain, and even trauma. Therefore, precisely because the interpretive stance of the setting is derived from differentiating processes in primary narcissism, analytic care as interpretation must be thought in relation to force or violence. And, in Freudian or Heideggerian terms, there would have to be a counterforce of evasion or concealment of the tension of interpretation.

Heidegger would probably contest any direct alignment of Nietzsche's understanding of active interpretation with his own understanding of the violence of interpretation. Nonetheless, both conceive differential relating (will to power, being) in flight from itself. This is why both understand interpretation in terms of force, and attempt to free it from objectivistic and subjectivist presumptions. Any psychotherapy that restricted itself to understanding interpretation as either objective correspondence (science) or subjective coherence (hermeneutics) would be engaged in the dedifferentiating, narcotizing, tranquilizing flight from pain or the uncanny. The psychoanalytic theories which only view care and concern in terms of *object* relations cannot think care and concern as differential *relating*,[10] and therefore remain mired in sterile debates about the objectivity or subjectivity of interpretation. And such theories would be incapable of understanding the temporality of difference *as* the temporality of interpretation.

Time, Finitude, Interpretation

For Nietzsche the temporality of will to power *is* eternal return, because difference is finite if one dispenses with the idea of an infinitely different God. Infinite past time and finite difference produce repetition of differentials of force, such that no permanent equilibrium can ever be reached. This is why "nothing is self-sufficient" and why there is no timelessness. Actively differentiating interpretation would have to be temporal in this sense. It cannot be grounded in any conception of atemporal, permanent truth or in any conception of truth as identity producing.

For Heidegger too, interpretation is inherently temporal, because it is phenomenological description of the possibility of *historicity.* Because Da-sein is historical, and is "in the truth" as unconcealment, it is as interpretation. Heidegger too grounds his understanding of time and interpretation in finitude. However, his conception of finitude is quite different from Nietzsche's.

The climax of *Being and Time* is the analysis of finitude as being-toward-death. Being-toward-death is grounded in Da-sein's being-in as being-outside, in Da-sein's always being ahead of itself. In this way, says Heidegger, Da-sein's not-yet belongs to Da-sein as possibility, as being-ahead-of-itself. To be essentially ahead of oneself is to be essentially toward one's not-yet, one's end. Death is the end of Da-sein as the not-yet. This is the possibility, the future, which Da-sein takes over as soon as it exists (1996, 228). Heidegger now says that being-toward-death, the essential finitude of Da-sein, the possibility of the impossibility of Da-sein, is Da-sein's "*ownmost nonrelational possibility not to be bypassed. . . .* Its existential possibility is grounded in the fact that Da-sein is essentially disclosed to itself, in the way of being-ahead-of-itself. This structural factor of care has its most primordial concretion in being-toward-death" (232). The *Angst* that discloses world as world, the primordial uncanniness of care, is being-toward-death—not as fear of one's own demise, but as the "ownmost," immanent possibility of care as being-ahead-of-oneself (233). Again and again, Heidegger insists that death as Da-sein's most extreme possibility reveals Da-sein's "wholeness" (239) as nonrelational, in that it is the most extreme individualization of Da-sein (243). This cannot mean individualization of Da-sein as a solipsistic subject to which world is then added. Grounded in care as anticipation, being-toward-death allows one to understand the end of being-in-the-world, the end of relational being. Heidegger says that anticipation of the nonrelational possibility forces the being that anticipates into taking over its ownmost being of its own accord (243). When anticipation frees Da-sein for its ownmost possibility as determined by the end, it understands itself as finite (244). Without such a nonrelational end, one could not conceive of the finitude of Da-sein, an essential component of primordial temporality.

Heidegger connects the readiness for the *Angst* of being-toward-death to existential guilt. Just as existential anxiety comes from everywhere and nowhere, existential guilt is not about a moral failure or lack, but about the "not-ness," the "nullity" that pervades Da-sein as being-toward-death (273). In authentic anticipation, in being-toward-death, Da-sein assumes *Angst* and guilt. Heidegger calls this "resoluteness" (274). As anticipatory, resoluteness provides insight into the authentic temporality evaded by the flight into the they-self and its "vulgar" understanding of time (281). Authentic temporality derives from *anticipatory* resoluteness, being-toward one's "ownmost" possibility, as "the primordial phenomenon of the *future*" (299). This is an "existential future," because it does not mean a not-yet actual *now*, but rather the "not-ness" intrinsic to being-toward-death as what one *is*. This "existential future" is Da-sein's coming-toward-itself as it has always already been: "Authentically futural, Da-sein is authentically *having been* . . . having-been arises from the future" (299).

Here, we must recall the structure of care as both being-ahead-of-oneself (now reinterpreted as the authentic future of being-toward-death), and as always already being-in-the-world (now reinterpreted as the having-been of historicity). How are these to be integrated with the third structural element of care, always being-together-with things and others?

Heidegger conceives a *resolute* being-together as active, as *making* present, as letting *what presences* in the world be encountered in action. *Temporality* is the unified phenomenon of a future that makes present in the process of having been. Temporality makes possible the authentic potentiality of being a whole of anticipatory resoluteness. *"Temporality reveals itself as the meaning of authentic care"* (300).

The structure of care as temporality (being-ahead of itself as future, already-being in as past, and being-together with as present) is not an earlier and later, a not yet and a no longer, in the vulgar sense of time. If it were, care would be something that occurs and elapses "in time" as objectively present (301). Heidegger can now make his fundamental point: "Temporality 'is' not a *being* at all. It is not, but rather *temporalizes* itself" (302). The phenomena of being toward, back to, and together with "reveal temporality as the ekstatikon par excellence. Temporality is the primordial 'outside of itself' in and for itself" (302). Future, past, and present are the *ecstasies* of temporality. Temporality is not a being that first emerges from itself: "its essence is temporalizing in the unity of the *ecstasies*." In vulgar time, on the contrary, time is a pure succession of nows without beginning and end. Vulgar time levels down the ecstatic character of primordial temporality (302). The pure succession of nows is endless, infinite, while Da-sein *exists finitely* (303). The finitude of primordial temporality does not mean that time does not go on, and does not mean empirical stopping. It is a characteristic of temporalizing as the toward *oneself*, i.e. as anticipatory resoluteness (303). Thus, Heidegger has integrated the temporality of finitude as anticipation, being-*in* as being-*outside*, and the critique of objective presence. If the temporality of "worldless" objective presence is the infinite series of now points, the temporality of being-in-the-world can only be the anticipatory, futural "outside itself." Because it cannot be thought in terms of objective presence, such time is a "process": it temporalizes itself. As anticipatory it has to be finite. As finite, as being-toward-death, however, *it is nonrelational in an existential sense.*

Does guaranteeing the finitude of time with being-toward-death compromise interpretation as differential *relating*? Would Nietzsche say that resolute assumption of "nullness" and death sneaks in the ascetic ideal by the back door? Wouldn't Nietzsche say that the question of finitude is a question of "being-toward-life": life as finite difference of force (will to power), life as repetition (eternal return), life as a "being-in-the-world" such that "nothing is self-sufficient" and nothing is timeless?

Such questions are actually too simple. Nietzsche, in *The Gay Science,* had defined life as a "very rare species of death" (1974, 183). In *The Will to Power* life as death is intrinsic to difference as connection-articulation, since every articulation is also a breaking down, a decay (1968, §655). Heidegger had written that just "as too little is presupposed for the ontology of Da-sein if one starts from a worldless I and provides it with an object, so too it is short sighted to make 'life' a problem, and then *occasionally also* take death into account" (1996, 291). Almost at the end of *Being and Time* Heidegger further specifies the way in which the everyday evasion of death is structurally related to everyday, vulgar time. He says that infinite now time is a flight from finitude, from being-toward-death, from authentic futurality (389). Inauthentic knowledge of fleeting time that always passes away derives from Da-sein's fleeting knowledge of its death (390). In other words, death as the most extreme *individualization* of Da-sein, its "ownmost nonrelational possibility," is the differential structure of the outside-itself, of time as the "ekstatikon par excellence," of being-in-the-world as care. Since being-in is understood as being-outside and being-open, it is the ground of Da-sein as disclosure, as interpretation. The existential understanding of death as nonrelational finitude is the full understanding of interpretation as care. Everyday time as the infinite succession of now points and everyday evasion of death are Da-sein's flight from the reality of care and death, from the *Angst* and uncanniness of finitude, from interpretation as temporally ecstatic: time as the possibility of being-outside-oneself.

Time, Resistance to Interpretation, Apparatus, Care

All of these concepts clarify the structure of resistance to interpretation. A patient's "objective" sense of the "subjective" nature of all interpretation produces both dismissal of what the analyst says and insistence on the "realness" of any perception about the analyst. Both are combined with a seemingly paradoxical willingness to stay in analysis "infinitely." Perceptual consciousness objectively assesses reality according to the principle of "I see it *now*." The dream as hallucination too, is governed by perceptual identity and temporal immediacy: if I see it now it is objectively real. For this reason there is no past and no future in dreams, only the "now" of perceptual identity and temporal immediacy. Moreover, the hallucinatory awakening of consciousness in dreams guarantees their economic function. A dream *is* a fulfillment of a wish, because the hallucinatory awakening of consciousness during sleep discharges tension through perception itself, instead of through the muscular apparatus, as in the waking state. In the analytic setting, a patient can discharge tension by the use of the dream mechanisms of perceptual identity and temporal immediacy: the "I see it now" which preempts interpretation. Analogously, the fetishist can use the immediate perception of an object to eliminate anxiety.

Here, though, we must recall "the paradox of the hungry baby." The baby can use hallucination to attempt to get rid of the tension of hunger, because of the prior, tension raising registration of the experience of satisfaction. As a process within primary narcissism, registration of the experience of satisfaction has to be both unconscious (differential "opening" of a pathway) and conscious (storage of a perceived object)—a possibility implicit to Freud's thought, but not specifically examined by him. The crucial point is that although conscious perceptual identity and temporal immediacy appear to ground the reality of the dream, every conscious hallucination is made possible because of a prior unconscious opening of a pathway.

The apparent absence of any temporal difference in dreams—the dream's hypercathexis of the conscious now—has been made possible through a splitting off of unconscious differential time. In fetishism per se the immediate perception of an object in order to relieve anxiety is a symptomatic response to the registration and repudiation of sexual difference. And in the dreamlike state of consciousness of the fetishistic transference the differentiating, opening function of interpretation is repudiated *because* it has been registered unconsciously. The apparent objectivity of infinite nowness is an evasion of differential time. In *Beyond the Pleasure Principle* (1920) Freud said that conscious time can be a stimulus barrier against unconscious time. Is this an example of conscious, objective, "vulgar" time as a flight from primordial unconscious time? The privileging of the infinite now as a symptomatic leveling of differentiating, finite, ecstatic time?

The analogy goes much further. Descriptive interpretation of disavowal of the interpretive process can liberate *Angst*-like "internalization anxiety." There is a characteristic use of subjective doubling to prevent integration with the uncanniness of the interpretive setting: "You're a jerk, just like me." Crucially, the patient defensively refuses analytic help, *analytic care*, while remaining in analysis. Is this an evasion of care not only as being-in-the-world, but as ecstatic time? Heidegger thinks that mood intrinsically makes Da-sein flee from its "ownmost" possibilities. In such flight, one form of time substitutes for another, and then is taken as time itself. Freud said almost exactly this when he described the equation of the conscious understanding of time with time itself, an equation that functions as a protective stimulus barrier. But this also means that empirical time can be understood symptomatically, like empirical care and empirical difference. Heidegger allows us to understand the integrated structure of this "symptom," clinically manifest in the flight from interpretive care in analysis. The compelling *need* for an infinitely static, uninterpretable transference is a defensive substitute for a finitely ek-static, interpretable differential relation. In Freudian terms, this is the use of the state of dream consciousness as a "stimulus barrier" against the differentiability and openness of the unconscious. It again takes us back to the question of need and self-preservation viewed in relation to the psychic apparatus.

Why does Freud conceive of a psychic apparatus? One usually thinks of an apparatus as a machine. Machines run on scientific, objective principles. Freud certainly did seem to want to install something like the tendency to inertia and breakdown of all machines in the idea of the pleasure principle. Initially, the pleasure principle was conceived as a primary tendency toward inertia (in *Project for a Scientific Psychology* [1895]), and it became the death drive (in *Beyond the Pleasure Principle* [1920]). In this sense, Freud would remain captive to an ill-advised attempt to guarantee the scientificity of his enterprise with objective, mechanical principles. In *Zollikon Seminars* Heidegger says that because Freud took scientific causality for granted, he wanted to transfer it to the psyche, and came up with the idea of a psychic apparatus (2001, 20).

But the psyche, and particularly the unconscious, is an apparatus for other reasons. It is a memory device in the sense of automatic, unconscious registration processes. It *is* such a device because of its openness, its differentiability. The automatic periodicity of bodily hunger cannot be divorced from the automatic periodicity of registration of the differentiating double—the mother of primary narcissism, the differential impression of a *relation*. Familiar, empirical *need* gratification is the structurally uncanny need to be "outside" oneself. When Freud thought about need empirically, he always referred to the prolonged "helplessness" of the human infant. Helplessness is empirical finitude. Helplessness is the need for empirical care.[11] The unconscious as memory apparatus is a question of differentiating finitude and differentiating care—ecstatic time. This is why it is a living machine, an uncanny apparatus. Therapeutic need for interpretive *care* compels the analytic setting to have just this kind of automatic structure. The unconscious dynamics of interpretive care, of the analytic setting itself, must be thought in terms of such an uncanny living machine.

Heidegger reinterprets "reality," as distinct from "the real," as care. He had said that everyday taking care of things is tranquilized with the merely real, such that being toward possibilities becomes mere *wishing* (1996, 182). Heidegger means "wishing" here in a nonpsychoanalytic sense. He calls wishing a "hankering after possibilities," possibilities that are conflated with the "real world." Symptomatically, however, he says that "wishing presupposes care" (182). Does Freud say anything else when he makes the experience of satisfaction the precondition of the wish? At the end of *The Interpretation of Dreams* Freud makes a statement that Heidegger doubtless would understand as metaphysical. He says that the wishing unconscious is the "core of our being," *das Kern unseres Wesens* (1900, 603). The statement is metaphysical in that as hallucination, the wish is structured by objective presence. But this is a symptomatically ontological statement, in that Freud "forgets" the condition prior to the wish, the unconscious differentiating registration of care. And once empirical maternal care is thought in relation to the living machine, care itself is a structure of primary narcissism, and of everything that follows (e.g. tension, uncanniness). This is what the concrete patient expresses symptomatically in the self-splitting from interpretation as differential *relating*. Concrete patients often combine resistance to interpretation with resistance to the time of the sessions.

Consider the following example. A young woman graduate student stubbornly resists all attempts to understand her conviction that she suffers from attention *deficit* disorder. In other words, she "objectively" lacks something. Psychological testing has revealed no neurological impairment and no evidence of attention deficit disorder. The patient applies to a very selective doctoral program in her field and is accepted. Eventually, she passes her comprehensive examinations and begins work as a teaching assistant. Now she *knows* that her deficit will lead to failure. She does have a few initial problems with her teaching, handled by constructive criticism in departmental meetings. In general, she gets positive reviews on her work. Her analyst and her husband constantly reassure her that the constructive criticism is part of the process of becoming a professor and is intended to help, but nothing dissuades the patient from her certainty that she will fail because of her deficit. One can understand this conviction of deficit in terms of the castration complex, but one immediately comes up against the problem of "the reality of castration."

Near the end of a particular session, the analyst had moved away from "objective reassurance." He had interpreted that the patient was afraid of losing her familiar sense of herself if she thought about her consistently good work. Note the descriptive quality of the interpretation. It certainly refers to conflict and anxiety, but makes no reference to events in the past, and it has a certain violence to it—it is not reassuring. In what the analyst thought was a rare moment, the patient said that his comment made sense. The analyst knew from long experience that the patient was very sensitive to the ends of sessions, and wondered to himself how she would react to an unusual opening as the time drew to a close. He made a remark to this effect. The patient looked at the clock as he spoke. The analyst thought that she was angry when he ended the session. The patient began the next session by asking the analyst for a change of schedule, complaining that all her academic obligations gave her no time to exercise. She spent the rest of the session saying that she knew that what the analyst had said toward the end of the previous session made sense, but that she couldn't hold onto it. She looked at the clock more and more insistently as she spoke, and finally walked out before the analyst ended the session. Fetishistic knowledge of "the reality of castration"—a deficit that cannot be interpreted—has something to do with the clock, with the time of the sessions.

When Heidegger asks more specifically how primordial finite time becomes vulgar infinite time, he considers the question of the "self." (The analyst in the example had interpreted the patient's fear of her loss of her familiar sense of her*self*.) Ecstatic primordial time temporalizes itself and makes possible the existential structure of care (1996, 304). To be able to say "I am," is to understand that one exists over time: "The ontological structure of the being I myself always am is centered in the self-constancy of existence" (305). Grounded in existence, the self cannot be an objectively present substance or subject. Rather, it is a function of the structure of care, and thus of temporality. In other words, the familiar, objective constancy of the self is a flight from ecstatic time. Ontologically, *to exist over time is always to be outside oneself*. The "self-constancy" of existence means that one "is" as the ecstatic opening to each other of past, present, and future. This is Da-sein's *historicity* (305). Future as anticipation is the link of historicity to care.

The patient in our example begins to open herself to interpretive care. This opening takes her into the unfamiliar realm in which objective presence and absence are "historicized," i.e. temporalized. Her perception of an unmodifiable objective absence, attention *deficit* disorder, becomes symptomatic. The patient is a bit shaken in her everyday sense of "I" during the time of the session. As this occurs she becomes more and more preoccupied with the clock. She seems to want to have objective control over the time as an interpretive process takes her outside herself. In the next session she wants to change the time of the session, talks about her repudiation of analytic care, and then ends the session herself. What is the time of the session? Is it a succession of now points? And what is the "self" in analytic time?

As the possibility of history, Da-sein does not occur objectively within history. This again explains why resistance to interpretation cannot be interpreted in terms of repetition of the past in the usual sense. However, everyday Da-sein is preoccupied with taking care of things, the taking care which takes time. In this way, Heidegger says, Da-sein uses time and develops a measure of time. The linkage of taking care, taking time, and measure is why measurement of time is constitutive of being-in-the-world (306). In other words, measured time has a symptomatic relation to ecstatic time. Heidegger calls measured time "within time-ness." The relation of within time-ness to ecstatic time is the relation of everyday care to existential care. Therefore, "the time 'in which' objectively present things come into being and pass away is a genuine phenomenon of time" (306). The familiar measured time of the analytic session is inhabited by unfamiliar ecstatic time. In ecstatic time past, present, and future are open to each other. This means that *the present is never simply the now.*

For Heidegger the future has an essential role as the possibility of interpretation. Our patient registers and repudiates an interpretive opening that would give her a future that she already is: in the everyday sense, her good work is the continuation of her demonstrated capacities. But because her good work has a differentiating function, she splits it off, so that she has no future, only the infinite repetition of allegedly objective perception of her "deficit" *now.* When descriptive interpretation opens the unfamiliarity of a differential space, the patient becomes preoccupied with the clock. Recall the analysis of the Da- of Da-sein, the "there" as disclosure, clearing, opening. Heidegger says: *"Ecstatic temporality clears the There primordially"* (321).

To be in analytic time is to be in historicity. It is to anticipate interpretive care as differentiating integration with what one always already has been, but has evaded through self-splitting. This is the "ontological" understanding of registration and repudiation of difference *as* the splitting of the ego in the *process* of defense. It shows why self-splitting is as spatial as it is temporal. Despite the objective presence together of analyst and patient, concrete patients' resistance to analytic time is equally a resistance to analytic space as a finite, differential "clearing." The patient walks out of the session in which she oscillates between opening and closing the space of interpretation. By preempting the analyst's empirical reference to clock time at the end of the session—her "now" ends the session—the patient gains (illusory) control over the ecstatic time-space of the interpretive setting.

The natural processes studied by the sciences and the events studied by history occur "in time." Heidegger says that everyday Da-sein's "reckoning with time," "taking time," *measuring time* are more fundamental than the time presumed by science and history. This reckoning itself, says Heidegger, precedes the use of any measuring instruments. Rather, the clock itself is made possible because of the linkage of time and care, to which must be added the *apparatus-like unconscious structure of care*.

Winnicott (1954) understood empirical care in terms of empirical time. He had the insight that integration of care and instinct holds open the transitional space of historicity, of "doing something about something." This is an important intuition, whose fuller, nonempirical significance can be understood in terms of the periodicity of need in interaction with unconscious differentiation. The relation of the clock to psychoanalytic care is a function of this "body-mind" interaction, of the unconscious as memory-apparatus open to the (not) me of primary narcissism.

The measurement of the time of the session would have to be related to the fixing of the time of the appointment. Heidegger calls the seemingly self-evident relational structure of the future then, the past before, and the present now *datability* (374). Datability is made possible in three ways. One: the simultaneous understanding of world and the self-understanding of care: "temporality, recognizable as ecstatically open, is initially and for the most part known only in this *interpretedness* that takes care" (375;

emphasis added). Datability is the "reflex" of the *ecstatic* constitution of temporality. The interpretive expression of "then," "before," and "now" is "the most primordial way of *giving the time*" (375). The ecstatic unity of temporality is unthematically and unrecognizably presumed along with databilty. Two: the "extension" of the time that Da-sein takes and gives. Heidegger makes a typically complex statement about extension: *"Factically thrown Da-sein can 'take' and lose time for itself only because a 'time' is allotted to it as temporality ecstatically stretched along with the disclosedness of the There grounded in that temporality"* (377). To paraphrase: ecstatic temporality is primordially finite. In the everyday sense this means that Da-sein's time to exist has a certain extent, and Da-sein always understands this. One always knows that one has a limited amount of time stretched out before one, a span. But this is how Da-sein exists in everyday time, and how a preontological understanding of finitude is implicit to everyday time. Giving and taking time, using and losing time, dating the "span" of time is the "symptomatic reflex" of ecstatic, finite time. Three: datable time is public, is always "in the world." The they-self uses time collectively in everyday care (378). For example, analyst and patient share the same everyday time and can make datable appointments to see each other. But just as measure of time is constitutive of being-in, being-open, and *ek-stasis,* so the worldly character of datable, public time is dependent on the existential link of finitude and interpretation.

Usually, neither analyst nor patient gives much thought to the dated, measured time of analysis. Freud thought that this was the most reasonable way to practice a psychotherapy in which resistance can produce nonattendance and transference can produce reactions to time that are to be interpreted, not gratified. The patient's "rental" of the dated time of measured sessions helps to guarantee the analyst's neutrality. But just as Freud could not conceive the dynamics of resistance to interpretation, he could not think about the dynamics of the measured, dated session. Clinically, one finds a connection between the concrete patient's resistance to interpretation and extreme sensitivity to analytic time. Heidegger and Freud in their respective ways help us to understand that insistence on the "nowness" of "perceptual identity" and "temporal immediacy" is a registration and repudiation, a revealing and concealing, of differential time. Heidegger says that looking at the clock and orienting oneself toward time is essentially saying "now." The "now" is always already understood as datable, spanned, and worldly (382). In measurement, time is encountered as "now and now and now"—a universally accessible, objectively present multiplicity of nows (383). If the analyst can understand that conscious time is also the dream time of hallucination, the analyst can also understand how and why a patient's resistance to interpretation becomes an insistence on infinite repetition of objective perceptual identity: I *am* defective *now and now and now*; you *are* a jerk *now and now and now*; I control the interpretive setting by ending the session *now*.

What Heidegger emphasizes, though, is that time thought outside the now-structure is time thought outside the subject-object structure. Within-time-ness, the time "in which" objective things move is itself not objective; time itself is not an objectively present being. But, as always, this does not mean that it is subjective:

> The time "in which" objectively present things move is not "objective," if this means the objective presence of beings encountered in the world. But it is not subjective either, if that means objective presence and occurrence in a "subject." *World time is more "objective" than any possible object because, with the disclosedness of the world, it always already becomes ecstatically and horizonally "objectified" as the condition of the possibility of innerworldly beings. . . . But world time is also "more subjective" than any possible subject since it first makes possible the being of the factical existing self, that being which . . . is the meaning of care.* "Time" is neither objectively present in the "subject" nor in the "object," neither "inside" nor "outside," and it is "prior" to every subjectivity and objectivity, because it presents the condition of the very possibility of this "prior." Does it then have any "being" at all? And if not, is it then a phantom or is it "more in being" than any possible being? (384–85)

Primary narcissism, the differentiability of the unconscious, and care as the prior condition of the wish are all conditions of each other. They are temporally grounded in the periodicity of need. Need itself *is* finitude. Unconsciously, need is difference, need is repetition. Because there is not a subject-object structure in primary narcissism, need, difference, and repetition cannot be said to be "inside" or "outside." How do they occur? As what one might call an unconscious environment, a surround, a surface—a world. The analytic setting itself, as a function of unconscious need, difference, and repetition, *is* such a surface surround. One usually thinks about the unconscious in terms of something "buried in the depths," but "burial" and "depth" already imply inside and outside. Inside and outside become relevant categories when the difference and repetition of need are repudiated, creating the wish and its now-structure of objective presence. Psychoanalytically, there is a way of thinking "primordial time" that is neither objective nor subjective, because it is "prior" to the now-structure. This is the ecstatic-relational *time* of the setting as a *space* of interpretation.

But the setting is also a function of the differentiability of the psychic apparatus, which itself is "always already" in transitional time-space. The dated, measured, interpretive structure of the setting immediately situates the patient "in" this transitional area. Heidegger spoke of being-*in* as being-*outside* and being-*open*. In relation to the setting we can now also say that being-*in* its environment is being-*on* a surface. But this surface is unconscious. In *Zollikon Seminars* Heidegger notes that Freud's repression model assumes "a physical or psychical *container*, into which what is forgotten can be thrown" (2001, 170). When one is thinking in terms of unconscious registration and repudiation of differential time-space, one cannot think of a "buried container." One is dealing, rather, with *automatic, machine-like, but alive, transitional interactions between two surfaces: world (environment, setting) and unconscious.*

When Heidegger spoke of the relation of the clock and datability to primordial time, he did not speak of the *intervallic* structure of the "now and now and now." By definition, differential repetition is intervallic. Nietzsche called it "rhythmic," as did Freud in *Beyond the Pleasure Principle.* The differential time of need is itself intervallic, periodic. This is where psychoanalysis might provide a rejoinder to Heidegger's understanding of finitude in terms of death. Empirically, there is no periodicity of death, as there is of need. Heidegger looks for a linkage between the empirical time of the infinite now and finite primordial time. He states that datable, extended, public time is made possible by the natural clock of the sun, just as the use of the clock itself is grounded "in the temporality of Da-sein that makes possible a dating of time taken care of with the disclosedness of the There" (1996, 381). But this makes finitude and death existentially *nonrelational* as Da-sein's "ownmost" possibility. Finitude and need are existentially *relational* as structures of primary narcissism. This makes the psychic apparatus a kind of intervallic "clock," a clock that functions both according to unconscious time (differential opening) *and* objectively present conscious time (I see it now). Once registration and repudiation of difference is the basic unconscious process, the psychic apparatus provides a more integrated model of two times (differential time, now time) and their relation. Unconscious differential time is itself the possibility of the space of interpretation—the opening, the "clearing." Does it not then provide a more consistently *relational* account of interpretation?

Heidegger has given an existential account of self-preservation in relation to ecstatic, differential time. But because he thought finitude in relation to death, and because, like Nietzsche, he would dismiss any conception of a psychic "apparatus," he had to ground finitude and interpretation in a nonrelational possibility. This does not mean that he does not think death in terms of difference. But it does mean that death as difference has a strained relation to the structure of articulation as relation, *connection*. Certainly death as difference individualizes Da-sein, is a structure of being-in-the-world, and is ecstatic as anticipatory. But Heidegger also insists that the present is never simply the now. If it were, there would be a nonrelational aspect of time, a lapse into objective presence. Can being-toward-death as existentially nonrelational be integrated with a fully relational account of time? In terms of the psychic apparatus, the temporality of need explains the *ek-stasis* of the present, in which I *am* the other, and also explains that this ek-static present will always be leveled down into a now not open to past or future, as in dreams. Further, the unconscious machine is itself uncanny in several ways. The machine maintains a differential relation of life (self-preservation) and death (apparatus). It is not conscious, but functions as a surround, a surface. As a "surface device" that operates without a subject-object structure it registers the differentiating tension of the uncanny *relation* to that which is (not) me. The psychic apparatus is a "relational machine." There would be no nonrelational aspect of the unconscious as Heidegger contends there is of Da-sein (in *Being and Time*).

Tension, Self Preservation, Language

In the *Zollikon Seminars* session of March 1, 1966, Heidegger revisits the question of preservation of life and being-in-the-world. Now he speaks of relationality itself *as* tension—without reference to being-toward-death. He asks: "Why does a certain amount of stress result in the preservation of life?" The answer is "grounded in the . . . ecstatic relationship." Heidegger is thinking self-preservation, tension, and time together. The "stress of *ek-stasis*" is intrinsic to being-in-the-world, the "openness according to which the human being is always already addressed by beings other than himself. The human being could not live without this being addressed. 'Stress' is something that preserves 'life' in the sense of this necessity of being addressed. As long as we think of the human being as a world-less Ego, the necessity of stress for life cannot be made intelligible" (2001, 137).

Opening is always a question of interpretation for Heidegger, and thus he returns to the interpretedness intrinsic to the "stress of *ek-stasis*":

> Stress has the basic character of being claimed by something as a being addressed. Such a thing is only possible on the basis of language. . . . Insofar as the human being is being-with, as he remains essentially related to another human, language as such is conversation . . . stress belongs to the essential connection of address and response, that is, to the dimension of conversation . . . conversation forms the fundamental domain within which an interpretation becomes possible. Thus, the "hermeneutical circle" is not a *circulus vitiosus*, but an essential constitution of being human. It characterizes the finitude of the human being. (139–40)

As in *Being and Time* (1996), openness and finitude make interpretation—the "hermeneutical circle"—a basic structure of Da-sein. This structure now implies "stress" as well as *Angst* and uncanniness. This stress is intrinsic to language itself as being-with. Interpretation—in the address and response of the "talking cure"—*is as self-preservative tension*. On the unconscious surface interpretation is both care and force—a care and force that will always provoke evasion and self-splitting.

How does one then conceive "interpretation" as "analysis"? Heidegger called his method of phenomenological description both "interpretation" and "analysis of the existentiality of existence" (1996, 34). In *Zollikon Seminars* (November 23, 1965) he further clarifies what he means. He mentions some of the early Greek senses of *analuein* (Penelope's unweaving, the loosening of chains, liberation from captivity, dismantling of tents), and then jumps to Kant's sense of analysis. This is not a reduction into elements, he says, but the tracing back to the unity, the a priori synthesis, of the possibility of objects of experience. Heidegger calls this "the articulation of the unity of a composite structure," and says that this is "essential in my concept of the 'analytic of Da-sein'" (2001, 115). He then contrasts the "analytic of Da-sein" to psychoanalysis, and states that "symptoms are not reduced to elements in the manner of Freud. Rather, the quest is after those traits characterizing the being of Da-sein regarding its relation to being in general. . . . The interpretation of the primary structures constituting the being of Da [opening, clearing, *ecstasis*] understood as such . . . is the existential analytic of Da-sein" (120–21).

The interpretation of the Da is the interpretation of the possibility of meaning, the "as structure." Psychoanalytically, the "as structure" is close to the idea of transitional phenomena, which are linked to historicity, the open relation of past to present. The timed interpretive space of analysis is itself grounded in this historicity, in transitionality. The resistance to interpretation is a self-splitting motivated by the tension, anxiety, and uncanniness of being-in the setting. Description of this process, grounded in the articulation of being-in as being-outside, -open, and -on—the primary structures of the Da—is the countertension of interpretation. This is noncausal, phenomenological description, *and* analysis in the Greek senses of unweaving, dismantling, liberating—unbinding. Unbinding itself, however is not simple, precisely because it is interpretive. Interpretation as the differential relation of the address-response nature of language is binding. This is another way of thinking interpretation in relation to being-in-the-world, to primary narcissism. It is a transitional process in which unbinding (liberation) and binding (interpretation) are conditions of each other. As a transitional process, it is not simply intrapsychic or interpersonal. Analysis of the resistance to interpretation is, rather, noncausal description of processes which occur between patient and analyst and within the patient—simultaneously. The self-splitting which evades the opening of interpretation occurs in relation to being-in the transitional time-space of the interpretive, binding-unbinding, setting.

Time, Transitionality, Drives

In *Kant and the Problem of Metaphysics,* the immediate successor to *Being and Time*, Heidegger comes to conclusions directly relevant to the transitionality of the analytic setting. He focuses on the two stems of knowledge in the Kant's *Critique of Pure Reason*: sensory reception and understanding. For Heidegger, Kant's innovation is to ground understanding in sensory reception, intuition. Because Kant is engaged in a transcendental, i.e. experience-free, analysis of the possibility of knowledge, intuition itself has to be examined transcendentally. Hence the *Critique* begins with the transcendental aesthetic (from the Greek *aisthesis,* "sensory").

The transcendental forms of intuition are space and time. Space is represented in advance in everything that affects the external senses; time, the succession of mental states, is the form of the inner sense. Time quickly takes precedence, because it is the a priori condition, the universal pure intuition, which makes pure knowledge and transcendence possible.

Kant also posits "pure imagination," or the "transcendental imagination," as the possibility of the synthetic unity of intuition and understanding (1962, 41). Once he does so, Heidegger says, there has to be a structural connection between the transcendental imagination and time. The connection is in the idea of connection or "linkage"—binding—itself. The transcendental imagination has the power of forming relations; time as universal pure intuition is the medium in which making connections is possible. In Heidegger's reading, the transcendental imagination, as neither sensory reception nor intellectual understanding, is also the condition of possibility of time itself as synthesis, relation, *Bindung*. The emphasis is clearly on a fully relational account of primordial time; there is no mention of being-toward-death.

The transcendental imagination as *Bindung* is akin to being-in-the-world. Just as Da-sein is not a subject which is then brought into relation with objects but only exists as being-with, so the transcendental imagination does not join together intuition and understanding as two extremities. Rather, as the "root" of the two stems, as *Bindung*, the transcendental imagination is the possibility of their connection and differentiation. Time, then, can be thought as the process of connection and differentiation itself.

Heidegger contends that Kant "recoiled" from his analysis of the transcendental imagination—it was downplayed in the second edition of the *Critique of Pure Reason*—because it brought him to the "abyss" of metaphysics (1962, 173). This is the point at which pure reason is made possible by the intermediate "faculty" of imagination, which in turn implies a rethinking of time. We are very close to Freud's singular remarks about an unconscious time from which there would have to be a "recoil," because it raises tension—as does Eros (*Bindung*) itself. And unconscious time gives Freud the possibility of rethinking "the Kantian theorem that time and space are 'necessary forms of thought'" (1920, 28). Freud's *Bindung* is the prior condition of the pleasure principle, and is conceived in terms of pleasurepain and time as periodicity. It too is the "prior" as intermediate, as transitional.

In *Kant and the Problem of Metaphysics* time as pure intuition and as *Bindung* forms the present, reproduces the past, and anticipates the future, such that present, past, and future only exist together, as syntheses. Not surprisingly, Heidegger privileges the future as the third synthesis of time that anticipates the other two as coexisting (1962, 184–90). The third synthesis is the first. The intermediate has to be the prior for the transcendental imagination, just as *Bindung* is the transitional, intermediate, prior condition of the pleasure principle. Since primordial time, the *ekstatikon* par excellence, is neither subjective nor objective, Heidegger said in *Being and Time* that "time temporalizes itself." In *Kant and the Problem of Metaphysics,* he calls this "time as pure self affection" (1962, 201–5). "Self" here cannot mean any permanently existing subjectivity. The self as temporal is ek-static, outside itself, as a condition of possibility of its historicity. In psychoanalytic terms, time is the "tension of *ek-stasis*" in relation to primary narcissism: one *is* the other in all unconscious differentiating registrations without a subject-object structure. Such registrations are "self-affective" in the same way that Heidegger says time temporalizes itself. Transitional time-space, the time-space of interpretation, is autoaffective. This explains the overall psychoanalytic conception that the most effective interpretations are the ones made by the patient, as the result of internalization of the analytic process.

Such theorizing about the time-space of interpretation can appear to ignore the body and sexuality. However, there is a specific instance in which Freud conceives an intermediate, transitional state in relation to the theory of sexuality and to time as periodicity. In "Instincts and Their Vicissitudes" (1915c)—the title is an unhappy rendering of "Triebe und Triebschicksale," "Drives and Their Fates"—Freud expands the theory of infantile sexuality. He had already said in the *Three Essays on the Theory of Sexuality* (1905) that the component drives of infantile sexuality occur as pairs of opposites, i.e. in active and passive versions. Here he is interested in the "genealogy" of these pairs of opposites. He first examines sadomasochism, and says that originally the child simply has wishes to "exercise violence or power upon some other person as object" (1915c, 127) in a nonsexual way. This nonsexual, active aim to hurt is then turned around upon the subject, and the object is given up. The active wish to exert violence or power becomes autoaffective: one hurts oneself. In a third stage, an extraneous object is sought to inflict pain upon oneself; Freud calls this masochism proper. He notes that in the second stage, originally active sadism is not yet passive. Rather, the "active voice is changed, not into the passive, but into the reflexive, middle voice" (128). The middle—intermediate—voice can be called the voice of self-affective processes. But it is not yet primary.

The critical moment comes when Freud examines voyeurism-exhibitionism. Initially, he finds the same structure as in sadomasochism. An active wish to look is turned around upon the subject, setting up the passive aim of being looked at; then one seeks an extraneous object who looks at one—voyeurism has become exhibitionism. But, says Freud, this is actually not right, because there is a stage prior to the active wish to look. He calls this the "autoerotic," original moment of voyeurism (scopophilia). Freud here distinguishes between the genealogy of sadomasochism and voyeurism-exhibitionism: the former is not originally sexual, while the latter is. Once voyeurism-exhibitionism is originally sexual, however, it has to be thought in relation to autoerotism, the essence of infantile sexuality. So, says Freud, "the scopophilic instinct is autoerotic; it has indeed an object, but that object is part of the subject's own body." Moreover, the "preliminary stage is interesting because it is the source of *both* the situations represented in the resulting pair of opposites" (130; original emphasis). In the "preliminary stage," "oneself looking at a sexual organ" equals "a sexual organ being looked at by oneself" (130). The first half ("oneself looking") of the equation becomes active looking at "an extraneous object" (voyeurism), while the second half ("at a sexual organ") becomes a part of oneself passively being looked at by an "extraneous person" (exhibitionism) (130). The preliminary stage then, is one in which the oppositions subject-object and active-passive do not hold. It can rigorously be called transitional. Freud himself calls it "intermediate" (131).

This "autoerotic stage of scopophilia" might seem to be a purely theoretical inference. However, the idea that oneself looking at a sexual organ equals a sexual organ being looked at by oneself exactly describes the situation of the infant and the breast in primary narcissism. The infant *is* the breast which it sees, making this a reflexive, autoaffective seeing. The registration of the experience of satisfaction takes place within this structure. Unconsciously, this process can be described as: "In seeing myself as the other which I am, I (am) open(ed by) a differentiating memory trace." This is originally unconscious thought: the nonverbal registration of a tension-raising relation. It is *Bindung*—a prior synthesis as articulation-connection that is also the root, the condition of possibility of subjective, active voyeurism and objective, passive exhibitionism. It also links "conscious" and "unconscious." It is perception (seeing) *and* memory (opening of a pathway), or rather perception *as* memory; it is self-preservative *as* libidinal.[12] Like the transcendental imagination, it is simultaneously passive and active, receptive and spontaneous (162, 159). Does it then, like the transcendental imagination, also have a relation to finite time?

Finite time for Freud is always a question of periodicity, a question which emerges immediately in relation to "primary scopophilia." Freud is attempting to account for the way in which voyeurism can be succeeded by exhibitionism, because both derive from "primary scopophilia." He writes:

> The only correct statement to make about the scopophilic instinct would be that all the stages of its development, its auto-erotic, preliminary stage as well as its final active or passive form, co-exist alongside one another. . . . We can divide the life of each instinct [*Trieb*, drive] into a series of separate successive waves, each of which is homogenous during *whatever period of time it may last*, and whose relation to one another is comparable to that of successive eruptions of lava. We can then perhaps picture the first, original eruption of the instinct [*Trieb*] as proceeding in an unchanged form and undergoing no development at all. The next wave would be modified from the outset—being turned, for instance, from active to passive—and would then, with this new characteristic, be added to the earlier wave, and so on. If we were then to take a survey of the instinctual impulse from its beginning up to a given point, the succession of waves which we have described would inevitably present the picture of a definite development of the instinct [*Trieb*]. . . . This reference to the developmental *history* of instincts [*Triebe*] and the *permanence of their intermediate stages* should make the development of instincts fairly intelligible to us. (130–31; emphases added)

Freud claims that the permanence of the intermediate stages of the drives makes their developmental history "intelligible." How? One can read Freud to say that because the active and passive forms of looking derive from the preliminary phase, all the phases actually coexist. Certainly either the active or passive form can appear to dominate a given *period* of drive activity, like a discrete eruption of lava. The collection of discrete eruptions is the history of the drive. But the source of the lava is the primary, intermediate phase, which is permanent. Otherwise, there would be no eruption at all. Nor would one have a way of explaining how and why a phase of exhibitionism can succeed a phase of voyeurism, despite their apparent opposition. The permanence of the intermediate stage is the permanence of its periodic repetition, a kind of eternal return. Note that as the volcanic source of periodic eruptions, the repetition of the primary intermediate phase is a disruptive force.

Freud here does not link periodicity to the periodicity of need. Once one interprets primary scopophilia as the "seeing" intrinsic to the experience of satisfaction, however, there is good reason to do so. In terms of the psychic apparatus, the periodicity of need is the relation of repetition to difference. Freud has actually given us a way to think an intermediate, transitional organization of the drives as a condition of finite, differential-relational time. The intermediate, prior condition has to be repeated if there is to be an intrinsic relation between the active and passive, subjective and objective forms of the drive. If there is a developmental *history* of the drive—the "successive eruptions"—the primary, intermediate form is the condition of possibility of this history, its historicity. Thus, we have a way of thinking the drives and the body in terms of transitionality[13]—but, unusually, a "volcanic," sexual–self-preservative, transitionality.

Freud's initial project historicizes sexuality: neurosis as a question of memory is also a question of sexuality. Deferred action explains how repressed memories of infantile sexuality produce adult symptoms. Infantile sexuality itself changes the history of sexuality: reproductive sexuality becomes the product of a development rooted in autoerotism. The "primary, autoerotic, intermediate" phase of scopophilia itself becomes the condition of possibility of the historicization of sexuality in this singular passage. Just as Freud stumbled onto an analysis of *Bindung* as a prior condition of the pleasure principle, so he here stumbles onto an account of an autoaffective, transitional, periodic, prior condition of possibility of a history of the drives. And once the primary phase of scopophilia is integrated with the registration of the experience of satisfaction, it implies the differentiating trace of the other which I am (not). As autoaffective it is structurally heteroaffective.

Clinically, we have already seen that the patient who resists interpretation insists upon subjective doubling—"you're a jerk, just like me." This is a disavowal, a registration and repudiation, of opening, i.e. the nonsubjective doubling in which interpretation integrates the differential elements which the patient always already is. Interpretation in this transitional area, interpretation of historicity, interpretation of opening, is made possible by the primary phase of scopophilia. This is the rigorous sense in which analysis aims at making a self-analytic process possible. Resistance to interpretation is resistance to a "seeing oneself" that differentiates, i.e. resistance to the auto-(hetero)-affective time of the interpretive setting. The primary, intermediate phase of scopophilia grounds this possibility in the historicity of sexuality. Primary scopophilia *as* registration of the experience of satisfaction is a drive description of the autoaffective seeing intrinsic to interpretive care. In this sense, is the psychic apparatus akin to Heidegger's understanding of the transcendental imagination? Both are related to the autoaffective structure of the primary intermediate.

In general, Heidegger is as dismissive of the theory of the drives as he is of the theory of the psychic apparatus. In the *Zollikon Seminars* he says that Freud used the drives as causal explanations, such that the joint conceptions of drive and psyche can never arrive at the "structure of care" (2001, 172). He did not seem to know that the theory of the drives and of the psychic apparatus contained moments such as primary scopophilia (Eros, *Bindung*, originally unconscious thought, and primary narcissism), which open onto the structure of care, and do so in a way that accounts for the historicity of the body. And while Heidegger notoriously says very little about sexuality itself, he is a thinker of the body. In *Zollikon Seminars,* as in many other places, he says that we do not simply "have" a body, but that we "are" as body (28, 87). To think the body existentially would be to think it temporally and to think it transitionally, such that mind is not equated with subject and body with object. Heidegger did not encounter Freud deeply enough to see that there are moments in the theory of the drives that accomplish just this aim.

The New Interpretation of the Sensuous

The closest Heidegger may have come to a rethinking of sexuality is in volume 1 of *Nietzsche.* There, his major preoccupation is Nietzsche's conception of the will to power as art. Because art is the countermovement to the nihilism of the ascetic ideal, Nietzsche understands it in terms of the body. He calls "rapture" the basic aesthetic state, the physiological precondition of art (1979–1987, 96–97). Heidegger immediately emphasizes rapture as will to power: it is an enhancement of corporeal force, like sexuality itself for Nietzsche. Again he says that we *are* as body. Nietzsche's rapture becomes for him a way of thinking how we *are* as body in relation to beings as a whole. It becomes for Heidegger a mode of attunement, and as such, a form of being-in-the-world. Nietzsche's rapture as will to power is an "interlacing" (relating, binding) of all enhancements (97–98). Such enhancement as art cannot be conceived in subject-object terms: rapture "explodes" the subjectivity of the subject, brings the subject out of itself ek-statically; and rapture "breaks through" the distance of objectivity, of art as an object of representation (123). For all these reasons, Heidegger says that Nietzsche's aesthetics is actually a metaphysics, a statement about the being of beings (131). This is like the way in which he made Kant's transcendental imagination an opening to a rethinking of time. Here, precisely because of Nietzsche's emphasis on rapture, it is sexuality that would have to be thought in terms of being. Or, in Heidegger's terms, sexuality is *already* thought in terms of being when rapture is the "interlacing," the binding, of all enhancements.

Heidegger then turns to Nietzsche's famous statement that "art is worth more than truth." This statement is part of Nietzsche's project of "inverting Platonism." For Plato, truth is supersensuous, removed from the transience of the sensuous. Nietzsche always attacks this idea: the transvaluation of Platonic-Christian morality would then value the sensuous. If art as rapture is worth more than truth, says Heidegger, art for Nietzsche is more in being than truth, is the basic occurrence of being (140). Heidegger then asks, what does being mean if the sensuous is more in being? What does *sensuous* mean?

To answer, Heidegger makes the kind of argument that will dominate all four volumes of *Nietzsche*. He says that Nietzsche's statement on art and truth does not arrive at the proper question of truth, but presupposes as self-evident that truth is knowledge. This is the basic Cartesian innovation: truth is certitude. Therefore, despite all his deconstructions of the metaphysics of subject and object, Nietzsche does not emerge from the metaphysics of modernity (148–50). Heidegger then compares truth in Platonism and truth in modernity. For Plato, true knowledge is in supersensuous Ideas. True knowledge measures itself against Ideas (151). For modernity, true knowledge is also a measuring, but upon the sensuous. This is the metaphysics of modern science, of positivism (152). Positivism inverts Platonism: it puts the sensuous in the place of the nonsensuous. A large strand of Freud's thought conforms exactly to this way of thinking. Freud wanted the theory of sexuality to be the scientific justification for psychoanalysis in the positivist sense. His claim to have constructed a nonmetaphysical theory of unconscious processes grounded in sexuality can easily be seen as a positivist inversion of Platonism, and well within metaphysics.

However, Heidegger knows that Nietzsche cannot simply be confined to modern metaphysics. First, because Nietzsche cannot be seen as a positivist; everything in his late work speaks against the positivist "faith" in truth. Second, because Nietzsche's overturning of Platonism is not simply a mechanical exchange of the sensuous for the supersensuous. For Nietzsche the true is the sensuous not in the sense of positivism, but as the countermovement to the nihilism of the ascetic ideal (160–61). But a basic question remains: does Nietzsche's nonpositivist *inversion* of Platonism still maintain the above-below structure of Platonism? Nietzsche himself examined this question in his "History of an Error" (in *Twilight of the Idols* [1990]). After the substitution of positivism for Platonism, one must twist free of Platonism altogether by abolishing any possible distinction between the "true" (above) and the "apparent" (below) worlds (1979–1987, 201). Thus, says Heidegger, if the sensuous is to be freed of Platonism, there must be "a new interpretation of the sensuous on the basis of a new hierarchy of the sensuous and the nonsensuous. The new hierarchy does not simply wish to reverse matters within the old structural order" (209). This new structure "derives the force and direction of its motion from the new inquiry and the fundamental experience in which true being, what is real, 'reality,' is to be defined afresh" (211).

Looping back to the discussion of rapture, Heidegger says that art as sensuous-corporeal, as will to power, is always the "beyond," the outside oneself, i.e. the "ek-static" (although he does not use the word here). This is how the sensuous constitutes reality proper for Nietzsche (212). But, says Heidegger, just as Nietzsche does not rethink truth itself, his opening onto a new interpretation of the sensuous lapses into the "timeworn schema of Being and Becoming" (219), i.e. does not rethink time. Kant may have recoiled from the temporality of the transcendental imagination linked to the transcendental aesthetic, but Nietzsche did not even reach the point of having to rethink the sensuous in terms of time. Nietzsche's objection to timelessness still isolates time from the question of being. In volume 4 of *Nietzsche,* Heidegger will call Nietzsche the "last metaphysician" for just this reason: his emphasis on the body and becoming participates in the metaphysical forgetting of being.

Heidegger may not be correct about Nietzsche here. Deleuze contends that eternal return as repetition of difference *does* rethink time as articulation-connection, the basic structure of being. Freud did not formally join such issues. Nonetheless, they do emerge when he considers unconscious registration, the drives as autoerotic, the before of the pleasure principle, periodicity, and *Bindung*. The conception of "originally unconscious thought" can itself be understood in terms of a "new structure" of the sensuous and the nonsensuous: thought as nonsensuous cannot be divorced from the sensuous as libido, self-preservation, autoerotism, tension, binding, and differential registration. (Recall the patient with the fibrillating brain.)

David Krell, the general editor of the English edition of *Nietzsche*, contends that the "new interpretation of the sensuous" is the work's most essential question, but is never really pursued by Heidegger—or by Nietzsche (1979–1987, 3:274–75). Would not Freud's momentary incursion into "self-affective seeing" be the opening to such an interpretation? An interpretation that, as Heidegger says, has to change what we think of as "reality"? A reality that can be conceived in terms of a psychic apparatus both sensuous and nonsensuous, an apparatus whose intermediacy cannot be divorced from tension and uncanniness? A reality repeated in the setting of interpretive care?

Opening and Interpretation in Heidegger's Later Works

Heidegger's understanding of care, time, and interpretation in relation to *Angst*, uncanniness, and stress helps to explain how and why *some* patients almost all the time, and *all* patients at some time, disavow the self-preservative need for analytic care. Interpretation of the process of defense against the registration and repudiation of the *reality* of the setting has to be phenomenological description. Such description, despite its seeming simplicity and obviousness, is intrinsically "violent" in its opening of transitional space. It binds to unbind. As heteroaffective in the intermediacy of primary narcissism it is autoaffective.

Acute clinicians have sometimes grasped this process without being able to account for it. In the last clinical example in *Difference and Disavowal*, Michael Feldman, a contemporary Kleinian, was able to think beyond the usual conception of projective identification—the splitting off of "bad" parts of oneself and projecting them into the analyst. Feldman (1997) cited the case of a persistently concrete patient. He thought that the patient was pressured to create *identities* in order to defend against what he called the "alarming space" of possible interpretation. When he used such (non-Kleinian) thinking, and described this process to his patient, she responded that she always spoke to him in order "not to give him an opening." To understand the unconscious dynamics of why a patient in analysis would speak in order to avoid "opening" requires thinking concreteness in terms of registration and repudiation of difference, thinking difference itself as will to power and eternal return, and thinking "identity" as a flight from the *Angst* and uncanniness of interpretation as disclosure—Heidegger's existential analytic. All illuminate why interpretation implies opening as alarming space—and time.

The theme of "opening" dominates Heidegger's later works. Toward the end of his life he published an essay called "Time and Being," accompanied by the account of a seminar (1972). There he stated that *Being and Time* interprets Da-sein's temporality, "as the ecstatic element which in itself already contains a reference to truth, to opening up, to the unconcealment of being qua being, even though this is not explicitly named in the part of *Being and Time* which was published" (28). In other words, the interpretation of time limited to the analytic of Da-sein does not mention the temporal character of being itself. The thinking of difference as articulation-connection and as opening become ways of thinking being more radically. This also means thinking being as relation; at the end of *Nietzsche,* Heidegger had said that *being as relation* is the unthought of metaphysics (1979–1987, 4:208). Simultaneously, he is more concerned with difference as pain and tension, and with something like a "registration and repudiation" of opening itself. Several examples:

1. In his essay on "Language," Heidegger says that difference is neither distinction nor relation as independent characteristics, but as opening (1971, 203). He comments on a line in a poem by Trakl that reads: "Pain has turned the threshold to stone" He asks what pain is:

> Pain rends. It is the rift. But it does not tear apart into dispersive fragments. Pain indeed tears asunder, it separates, yet so that at the same time it draws everything to itself, gathers it to itself. Its rending, as a separating that gathers, is at the same time that . . . which . . . joins together what is held apart in separation. Pain is the joining agent in the rending that divides and gathers. Pain is the joining of the rift. The joining is the threshold. It settles the between, the middle of the two that are separated in it. Pain joins the rift of the difference. Pain is the difference itself. (204)

Ontologically, Heidegger now sees the kind of relation between difference and pain we have already seen in Nietzsche and Freud. Ontological difference-as-pain of course is not the experiential pain avoided by the herd, or the intrapsychic pain of raised tension levels. Pain here is no longer even an existential "mood" in the sense of *Being and Time,* because mood was the everyday experience of being-in-the-world. Just as difference is the difference between being and beings, pain is the mode in which being and beings are always separate, as in the entire history of metaphysics, and yet joined. Ontologically, difference as articulation and connection *is* pain. One would misunderstand Heidegger if one thought he was saying that metaphysics is not capable of thinking difference because it avoids pain. It is rather that difference as the unthought of metaphysics can only be as pain.

But just as one can always ask about the relation of empirical difference to ontological difference, so one can ask about the relation of empirical pain to ontological pain. The "place" where empirical and ontological pain are themselves separated and joined *is* the differentiability of the unconscious. One can think of the registration and repudiation of this differentiability empirically, in fetishism for example, but one can also think of the painful separating and connecting of registration of difference in primary narcissism. When difference as pain in primary narcissism is *repudiated*, it is "unthought." But the repudiation of difference in primary narcissism is also the painful point of articulation and connection of the thought and the unthought, of empirical and ontological difference. The empirical pain expressed in resistance to interpretation, and empirical difficulties with the measuring and dating of sessions, is likewise the painful point of articulation between the empirical setting of analysis and its ontological possibility. The analyst, who provides and maintains the setting, *is* this pain, like the mother of primary narcissism who *is* the pain of difference.

Here, one might rethink Freud's conception of primary masochism. In "The Economic Problem of Masochism" (1925b) he reverses the position he took in "Instincts and Their Vicissitudes" (1915c) and posits a primary masochism akin to primary scopophilia. He understands primary masochism as that part of the death instinct, the drive to self-destruction, that always remains self-directed. "Pain" itself is implicit to the relation to the caretaking mother of primary narcissism, and to the analyst in the setting—the inevitable stress or tension of "the preservation of life" (2001).

The pain implicit to the autoaffective seeing of primary narcissism opens the "alarming space" of interpretation. Perhaps primary masochism as the drive to self-destruction is directed against "self-preservation" as the pain of autoaffective differential opening. This would be pain against pain, just as there is (castration) anxiety against (internalization) anxiety.

2. In *Identity and Difference* (1969) Heidegger returns to his preferred fragment from Parmenides, which roughly says that thinking and being are the same. Heidegger typically tries to convey an understanding of a pre-Socratic way of thinking that is not yet metaphysical, not yet dominated by the forgetting of being. He says that metaphysics symptomatically forgets being when the principle of identity, A *is* A, is assumed to mean A = A. The question about Parmenides' fragment becomes: is thinking *identical* to being, does thinking *equal* being? Or does Parmenides mean something else when he says that thinking and being are *the same*? Heidegger of course thinks the latter, because Parmenides would not yet be thinking in terms of the metaphysics of identity.

Heidegger writes: "In the merely identical, the difference disappears. In the same the difference appears, and appears all the more pressingly" (1969, 45). The matter of thinking is difference *as* difference—now the "as" structure of difference itself, rather than the "as-structure" of something as something. But just as for pain, to think difference *is* to think the unthought, the difference between being and beings. Thus the "matter for thought" is equally the oblivion of difference: "The oblivion belongs to the difference because the difference belongs to the oblivion. The oblivion does not happen to the difference only afterward, in consequence of the forgetfulness of human thinking" (50). To think the oblivion is to think how the same inevitably becomes the identical. Psychoanalytically, it is to think how repudiation of difference "belongs" to its registration, how the uncanny, tension raising sameness of primary narcissism—I am (not) the other—produces the tension reducing identity structure of the wish. But this also means that human forgetfulness, even psychoanalytically conceived as repression, is not the sole reason for oblivion. Rather, repression, like the wish, has a prior condition in the repudiation that belongs to the registration of difference. The splitting of the ego in the *process* of defense is potentially the nonmetaphysical prior condition of repression. In the repression theory difference remains unthought.

Just as Heidegger thought of difference as pain, he now thinks of it as tension. This tension is also the tension between being as ontologically prior and the usual metaphysical conception of a prior condition as cause. As always, for Heidegger, phenomenological interpretation is not causal. However, just as being and beings are separate and joined, so too ontological grounding and metaphysical causality are separate and joined—hence the tension. Heidegger says that in stepping back from the oblivion of difference, we allow the "essential past to speak inasmuch as we are thinking of unconcealing and keeping concealed" (67). Because this past is difference as the unthought, it is about something all-pervasive, but not in the metaphysical sense of "something universal, valid in all cases, nor a law guaranteeing the necessity of a process in the sense of the dialectical" (68). The unthought essential past "grounds," but does not cause. Being grounds beings; beings effect causes. However, past as ground and past as cause exist together, precisely because beings *exist*, beings *are*.

Heidegger calls the existing together of ground and cause *perdurance*. Of it he says: "The perdurance of that which grounds and that which is grounded as such not only holds the two apart, it holds them facing each other. What is held apart is held in the *tension* of perdurance in such a way that not only does Being ground beings as their ground, but beings in their turn ground, cause Being in their way. Beings can do so only insofar as they 'are' the fullness of Being: they are what is most of all" (68; emphasis added). Psychoanalytically this means that one must think of a tension between past as ground and past as cause. This is the tension between registration and repudiation of difference (ground) and repression (cause). This means that interpretation of the past itself contains a tension between phenomenological description and objective causality. This tension is as intrinsic to the psychoanalytic setting as is the pain of difference.

In *Identity and Difference* Heidegger speaks of metaphysics as ontotheology. He means that metaphysics *onto*-logically assumes the possibility of universal principles, valid everywhere (e.g. beings are what is objectively present, time is an infinite succession of now points); and *theo*-logically makes these principles the highest principles. As ontotheology, metaphysics cannot think the "the active nature of being" (1969, 66). This is the activity of the "same" in which "difference appears," versus the identical in which "difference disappears." But of course difference as activity cannot "appear" as something present. Anything that can appear as something present can be re-presented. The thinking of difference as active process cannot be representational (62). To think difference representationally would reduce difference to a "distinction," a relation that our understanding adds to being and beings.

Here we have an extremely difficult point for psychoanalysts. Just as difference is not causal, it is not representational. Repudiation of it will be put in causal, representational terms, e.g. I know that you are angry at me *because* I am *late*. If the analyst assumes only causal, representational thinking, the analyst will not be able to conceive the noncausal, nonrepresentational repudiation of difference as active process implicit to such a statement of perceptual identity. Almost all psychoanalytic theory presumes representation, from Freud to the present.[14] Repression always works on representations; object relations are mental representations.

Neither Loewald (1980), in his conception of internalization of a differential, nor Winnicott (1951), with his conception of transitional space, give specific attention to the presumption of representation. But Heidegger importantly allows us to think that representation, like identity, belongs to the oblivion of the active nature of difference as "all pervasive" ground. Representation can be a "symptom." Heidegger writes: "Since metaphysics thinks of beings as such as a whole, it *represents* beings in respect of what differs in the difference, and without heeding the difference as difference" (1969, 70; emphasis added). When metaphysics thinks of beings in terms of the universal ground of beings, it is logic as onto-logic. When it thinks beings as a whole in terms of the highest being which accounts for everything, it is logic as theo-logic. Fetishism is onto-theology: it *represents* (sexual) difference in terms of objective presence and absence. Concreteness operates onto-theologically: it cannot heed the active differentiating process of interpretation, and replaces it with perceptual identities. Transference becomes an apparently objective repetition of the past that is actually the oblivion—the repudiation—of the "essential past." But difference as pain *is* as the tension that holds separate and connected the representational and nonrepresentational past, the past as cause and the past as ground, the past that can be spoken of objectively and the past that can only be described as *process*.

3. In "Time and Being" (1972) the essential past as process, as open*ing*, becomes the fourth dimension of time. Familiarly, Heidegger says that since time is nothing that is, one can never say that future, past, and present are before us simultaneously. Rather, they are interrelated as

the presencing that is given in them. With this presencing, there opens up what we call time-space. But with the word 'time' we no longer mean the succession of a sequence of nows. . . . Time-space now is the name for the openness which opens up in the mutual self-extending of futural approach, past and present. This openness exclusively and primarily provides the space in which space as we usually know it can unfold. (14)

Time-space as opening is presenc*ing*, a phenomenological process. This process demonstrates that "the unity of time's three dimensions consists in the interplay of each toward each. This interplay proves to be the true extending, playing in the very heart of time, the fourth dimension. . . . True time is four dimensional" (15). As a discipline grounded in time and interpretation, psychoanalysis is set in this fourth dimension. In *Kant and the Problem of Metaphysics* the third synthesis of time (the future) was linked to the intermediate as prior. Now, one would have to amend that idea, and say that the fourth dimension is really the first. Opening is what Heidegger in *Being and Time* called the prior, or the essential past as pervasive ground. Recall his questions about the prior in *Being and Time:* "Does it then have any 'being' at all? And if not, is it then a phantom or is it 'more in being' than any possible being?" (1996, 384–85).

In a new approach to opening as the "fourth-first" dimension of time (space), Heidegger thinks about the German expression for "there is," *Es gibt,* "it gives." As the condition of possibility for being able to say "there is being," "there is time," Heidegger wants to think the opening in terms of the "it gives." What "it" gives is being *as* time, in a relatedness that is not "retroactively superimposed" upon them (19). Opening is a relatedness that precedes any things related. This relatedness is as pain and tension. Heidegger calls it the "event of appropriation," the relatedness such that being and beings "belong" to each other. Such an event, he says, must not be thought as an occurrence and a happening, but as the "extending and sending" which opens and preserves being *as time* (20).

Sending is Heidegger's word for the history of being. In different eras, being has a different destiny (*Schicksal*), is sent (*ge-schickt*) in different (symptomatic) forms—forms that reveal and conceal it, e.g. objective presence in the modern age. There would be no destining, no sending of being without the event of appropriation of the "it gives." But because being is sent such that the opening is always concealed and being is forgotten, Heidegger says that expropriation belongs to appropriation (23). Being is sent such that it expropriates itself of itself. Symptomatically, then, expropriation "preserves what is its own" (23). This preservation is not a preservation of something represented. Rather, representation itself is the preserving expropriation of nonrepresentational difference. Here we have the difference between the forgetting that preserves representations, i.e. repression, and the repudiation that belongs to registration of difference, preserving difference in representation and identity. As phenomenological description, to say "Es gibt Sein, Es gibt Zeit" is not to put the *Es* in the position of a subject that gives an object. It is rather a *giving as opening* (19).

The *Es* of *Es gibt* is more impersonal than Nietzsche's or Freud's *Es*. For Nietzsche and Freud, the id is the impersonal force of the drives, the passions beyond conscious control. Although Nietzsche states that there is no timelessness of the unconscious, Heidegger contends that he simply evades the question of time altogether, as when he speaks of time as becoming, of an id always in flux. Freud mostly speaks of the timelessness of the unconscious, but the id, as unconscious, is a question of memory as well as drives.[15] Memory means "time." And once unconscious memory is itself a condition of differentiability, of difference as active process, there would have to be time as opening "in" the unconscious. Does the event of appropriation also give the id in this sense? *Es gibt "Es"*? This might not be as nonsensical as it sounds. For Heidegger, from *Being and Time* on, time temporalizes itself, because is not a present being. This is time as the ek-statikon. The giving of the *Es* is a giving of itself, an autoaffective—temporal—giving. Here we can recall that Freud's *Es* also gives "primary, intermediate" phases that are neither active nor passive, and that always "accompany" the developmental history of the drives. This synthetic-differentiating, temporalizing process, makes it possible to say *Es gibt "Es."* In the seminar portion of "Time and Being" (1972) Heidegger comments that the "It" of "It gives" "does not name the availability of something which is, but rather precisely something unavailable, what concerns us as something uncanny, the demonic" (40). "It" gives the opening as differentiating double that is never present or absent, but is always "given," always active as autoaffective—the always returning primary intermediate.

Return is repetition. Is the repetition of *Es gibt* repetition of identity or repetition of difference? Heidegger allows us to think of the relatedness of the two forms of repetition, such that there could be no repetition of identity without repetition of difference. But the repetition of difference is uncanny, demonic, pain, tension. In specifically psychoanalytic terms, if transference is as repetition, it *is* because repetition has two modes: repetition of temporal immediacy and perceptual identity in tension reducing hallucinatory wish fulfillment; repetition of need in tension raising differential registration of the double in primary narcissism. Because need always returns, so too does the uncanny, the demonic, pain and tension.

Heidegger had asked in *Being and Time* whether being as the "prior," as primordial time, is "a phantom or is it 'more in being' than any possible being?" (1996, 384–85). Traditionally, transference as repetition has been spoken of "phantomatically": the reappearance of the ghosts of the past. Freud uses the image several times in *The Interpretation of Dreams* (1900, 421, 553), and so does Loewald (1980, 248–49), citing Freud. But transference as return of the ghosts of the past is not spoken of by either in terms of "the essential past," the always active, always *self-giving* opening of difference. Precisely because the essential past is the *giving* of itself, the self-temporalizing of the *Es gibt "Es,"* it is a "ghost" that can never be buried. The self-giving of the opening, of the *Es gibt*, would be phantomatic, demonic, uncanny, "unburiable" in just this sense. It is always there in the there, in the clearing, the opening. Therefore, it is always there in the analytic setting, and always there in the defensive, objectifying transference to the setting.

4. One of Heidegger's very last essays is "The End of Philosophy and the Task of Thinking" (1972). He contends that ours is the age of the completion of metaphysics, the global expansion of representational and causal thought inherent in technology. The decisive development of the sciences, within the field opened by the philosophies of Plato and Aristotle, inevitably led to their independence from philosophy. This might look like the dissolution of philosophy, but is actually the completion of the metaphysical project of thinking being *only* in terms of beings. Heidegger writes: "The sciences will interpret everything in their structure that is still reminiscent of their origin from philosophy in accordance with the rules of science, that is technologically. . . . The operational and model character of representational-calculative thinking becomes dominant" (57). He then asks whether there is a task for thinking concealed in the history of philosophy from beginning to end, "a task accessible neither to philosophy as metaphysics, nor, and even less so, to the sciences stemming from philosophy. . . . A thinking which can be neither metaphysics nor science" (59). Predictably, Heidegger speaks of the "opening" as the clearing for everything present and absent, so that the task of think-

ing is to become explicitly aware of the opening (65). The conception of temporality from *Being and Time* is now explicitly linked to the task of thinking the opening, because the opening is "that within which alone pure space and ecstatic time and everything present and absent in them have the place which gathers and protects everything. . . . But philosophy knows nothing of the opening" (66). Once ecstatic time is the opening of "pure space," i.e. the clearing itself, it is as the ontological relation of time and space.

Heidegger now characterizes the unconcealment of being as the "binding" character of the opening (68). Because concealment, *lethe*, belongs to unconcealment, *aletheia*, the opening is "the opening of presence concealing itself, the opening of a self-concealing sheltering . . . the opening of self-concealing" (71). In other words, opening as binding, as existential relatedness, conceals itself. This process is the task of thinking at the end of philosophy. Such thinking is neither science nor metaphysics and is "outside of the distinction of rational and irrational" (72).

In the appearance and disappearance in Freud's thought of unconscious processes not conceivable in subject-object terms, in the glimpses of a rethinking of unconscious time, there are several versions of "binding." Binding as "originally unconscious thought"—the registration of a tension raising relation. Binding as the before, the prior, of the pleasure principle, again linked to tension, pleasurepain, periodicity. Binding as articulating-connection in primary narcissism, such that there is the inescapable tie to what is (not) me, to the uncanniness of the time-space of interpretation, the opening of the analytic setting. A thinking that is neither science nor metaphysics, says Heidegger, has the task of thinking opening as binding, time as relation. And it has the task of thinking opening *bound* to its concealment, opening registered and repudiated. This is the task of psychoanalysis if it is to integrate its interpretive practice with a theory of its timed setting, the task of thinking the general structure of disavowal of difference.

fourth dimension of *time*. Opening, unthought by metaphysics and science, is the "binding" of space and time in the self giving of the *Es gibt*. Heidegger also says that "the unity of time's three dimensions consists in the interplay of each toward each. This interplay proves to be the true extending, *playing* in the very heart of time, the fourth dimension" (1972, 15). *Différance*, with its immediate reference to differing in time and space, says Derrida, is the "playing movement that 'produces' . . . effects of difference" (1982, 11).

There is a "common ground and *différance*" of the two interpretations of interpretation because *différance* is also a way of thinking articulation *as* connection. Deleuze had already pointed out that difference as articulation-connection is the shared theme of Nietzsche, Freud, and Heidegger. Derrida here speaks of the articulation and connection of the two interpretations of interpretation in relation to "historicity," a topic much discussed by Heidegger. *Being and Time* began by distinguishing historicity from the history of objectively present events. The possibility of history cannot be thought causally; in *Kant and the Problem of Metaphysics* (1962) it is intermediate, autoaffective—in psychoanalytic terms, transitional. Derrida too is saying that the nonmetaphysical interpretation of interpretation, the one that thinks beyond the traditional understandings of history and man, is nondeterministic, noncausal. But *as* historicity, as the possibility of the history of objective events, it is also the *différance* of causal, deterministic interpretation.

Freud, unlike Nietzsche and Heidegger, has no conception of noncausal interpretation. He assumes the possibility of historical interpretation, without thinking that one might have to interpret historicity itself. However, by situating Freud with Nietzsche and Heidegger on the displacement of the center, Derrida is asking us to think causal interpretation *with* noncausal interpretation. For Heidegger, "perdurance" holds together and apart interpretation as ground and interpretation as cause. For Derrida, noncausal interpretation, both different from *and* connected to causal interpretation, is their *différance* as play, the play of interpretation itself. The play affirmed by Nietzsche, and hinted at in Heidegger's fourth dimension of time.

Winnicott understood that the transitional space that makes interpretation possible is the *connection and separation* of past and present—historicity itself. Transitional space is also the possibility of play. Thus, Winnicott says that *"psychotherapy takes place in the overlap of two areas of playing, that of the patient and that of the therapist. . . . The corollary of this is that where playing is not possible then the work done by the therapist is directed towards bringing the patient from a state of not being able to play into a state being able to play"* (1971, 38).[16] But Winnicott does not discuss how and why someone might resist play. Loewald adds a crucial dimension when he says that therapeutic action *is* the internalization of the differential intrinsic to every interpretation. If registration and repudiation of difference is an ongoing unconscious process, then resistance to interpretation is resistance to play as transitional. Noncausal, active-descriptive interpretation opens the time-space of difference, makes possible the play of transitionality.

These psychoanalytic formulations of interpretation as play, however, do not address the essential metaphysical constraint on interpretation. In Heidegger's rethinking of interpretation as disclosure, interpretation does not make anything present, but analyzes presence itself as the flight from opening. Derrida's second interpretation of interpretation, interpretation as affirmation of play, would also have to be freed from the logic of presence. Clinically, this is difficult, but essential to understand. Defense against difference is *always* related to maintaining the traditional metaphysics of the real: subject and object, active and passive, inside and outside, as clearly defined, present opposites. To take such opposites as essences is to "recoil" from the nonpresent, intermediate states that make them possible. This "recoil" operates within the psychoanalytic theory of interpretation itself—for example, when interpretation is construed as *either* subjective *or* objective. In this sense, psychoanalytic interpretation as the search for origins conforms to Derrida's first interpretation of interpretation.

However, Derrida demonstrates that without knowing it, Freud placed radically nonpresent *différance* at the heart of his thinking. The initial understanding of the unconscious as memory depends upon the "spatial" opening of differentiated pathways (*Bahnungen*); the relation of past to present is one of "deferred effect." Moreover, Freud came to see the principle of delay as the relation of the pleasure principle to the reality principle (the latter as the deferral of the former), such that there is no absolute *opposition* between them (Derrida, 1982, 16–21). But Freud at no point sees that the centrality of spatiotemporal difference to the theory of the unconscious has to imply a critique of presence and causality. The large paradox of his thought is that it challenges the privilege of consciousness without challenging the privilege of presence.

For Derrida there is no possibility of a critique of consciousness without a critique of presence. He says that Freudian deferred effect cannot be thought as a past "present" that belatedly modifies a current "present." But this *is* Freud's basic understanding of deferred effect—precisely because Freud does not question presence. Derrida would have us think the deferred effect of a "'past' that has never been present" (1982, 21). This is akin to Heidegger's early notion of the "essential past," which has never been present in the sense of now-time, and his later notion of opening as time-space itself. Psychoanalytically, the "essential past that has never been present" can be thought in terms of differentiating registrations within primary narcissism, and in terms of the repetitive "permanence" of the intermediate, primary phases of the drive. Middle voice autoaffection *is* their structure, just as it is the temporality of the transcendental imagination (in Heidegger's reading of Kant). Since metaphysics "recoils" from such intermediacy, Derrida says that "the middle voice . . . may be what philosophy, at its outset, distributed into an active and a passive voice, thereby constituting itself by means of this repression" (9).

The "'past' that has never been present" is a phrase used by Emmanuel Levinas to describe "the trace and enigma of absolute alterity: the Other" (9). For Derrida, difference as the trace of the Other means that middle voice "self-affection" is in and of itself a relation to the Other: *self-affection is heteroaffection.* Thus, one can describe *différance* as "differentiating relation" (14), implying that *différance* is the process of opening to the Other—which is other than presence. Freud mainly thinks trace as storage of a past present. But in his primary-intermediate phases of the drive, autoaffection *is* heteroaffection; in primary narcissism autoaffection is the trace of the other I am (not). Freud does not begin to imagine that these two basic conceptions of trace—storage of a past present and differentiating registration—can be thought in a "differantial" relation to each other.

These two conceptions of trace also imply the two interpretations of interpretation. Interpretation of trace as storage of a past present presumes a history of objective events, the deciphering of origins; interpretation of trace as differentiating registration is interpretation of the intermediate play of the time-space of historicity. The former is interpretation of repression, defense against stored memory; the latter is interpretation of disavowal, ongoing defense against differentiating process. Although Freud certainly began to generalize disavowal at the end of his life, he had no time to think how it could change the model of interpretation built on the repression theory. Derrida implies that because *différance* was always at the heart of Freud's theory, he could have begun to think about something like the second interpretation of interpretation.

But since Freud never really questioned the metaphysics of presence, Derrida says that all Freud's "concepts . . . without exception, belong to the history of metaphysics, that is to the system of logocentric repression" (1978, 197). "Logocentric repression" was one of Derrida's most important early descriptions of metaphysics. It means the way in which the metaphysics of presence privileges spoken language: speech is the presence of language. "Logocentric *repression*" means that language as speech has to "forget" something with which it has a conflictual relation. Derrida found that even when speech is the privileged model of language, all such models inevitably refer to trace, inscription, and spacing at the origin. These nonpresent, differential, graphic elements—"writing" in Derrida's expanded sense—which make language possible, remain "unthought," or produce illogical, contradictory formulations—precisely because they undermine the privilege of presence. In his early work Derrida tends to look at the way the concept of "writing" becomes the "*symptomatic* form of the return of the repressed," the way in which "the metaphor of writing . . . haunts European discourse . . . [in] the systematic contradictions of the ontotheological exclusions of the trace" (197).

Derrida clearly wants to expand Heidegger's conception of metaphysics as ontotheology through his analysis of the logocentric repression of "trace." To describe the "ontotheological exclusions of the trace" in relation to "the symptomatic form of the return of the repressed" sounds psychoanalytic. But, says Derrida, "despite appearances, the deconstruction of logocentrism is not a psychoanalysis of philosophy" (1978, 196). Like Heidegger, for whom the forgetting of being is the largest question, Derrida thinks that the question of metaphysics *as* repression cannot simply be understood as the intrapsychic writ large. He writes: "logocentric repression is not comprehensible on the basis of the Freudian concept of repression; on the contrary, logocentric repression permits an understanding of how an original and individual repression became possible within the horizon of a culture and a historical structure of belonging" (196). But psychoanalysis and the deconstruction of metaphysics do meet in relation to the disavowal of difference. In *Group Psychology* (1921a) Freud noted, but could not explain, a general tendency to repudiate difference; Nietzsche's, Heidegger's, and Derrida's accounts of how metaphysics cannot think difference explain what Freud could not. The metaphysical tendency not to think difference as opening, articulation-connection, and intermediate, is the cultural-historical structure in which disavowal of difference becomes the most general intrapsychic question. Once this is so, one can rigorously speak of a *différance* of psychoanalysis and deconstruction. This is why Freud, and psychoanalysis in general, have always played such an important part in Derrida's thought.

"Freud and the Scene of Writing" and "Telepathy"

Originally published in 1966, "Freud and the Scene of Writing" is Derrida's first major statement of the role of psychoanalysis in his thinking. Ideally, it would be read in conjunction with *Voice and Phenomena* (1973), a study of Husserl, and *Of Grammatology* (1976). All these works pursue the metaphor of writing in philosophical discourse, and demonstrate the symptomatic incoherence which emerges when language assumed to be speech comes up against the question of its inscription. The incoherence is due to the fact that there could be no spoken language without a play of difference, and that writing itself is the trace of difference. In this expanded sense—trace of difference—"writing" is the condition of possibility of language. But writing is always considered *secondary* to the presence of spoken language. The privilege of presence encounters its limit: language as presence is made possible by what is other than presence. Freud is so significant for Derrida because he is always a thinker of trace, of writing as *primary*. For Derrida it is no accident that writing "will eventually invade the entirety of the psyche. Psychical *content* will be *represented* by a text whose essence is irreducibly graphic. The *structure* of the psychical *apparatus* will be *represented* by a writing machine" (1978, 199).

The early moment in Freud that makes possible the "invasion" of the psychic by writing is in the *Project* of 1895. Freud's great initial concern is to understand how memories not available to consciousness can produce symptoms. What is "mind" if not all memories are conscious, and yet have such powerful effects? Freud's first solution is to divide mind between perception and memory, seeing perception as conscious and memory as unconscious. In the imaginary neurophysiology of the *Project* there would have to be neurons for perception and neurons for memory, or a difference between neurons that accounts for conscious perception and unconscious memory. This difference is defined by Freud in terms of resistance to stimuli. Permeable neurons offer little resistance, and thus do not retain impressions permanently—conscious perception. Other neurons have "contact barriers" and offer resistance to excitation, but also retain an impression—unconscious memory. Derrida says that "this hypothesis is remarkable as soon as it is considered as a metaphorical model and not as a neurological description" (1978, 200).

What is remarkable in the metaphorical model can be explained under four major headings.

First, this origin of memory "presupposes a certain violence and a certain resistance to effraction. . . . Memory, thus . . . is the very essence of the psyche: resistance, and precisely, thereby, an opening to the effraction of the trace" (1978, 200–201). At the heart of Freud's initial conception, the unconscious is *open* precisely because it is memory; and because it is memory, it has to be conceived as trace, and as force.

Second, Freud immediately specifies that memory has to be thought "differentially." He says that if all contact barriers offered the same quantity of resistance, all memory pathways would be identical, and there would be no memory. Therefore, only the quantitative difference between the amount of resistance offered by the contact-barriers can account for differential pathways—that is, for memory itself. This is why Freud says that memory is represented by differences in the "breaching" (*Bahnung*, "facilitation" in the *Standard Edition*) of "psi neurons" (1895, 300). Derrida interprets: "Trace as memory is not a pure breaching [*Bahnung*] that might be reappropriated as simple presence; it is rather the ungraspable and invisible difference between breaches. We thus already know that psychic life is . . . the difference within the exertion of forces. As Nietzsche had already said" (1978, 201).

Third, Freud thinks that a principle of repetition is integral to differential breaching. He says that memory also depends upon the frequency with which the same impression is repeated (1895, 300). Derrida notes that frequency of repetition and quantity of excitation or resistance are heterogeneous, and that each repetition is discrete, finite. If finite repetitions are essential to memory, and heterogeneous to quantity, such repetitions can affect memory only "through the diastem which maintains their separation" (1978, 201). In other words, the interval between repetitions holds them apart and together, and itself acts with "the ungraspable and invisible difference between breaches." Repetition, then, "does not happen to an initial impression; its possibility is already there, in the resistance offered *the first time* by the psychical neurons" (202). This is like Deleuze's definition of difference as that which lies between two repetitions, and repetition as the differenciator of difference (1994, 76). Just as Nietzsche sees questions of empirical difference in terms of will to power and eternal return, so Derrida here is looking at Freud's "physiology of difference" in terms of the thinking of difference and repetition in general.

Fourth, the necessary violence of breaching immediately relates the question of differential pathways to pain. Freud himself says that "pain no doubt leaves permanent faciliations [*Bahnungen*]" (1895, 307). However, pain is trauma, and therefore must be deferred. Empirically, this is the essence of Freud's early theory. Painful, traumatic impressions are registered unconsciously, but there is an automatic attempt to defer their effect. Deferred effect—*différance*—is "irreducible," because memory is both the essence of psychic *life*, and yet linked to painful, traumatic disruption. Hence Derrida writes: "Life is already threatened by the origin of the memory which constitutes it" (1978, 202). He emphasizes that Freud calls all these processes "primary": difference, repetition, pain, and deferred effect are at the origin of the psyche. Thus, Derrida says, the classical conception of origin—which is differentiated and repeated only *after* its initial presence—becomes questionable.

But Derrida does not consider the ways in which difference and repetition in the *Project* have to be thought in relation to the registration of the experience of satisfaction. This is a critical issue, because registration of the experience of satisfaction is itself the articulation of psychic structure and psychic content. The psychic apparatus can register because it is "open to the effraction of the trace"; this is the condition of possibility of the wish, of psychic content. This openness of the apparatus always has to be thought in relation to primary narcissism, the way need and care imply "being-in-the-world." Satisfaction of empirical need—hunger—is bound to the pain of unconscious memory formation (the paradox of the hungry baby). Need, care, and self-preservation can be thought in terms of difference and repetition (will to power and eternal return).

Bahnung, including the registration of the experience of satisfaction, is itself the model for modification of the unconscious. Therefore it is essential to rethinking interpretation as differentiating process, rethinking therapeutic need and care. When Derrida says that "life is already threatened by the origin of the memory which constitutes it," he is thinking life in relation to the pain and tension of "opening to the effraction of the trace." Nietzsche saw the relation of life and difference in terms of pain; Heidegger came to see life as "stress" and difference as pain. Derrida goes one step further in his reading of the *Project* and says that "life must be thought of as trace before Being may be determined as presence" (1978, 203). The repetitive, differentiating registration of the experience of satisfaction includes the structural pain (tension) of primary narcissism. This *is* life as trace—again, the paradox of the hungry baby. But as the model for modification of the unconscious, it is also the essence of interpretive care. The general structure of disavowal of difference explains the inevitable "recoil" from life, trace, and care.

Automatic registration of difference implies a "device" for inscription; repudiation of difference implies that the device can "split itself." This conception integrates a theory of the psychic apparatus with something like Nietzsche's "life against itself" and Heidegger's "Dasein in flight from itself." However, Nietzsche lacked any conception of an unconscious apparatus and Heidegger simply dismissed it. Unlike Nietzsche and Heidegger, Derrida does think the psychic apparatus—because Freud himself represents it as a writing machine. Further, the interpretive structure of the psychoanalytic setting is itself a function of this apparatus. How to integrate a theory of interpretation with this strange conception of the unconscious as nonmetaphysical "machine"?

Derrida first addresses interpretation in relation to the psychic apparatus in terms of translation and energy. In *The Interpretation of Dreams* Freud demonstrates why translation of the manifest dream into its latent meaning can have no fixed key: interpretation emerges from the idiosyncrasies of the dreamer's associations. The psychoanalyst is in the position of the interpreter of hieroglyphics—the manifest dream as a picture language—except that each dreamer invents the hieroglyphics themselves. Actually, Derrida notes, Freud sets two limits on the translatability, the interpretation, of dreams. First, the materiality of the dream's pictographic writing itself cannot be translated, precisely because each dreamer creates his or her own idiom. Second, translation considered intrapsychically does not simply mean that something is taken from the unconscious and "moved" like an object into the preconscious or consciousness. Rather, as Freud explains, it is really a question of modifying relations of force and excitation. (Recall Ricoeur's insistence that for Freud hermeneutics is always energetics.) Derrida radicalizes both limits on interpretation. He says that unconscious writing cannot be considered as an "immobile . . . archive whose signified content might be harmlessly transported into the milieu of a different language, that of the preconscious or the conscious" (211). He then considers these limits in terms of the critique of presence:

> the value of presence can . . . dangerously affect the concept of the uncon-
> scious. There is . . . no unconscious truth to be rediscovered by virtue of
> having been written elsewhere. . . . There is no present text in general, and
> there is not even a past present text, a text which is past as having been pres-
> ent. . . . The unconscious text is already a weave of pure traces, differences in
> which meaning and force are united—a text nowhere present. (211)

One might accuse Derrida of overstatement here. For Freud there always seems to be an unconscious truth to be rediscovered, for just the reason Derrida rejects: the apparatus allows it to be "written" elsewhere. Yet the relation between historicity and registration of difference, the "essential past" that has never been present, means that Freud has lodged other processes within his assumptions about the presence of an unconscious text. Without such processes, there would be no present unconscious text (as in the relation between registration of the experience of satisfaction and the hallucinatory content of dreams; or the registration of sexual difference and the fantasies of phallic absence and presence). Derrida's statement about there being no present unconscious text holds on the level of historicity. Because truth and presence are not relevant categories on this level, interpretation itself is not a question of bringing truth into presence. Meaning itself is not primary. The unconscious as a "weave of pure traces" is an archival apparatus for "a meaning which was never present, whose signified presence is always reconstituted by deferral, *nachträglich*, belatedly, *supplementarily*: for *nachträglich* also means *supplementary*" (211; original emphasis). And Derrida immediately notes the contradictory double meaning of the verb *suppléer* (to supplement): to add what is *missing*, to supply something *extra*.

Supplementarity was an important concept for Derrida at this time. In *Of Grammatology* (1976) especially, he was captivated by Rousseau's descriptions of writing (and masturbation) as a "dangerous supplement." This became a prime example of the contradictions which always emerge when a thinker takes language to mean speech (because speech appears to be the living presence of language), and then attempts to conceive the relation of writing to speech. Writing is considered as *extra*, secondary, coming after the original living presence of spoken language. Yet writing is the differential play without which language would be *missing* that which makes it possible. This makes "writing" "primary," even though it must always be conceived as a "substitute," a supplement, for full speech. Consequently, such secondary supplementarity is at the heart of the primary.

Derrida, then, is demonstrating that Freud's use of scriptural metaphors to describe the functioning of the psychic apparatus, along with the irreducibility of deferred effect, mean that writing operates in the primary-secondary way of supplementarity. In fact, because one sense of *nachtrag* itself is "supplement," Derrida finds the expanded sense of writing, with its challenge to the metaphysics of presence, in the structure of Freud's discourse:

> That the present in general is not primal, but, rather reconstituted, that it is not the absolute, wholly living form which constitutes experience, that there is no purity of the living present—such is the theme, formidable for metaphysics, which Freud, in a conceptual scheme unequal to the thing itself, would have us pursue. This pursuit is doubtless the only one which is exhausted neither within metaphysics nor within science. (1978, 212)

In "The End of Philosophy and the Task of Thinking" Heidegger too had spoken of what is to be thought outside the domains of metaphysics and science: "opening as self-concealing" (1972, 72). Derrida is saying that "Freud's discovery" of the "irreducibility of the 'effect of deferral'" (1978, 203), with all its links to writing and difference, situates psychoanalysis exactly where Heidegger situates thinking at the end of philosophy. For this reason Derrida articulates another aspect of the dialogue between Heidegger and Freud. The irreducibility of the effect of deferral opens onto a thinking of time not dominated by the privilege of presence. Therefore, writes Derrida, the "timelessness of the unconscious is no doubt determined only in opposition to a common concept of time, a traditional concept, the metaphysical concept: the time of mechanics or the time of consciousness. We ought perhaps to read Freud the way Heidegger read Kant: like the *cogito*, the unconscious is no doubt timeless only from the standpoint of a certain vulgar conception of time" (215).

Freud *did* read himself the way Heidegger read Kant, in the singular passage on unconscious time in *Beyond the Pleasure Principle* (1920). There he said just what Derrida says here—that the unconscious is "timeless" only in opposition to conscious time, to the assumption that conscious time is time itself. Freud began to think unconscious time as trauma, calling for conscious time as a protective stimulus barrier. Thus, time is related to force, pain, tension. And Freud's conception of the primary, intermediate phases of the drives can be linked to the autoaffective temporality of the transcendental imagination—exactly what Derrida is referring to when he speaks of the way Heidegger read Kant.

Supplementarity is also Derrida's intervention into the question of finitude so essential to Nietzsche's thinking of difference and Heidegger's thinking of time. That which is *missing* something is finite, as is that which is *extra*. Trace as *supplement* of life, as the relation of *différance* to life, then has to imply finitude. The experience of satisfaction is itself a question of empirical finitude, need, and care—the essential helplessness of the baby, as Freud called it. But the *registration* of the experience of satisfaction is simultaneously a question of the apparatus and primary narcissism, of the mother-baby matrix and trace. Since the baby is not a subject and the mother not an object in this matrix, the registration of the experience of satisfaction *is* the trace of the other *as relation*. In terms of finitude and the apparatus, mother and baby are in a relation of supplementarity. And because registration of the experience of satisfaction is the model for modification of the unconscious, so are analyst and patient.

This is another way of thinking why the active-descriptive interpretations that address defenses against differentiation generally concern the splitting off of the *relation* between patient and analyst. It is also a way of thinking the relation of the apparatus to the interpretive setting. Derrida always reminds us that writing as supplement is construed as the "technique" for inscribing the presence of speech. Writing is always technological. Supplementarity at the origin puts the technological "before" the origin—"life must be thought as trace before Being can be thought as presence" (1978, 203). As the technology of trace, supplementarity describes a "living machine." As an "open" machine, a machine operating according to principles of difference and deferral, the Freudian unconscious is always in a relational structure that modifies it. Hence, interpretation itself as differential relation. This way of thinking about interpretation in relation to the psychic apparatus goes beyond the thinking of interpretation based on the repression model.

All of this comes together at the moment when the scriptural metaphors for psychic content become a scriptural metaphor for the psychic apparatus. In an apparently minor text of 1925c, "A Note on the Mystic Writing Pad," Freud says that he has found something he had been searching for since the *Project*: a writing apparatus that accounts for conscious perception and unconscious memory. As Derrida puts it, until Freud came across the *Wunderblock*, the "magic slate," there was no model for a "writing machine" that combined the essential characteristics of the psychic apparatus: "a potential for indefinite preservation [memory] and an unlimited capacity for reception [perception]" (1978, 222). Such a model would also have to be one in which preservation and reception are in different localities, which are nevertheless instrinsically related to each other. The three strata of the magic slate illustrate this idea perfectly. Its two upper layers—the transparent celluloid and the translucent waxed paper—rest upon a lower layer of wax. To write on the *Wunderblock* one uses a stylus. Freud first emphasizes the analogy of the two upper layers to the perceptual system. The impressions made by the stylus are visible because the transparent and translucent layers rest upon the wax. Since the lower ends of the two upper layers are not fixed to the wax, one has only to lift them to make the impressions disappear. The upper layers are then free for renewed inscription. Thus, the upper layers can always receive "fresh inscriptions"; and the uppermost, transparent celluloid layer also serves as protection. Freud says happily that the *Wunderblock* demonstrates the functioning of a perceptual apparatus which has an external shield against stimuli and a surface behind the protective shield which receives stimuli (1925c, 230).

Derrida makes two important comments about the comparison of the upper layers of the *Wunderblock* to the perceptual apparatus. First, the *Wunderblock* is "a stratification of surfaces each of whose relation to itself, each of whose interior, is but the implication of another similarly exposed surface" (1978, 224). Because a writing apparatus operates in terms of inscriptions on a surface, to compare the psyche to such an apparatus will have to upset the usual conceptions of "depth" and "surface." Once the metaphor of writing describes the *entire* apparatus—as will happen in a moment—not only perception, but memory too, will be a question of surface. The apparatus must be conceived as unconscious surface in order to account for its "being-in-the-world."[17] Second, Freud's emphasis on the protective function of the upper layer of the scriptural apparatus shows that there "is no writing which does not devise some means of protection, *to protect against itself,* against the writing by which the 'subject' is himself threatened as he lets himself be written: *as he exposes himself*" (224, original emphases). In his reading of the *Project*, Derrida had already said that the psyche, as "opening to the effraction of the trace," is threatened by the possibility that constitutes it. There it was a question of unconscious memory; Freud is now speaking of protection against external, perceptual stimuli. Within primary narcissism, however, memory, the "exposed surface of inscription," registers perception: where one cannot speak of inner and outer, memory *is* perception (as Loewald had already noted [1980, 254–55]). Thus the psyche's protection against "opening," "exposure," splits its intrinsic "being in the world" into conscious and unconscious, perception and memory. Nietzsche's life against itself and Heidegger's Dasein in flight from itself similarly split an intrinsic relation to "world" into subject and object.

Freud, assuming the split between conscious and unconscious, perception and memory, says that inscriptions can be erased from the upper layers of the *Wunderblock*, but are permanently retained in the lowest wax layer. Inevitably he compares the layer of permanent, but not visible, inscription to the unconscious. He says that the "layer which receives the stimuli—the system *Pcpt.-Cs.*—forms no permanent traces; the foundations of memory come about in other, adjoining systems" (1925c, 230). If the apparatus is to be capable of permanent storage while always remaining available for new inscriptions, Freud has here an almost perfect analogy to the idea that memory and perception must be in separate systems. And he has a model in which the unconscious makes consciousness possible, in which—as is always the case for Freud—the unconscious is the permanent, if mostly invisible, process, while consciousness is transitory: inscriptions come and go on the upper levels. But because Freud has said that the foundation—the possibility—of memory is in "other, adjoining systems," Derrida interprets that "writing supplements perception before perception even appears to itself" (1978, 224). The idea of differentiating traces implies "perception as memory," "conscious as unconscious," trace before presence—the functioning of a supplementary scriptural apparatus.

All of this opens onto the question of time. Until this point, says Derrida, "it has been a question only of the space of writing. . . . But there is as well a *time of writing*, and this time of writing is nothing other than the very structure of that which we are now describing" (1978, 225). Because Freud is describing what Derrida calls an "operation" (or a "process"), the interactions of the layers must be temporal. Derrida notes that Freud refers to "a discontinuist conception of time, as the periodicity and spacing of writing" (225); he links this reference to all the references to periodicity which stretch across Freud's work.

Periodicity implies finite intervals. Here, Freud links periodicity to the coming and going of consciousness, to intermittent reception of perceptual stimuli. He now attributes this intermittence to the periodic "cathexes" of consciousness from the unconscious. The unconscious stretches out "feelers" to sample the external world through consciousness. Whenever the cathexis, the feeler, is retracted, consciousness fades. Freud says that the "origin of our concept of time" is in the "periodic non-excitability" and "discontinuous method of functioning of the system *Pcpt.-Cs.*" (1925c, 231). Derrida comments: "Time is the economy of a system of writing" (1978, 226).

Freud concludes the paper on the *Wunderblock* by asking us to imagine one hand writing on its surface while the other hand periodically raises the uppermost layers to erase the inscriptions, keeping them fresh for new ones. This periodicity depends upon the periodic sampling of the external world by the unconscious. Because the question of trace cannot be divorced from the unconscious, and because consciousness has to be intermittent for Freud, Derrida writes: "Traces thus produce the space of their inscription only by acceding to the period of their erasure. From the beginning, in the 'present' of their first impression, they are constituted by the double force of repetition and erasure, legibility and illegibility" (1978, 226).

Careful reading might show an uneasy relation between Derrida's statement and Freud's thinking here. Despite the necessary scriptural metaphors, Freud is still thinking trace in terms of presence, the permanent retention of the present trace in the unconscious. His comments about periodicity emphasize *both* consciousness and the "sampling" of the external world by the unconscious. Certainly Freud uses the scriptural images of repetition and erasure, but none of this is integrated with Derrida's central idea that "the value of presence can . . . dangerously affect the concept of the unconscious" (1978, 211). Rather, the *Wunderblock* demonstrates how repetition and erasure in relation to temporary versus permanent storage account for the *presence* of unconscious traces. Ceding the difficulty, Derrida finally will say that Freud mostly conceives writing in terms of "empirical memories of a present truth outside of time" (227). Is there a gap between the *implications* of Freud's use of scriptural metaphors and the rest of his thinking?

To answer the question, Derrida looks at the "two-handedness" of the *Wunderblock*. He asks: "A two-handed machine, a multiplicity of agencies or origins—is this not the original relation to the other and the original temporality of writing, its 'primary' complication: an originary spacing, deferring, and erasure of the simple origin?" (226). Derrida is stretching Freud's conception of trace, so that it is always the trace of the other, always a *relation* to the other that is "other than presence." Difference as repetition, trace as erasure, have to *imply* nonpresent, spatiotemporal processes, but Freud would doubtless balk at the implication. The question of erasure is particularly important, because Freud compares the lifting of the upper layers of the *Wunderblock* to repression. Derrida says: "Writing is unthinkable without repression. The condition for writing is that there be neither a permanent contact nor an absolute break between strata: the vigilance and failure of censorship" (226). This is accurate: the *Wunderblock* works so well for Freud because "erasure," i.e. repression, accounts for an unconscious periodically in and out of touch with consciousness. But everything still depends upon presence for Freud: the repression of a present trace in consciousness guarantees its permanent presence in the unconscious.

Derrida, we have noted, does not consider the registration of the experience of satisfaction. However, to think trace "before" presence, to think "writing" as the hinge between psychic structure and psychic content, one has to. The registration of the experience of satisfaction literally concerns both conscious and unconscious: storage of an image, opening of a pathway. As a process within primary narcissism, however, it implies that conscious "is" unconscious, because, as Loewald said, in the mother-baby matrix perception *is* memory. In Nietzschean terms registration of the experience of satisfaction describes self-preservation as repetition and difference; in Heideggerean terms it describes the reality of care outside a subject-object structure. As conjointly conscious-unconscious, as "ecstatic," the registration of the experience of satisfaction must be thought as the articulating-connecting trace of the other. On this level, one can accurately think trace as nonpresent.

But Derrida is emphasizing that such traces must be thought in relation to the psyche as writing *machine*. He examines Freud's statement that the comparison of the psychic apparatus to the writing machine finally breaks down. Freud says that unlike the psyche, the *Wunderblock* cannot bring erased inscriptions from the wax back to the surface on its own, i.e. cannot bring repressed memories back into consciousness. "It would be mystic writing pad indeed if, like our memory, it could accomplish that" (1925c, 230). For Derrida, this is where Freud slips back into the metaphysics he had almost escaped. Freud's gesture here is Platonic: the writing of the "soul" is living; the scriptural machine is dead (1978, 227). But, says Derrida, everything that Freud had thought about the unity of life and death should have made him ask other questions here, and to ask them explicitly (227) If the metaphor of the writing machine is more than a metaphor, if it *is* the psyche, then the traditional opposition of the living soul to the dead machine itself becomes questionable. Freud does not engage this question explicitly. But the *inscription* of the experience of satisfaction in a context of primary narcissism concerns both "life" and technology, the unconscious as "living machine."

Derrida always thinks of spatiotemporal difference as this kind of intermediate technology— a great difference between his thought and Heidegger's. For Heidegger, technology is the inevitable end of philosophy. It is the planetary triumph of the metaphysical project which reduces being to beings, so that thought itself is exclusively representational-calculative. But Derrida, in his reading of Freud, finds a way to think technology as writing machine, technology as difference. Heidegger could dismiss Freud's conception of the psyche as a prime example of technological metaphysics, because he was unable to think the "strange machine" that Derrida finds in Freud's metaphor of the apparatus. The psychic apparatus cannot operate exclusively according to the entropic principle of tension reduction that describes the classical machine. It is a "living, differentiating machine" which increases its own tension levels repetitively, automatically. It is a "living machine" because it is in open relation to its environment. And it is a living machine that calibrates its own capacity for tension tolerance, protecting itself from itself. It closes itself, creating a picture of itself running exclusively on a tension reduction principle, when differentiating tension is traumatic. It even creates the illusion that conscious time is time itself. Derrida does not say all of this. But he does

locate in Freud's unconscious technology of writing and difference a way
to challenge Heidegger's conception of technology.

The interpretive setting, we have said, is a function of the psychic apparatus. Interpretation as differentiating process is technological in the way
Derrida asks us to think technology. The *relation* between patient and
analyst cannot be thought in strictly human, interpersonal terms. (Winnicott, in a flash, speaks of the "mother's technique" [1954, 263].) If the
analyst does not maintain the differential of the interpretive stance, the
analyst disavows the uncanny reality of "unconscious" processes as intermediate technology. For Heidegger, being-in-the-world is itself uncanny;
it is the "outside of oneself" as care, as temporal-ecstatic. This essential
uncanniness as care becomes being-toward-death as "Da-sein's ownmost
non-relational possibility" in *Being and Time*. Derrida is providing the
means to think an essential uncanniness of the living-dead machine as
relational. The relation, however, is not strictly human: it is a relation
to what is other than presence, to difference, to intermediate time-space
between life and death, between man and machine, to the "technological"
mother of primary narcissism. If one were to read Heidegger on Kant the
way Derrida reads Freud, one would have to think of the *technology* of the
transcendental imagination, the technology of time.[18]

Years later, Derrida returned to the question of the technology of the
transcendental imagination in "Telepathy" (1981). His reading of Freud's
unusual essays on telepathy is akin to his reading of "A Note on the Mystic Writing Pad" (1925c). He deliberately looks at the way in which certain
technological metaphors in apparently minor writings of Freud produce
some of the most radical openings to nonmetaphysical thinking. Derrida's
analysis of telepathy in fact leads him to say that the "analytic situation"—
the timed, interpretive setting—itself has to be conceived in terms of a
"new metrics of time . . . as well as another reading of the transcendental
imagination" (1981, 243).

Freud examines telepathy in the 1920s (1921b, 1922a) in the same spirit
in which he approached dreams. The popular tradition had always found
dreams meaningful; science had mostly thought of dreams as meaningless.
The popular tradition, of course, had no conception that the meaning of
dreams was a result of unconscious processes; and science itself, for Freud,
always equated mind with consciousness. To create a scientific theory of
the unconscious was to find the truth hidden in the popular beliefs about

dreams. Analogously, there has always been a popular tradition of belief in telepathy—the belief that one can somehow "know" what is going on in someone else's mind, or that one can "know" things in unconventional ways. Is not the psychoanalyst someone who "knows" what is going on in someone else's mind? At least metaphorically, the possibility of telepathy would be the possibility of psychoanalysis. Freud supports his gesture here by comparing psychoanalysis to such scientific advances as the discovery of radium and the theory of relativity: both allowed science to understand things previously rejected as "occult"—"alchemical" transformation of one element into another; malleability of time and space. Both discoveries, says Freud, ran the risk of seeming to undermine science, but really expanded it (1921b, 177–78). He wants to examine telepathy in just this way. Derrida paraphrases: "It is difficult to imagine a theory of what they still call the unconscious without a theory of telepathy. They can neither be confused nor dissociated" (1981, 247).

Strictly speaking, Freud had already envisaged something like telepathy in a familiar passage of one of his papers on technique (1912). There he said that the "fundamental rule" of psychoanalysis—free association—has to be complemented by the analyst's "evenly suspended attention." Just as the patient has to say whatever comes to mind, so the analyst has to give equal weight to everything the patient says *and* to whatever comes to his or her mind while listening to the patient. Freud used the—technological—image of the telephone to describe the interaction between patient's and analyst's free associations. At one end of a telephone conversation someone speaks. The wires transport physical energy, sound waves, which are reconverted back into words by the listener at the receiving end. By giving equal weight to everything the patient says, and by being open to all his or her own responses, the analyst is *unconsciously* picking up the "energic" underpinning of what the patient is saying, and then reconverting this "energy" back into thoughts, interpretations. The whole analytic process depends upon the possibility that one unconscious can affect another without going directly through consciousness (1912, 115–16). In the first paper on telepathy, Freud rebaptizes this process "thought transference" (1921b, 184). He concludes the second telepathy paper by saying that the entire question of telepathy is nonproblematic if considered as an unconscious phenomenon (1922a, 220). There was always "thought transference" for a "telephonic" unconscious.

What is important for Derrida is that Freud is describing an unconscious technology of teletransport and conversion—literally transport of energy and reconversion into words. In "Freud and the Scene of Writing" (1978) Derrida examined how these technological metaphors function as more than metaphors. Here, he is most interested in the *transport*, because "transport" itself is the technical means of carrying over (trans-) a distance (tele-). The etymologically linked words "trans-lation" (*latus* is the past participle of *pherein*, "to carry over"; *Ubersetzung*), "meta-phor" (same derivation; *Uber-tragung*, "carrying over"), and "trans-ference" (again same derivation; again *Ubertragung*) all *literally* depend upon what Derrida calls "telematic *tekhne*," transport over (spatial) distance. This is also a radically "relational technology": Derrida notes that Freud says that unconscious telematic technology is "always plugged in" (1981, 253). The entire theory of the unconscious, Derrida says, implies that it is "difficult to imagine that one might think something within oneself without being surprised by the other, without the other even being aware of it on the spot" (247). Not only is there an "interpersonal" unconscious technology of transport, the "intrapsychic" *is* this technology. It is always a question of *trans*-port and differential distance (*tele-*).

But how does this lead to the postulation of a "new metrics of time" and "another reading of the transcendental imagination"? Freud concludes the second telepathy paper with a hint about why telepathic unconscious processes also demand a rethinking of time. He calmly—and shockingly—asserts that it is possible to receive "telepathic" knowledge of events taking place at some distance in time and space in sleep. This knowledge can then be integrated into a dream (1922b, 219). (He gives the example of a man whose dream seemed to demonstrate foreknowledge of the birth of his grandchildren, knowledge that objectively could only have reached him the next day.) Freud's stance here is complex. On one hand, he casually gives to telepathic phenomena in dreams the status of something as ordinary as the perception of physical needs during sleep, or the appearance of the day's residue in the dream. On the other, he asks about the status of the *reality* of the event telepathically received in the dream and links it to the possibility of unconscious time. He says that dream interpretation—which in the case of the unconscious reception of the news of the birth also proceeds along traditional lines, integrating the telepathic event with the dreamer's Oedipal conflicts—both maintains and negates the difference between the dream and the event. In other words, if the *reality* of the telepathic event occurs in a dream, reality itself cannot simply be the "objective reality" of consciousness. Then Freud says that the time of telepathic reality cannot be "astronomical," "objective time," because the "technology" of transport over distance implies a time *delay* (1922a, 220). Derrida comments: "With the help of psychic temporality, of its nonsynchronicity, its time differences if you will . . . one can peacefully envisage telepathic probability" (1981, 265).

Here we have a complex technology. The telephone "explained" the transport and reception of telepathy. Now this transport and reception take us into a reality of differential time, Derrida's "new metrics of time." This is the differential time that is as "real" as "astronomical time," and is inherent to it. (Recall Freud's singular remarks about the unconscious time symptomatically inherent to conscious time from *Beyond the Pleasure Principle*.) As a technology of receptivity, telepathy depends upon both the unconscious receptivity Freud had already compared to the telephone *and* upon differential time. This conception radicalizes deferred effect, demonstrating that it is not *only* a defensive response to trauma, but is always part of communication "between" one unconscious and another, and "within" the unconscious. The reality of such communication depends upon "deferred receptivity," a receptivity which cannot be isolated in "astronomical time." However it occurs —whether as telepathic event, analytic interpretation, intrapsychic process—it implies a receptivity that cannot be consciously willed: this is why the analyst's "evenly suspended attention" is the necessary complement to free association. Thus Freud speaks of the "receptive and passive" aspect of telepathy. Derrida here "regrets that [Freud] did not read a certain Kantbuch which was being written just when he changed his mind . . . about the possibility of telepathy" (1981, 264). Why? Heidegger describes the "autoaffective" temporality of the transcendental imagination as "pure receptivity" (1962, 195). "Pure" here means transcendental, which for Heidegger always becomes "ontological." "Pure receptivity" also "reaches out," is the essence of synthesis, binding, relation. The receptive relationality of the transcendental imagination, integrated with a "telephonic" unconscious, is the technological possibility of telepathy.

In discussing *Kant and the Problem of Metaphysics* (1962), we emphasized that processes in primary narcissism can be described as autoaffective in a nonsubjective sense. The registration of the experience of satisfaction within primary narcissism can be described as a "receptive, passive" unconscious differentiation. Freud even envisaged "originally unconscious thought" as the tension-raising "impression" of a relation, which can only occur within the context of primary narcissism—another kind of "passive reception." But primary narcissism is the area of the intermediate, just as the transcendental imagination is "transitional." Just as Heidegger envisaged a receptive spontaneity of the transcendental imagination, so Freud briefly glimpsed the "primary phase" of the drive as the *possibility* of its active and passive versions. Again, the *active receptivity* of telepathy and of the transcendental imagination is not consciously willed. Analogously, the analyst's apparently "passive, receptive" stance makes interpretation possible. Derrida is linking Heidegger's autoaffective receptivity to Freud's intuition about differential temporality and telepathy. But, as always, Derrida is thinking technologically. His references to *Kant and the Problem of Metaphysics* mean that the telepathic technology of the unconscious is structurally related to the temporality of the transcendental imagination.

There is a long psychoanalytic tradition of thinking the mother-infant matrix in terms of unconscious communication, with an emphasis on transmission of affect. Derrida's emphasis is on the "technology" that would make such unconscious communication possible. Not only is the psyche a "writing machine" that operates on a principle of differential time, it is now a "telepathic" machine operating on the same principle. Derrida says that the thinking of telepathy has to free itself from the "Oedipal code" which coexists all too easily with traditional assumptions about reality, time, and space. As in the discussion of the structural *repetition* of the "primary phases" of the drives, one can say that all processes of differentiation unconsciously occur in primary narcissism, in transitional time-space. This "primary, intermediate" time-space" *repeats itself*. It coexists with "Oedipal reality." It is the possibility of "telepathic" registration of difference.

The technology of the clock, the nonsynchronicity of its apparent synchronicity, is "telepathic" in this sense. The "new metrics of time" of the analytic situation means thinking clock time in relation to ecstatic time. Ecstatic time is the structure of care and interpretation. It is a *relation* to what is other than presence, to differential time-space. Derrida does not specifically think "care" the way Heidegger does. But all of his thinking about technology as transitional life-death allows an understanding of the psychic apparatus as "relational machine." The "new metrics of time" linked to "another reading of the transcendental imagination" is not literally another way to measure time, so that the analytic session itself might not be timed. Rather the measure of time itself always contains the "other metrics" of the transcendental imagination technologically conceived. Again, the psychic apparatus is a kind of intervallic "clock," a clock that functions both according to differential unconscious time (disjunctive telepathic-receptive time) *and* objectively present conscious time (classically uniform astronomical time). Thus a patient can simultaneously resist the opening of interpretive care while attempting to control clock time. The patient is attempting to disavow the reality of the other metrics of the timed interpretive setting. Just as the analyst must understand why apparent passivity is an activity that makes the transitional *space* of interpretation possible, so too the analyst must understand that use of the clock to measure the session depends upon differential, nonsynchronous time, the time of tele-transport. This is the temporality of unconscious communication, the possibility of psychoanalytic interpretation.

Fetishism and Specters

> Ghosts used to be either likenesses of the dead or wraiths of the living. But here in the Zone categories have been blurred badly.
> —Pynchon, *Gravity's Rainbow* (1973)

The description of intermediate states demands locutions like "active-passive" or "living-dead." These expressions contain intermediacy within themselves. Derrida early on found a pattern of blind use of words with intermediate, double meanings to describe writing itself (e.g. "supplement" in Rousseau; *pharmakon*, "remedy-poison," in Plato). He saw such blind self-contradictions as symptomatic expressions of the "ontotheological" exclusion of the trace. Since writing, as trace, is itself for Derrida the play of difference, he coined a term whose double meaning itself describes this play. *Différance*, of course, is not simply a neologism. As an actual word it means the act of deferring. This temporal sense of the word, combined with its phonic indistinguishability from *difference*, becomes a description of how double meaning words themselves function: they are different in themselves, deferring any decision about a singular meaning. Derrida calls such words "undecidable." Suspensive undecidability is the "play of *différance*" which "creates effects of difference." Wherever there is an effect of difference, there is always also a question of undecidability.

Undecidability is oscillation. Freud's theory of fetishism brings oscillating structures into psychoanalytic theory, because the fetish oscillates between registration and repudiation of reality. Derrida undertakes an analysis of fetishism in *Glas* (1986) to demonstrate how Freud brushes up against nonmetaphysical thinking without quite realizing it, when the oscillation of the fetish leads to undecidability. Ultimately, Derrida finds in Freud a possible generalization of fetishism that cannot be contained within a decidable logic of opposition. This means that there are "heterogeneous elements in Freud's text, i.e. decidable and undecidable statements, and a non-closure of the text on itself" (1986, 209).

Derrida himself seems unaware of Freud's own generalization of fetishism at the end of his life. Is there a relation between Derrida's "general fetishism" as a potential logic of oscillating undecidability and Freud's own generalization of fetishism? Between what Derrida calls the "nonclosure" of Freud's text on itself and psychoanalytic practice? Such questions guided the rethinking of registration and repudiation of reality in *Difference and Disavowal* (2000). Freud, we know, embroiled himself in the illogic of a registration and repudiation of "the reality of castration." This contradiction was resolved by postulating a registration and repudiation of the reality of (sexual) difference. Castration and noncastration, phallic absence and presence, are then substitutes for the split off reality of sexual difference. Freud did not see the double oscillation in fetishism: between registration and repudiation of difference, i.e. between reality and fantasy; and between the phallic absence and presence that replace the reality of difference, i.e. between two fantasies conflated with reality. How does Derrida's analysis of the undecidability of fetishism in *Glas* intersect with all of this?

At first, Derrida takes pains to demonstrate that in terms of truth and decidability fetishism has to be understood as a form of the castration complex. Here, the emphasis is on Hegel and Freud. Castration itself, Hegel and psychoanalysis agree, while not a real event, is about law, conceptuality, and the all-encompassing dialectical process of *Aufhebung*—negation, conservation, "raising up" to new synthesis. If fetishism is to depart from metaphysics, it cannot be on the basis of a logic of castration which is easily accommodated to speculative dialectics (1986, 43).

Derrida finds in Hegel's discussion of the fetishism of African religions the beginning of a "resistance" to dialectical logic. Hegel himself says that African religion has no history, is "unconscious," in the sense that it is not governed by the "motor" of consciousness as negation (1986, 207). But eventually the African "unconscious" does become "conscious," does enter history, does dialecticize itself (209). Therefore, one might view the fetishism of African religions as that which resists dialectics, or as a resistance to dialectics that is its negative—and therefore dialectizable. Thus Derrida's first major point: something about fetishism leaves it suspended between decidable dialectics and undecidability itself: "A certain undecidability of the fetish lets it oscillate between a dialectics (of the undecidable and the dialectical) and an undecidability (between the dialectical and the undecidable)" (207).

To specify the undecidability of the fetish, Derrida analyzes its structure more precisely. He says that wherever it appears, whether in Hegel, Marx, or Freud, the fetish is always understood as a *substitute* (209). The fetish is a substitute for

> the thing itself . . . , the origin of presence . . . , what occupies the center function in a system, for example the phallus in a certain phantasmatic organization. If the fetish substitutes itself for the thing itself in its manifest presence, in its truth, there should no longer be any fetish as soon as there is truth, the presentation of the thing itself in its essence. . . . Something—the thing—is no longer itself a substitute: there is the non-substitute, that is what constructs the concept fetish. . . . If what has always been called fetish . . . implies the reference to a nonsubstitutive thing, there should be somewhere—and that is the truth of the fetish, the relation of the fetish to truth—a decidable value of the fetish, a decidable opposition of the fetish to the nonfetish. (209)

The allusion to "the center function in a system" takes us back to "Structure, Sign, and Play," where Derrida demonstrated that at the center of every structure there is always play and repetition, difference where one assumes there would be full presence. He is now saying that the psychoanalytic theory of the castration complex itself presumes the presence of the phallus as its structuring center. The fetish, as Freud insists, is a substitute for the missing maternal phallus, presumed to be absent because it was once present. The "reality of castration" is an effect of full presence at the center of a fantasy organization. All conceptions of fetishism, including Freud's, assume that the fetish is the secondary substitute for the original presence of the thing—e.g. the phallus. If there is presence at the center, the fetish as substitute is *decidably opposed* to the "real thing."

Derrida's thinking of difference as trace is always concerned with the idea of the "secondary" substitute—e.g. writing as the substitute for speech. For Freud the fetish is decidably opposed to the presence it replaces. But because the fetish *is* a substitute, might it function as an "original substitute," which undermines the decidable relation between the thing itself and its substitute (like writing and spoken language)? Clinically, Freud notices "the divided attitude" of the fetishist: the woman is both castrated and not castrated (rephallicized). This divided attitude produces an oscillating structure. Freud demonstrates this oscillating structure with the "particularly subtle" case in which a man used his fetish to place someone in the castrated and someone in the phallic positions, regardless of biological sex. Such a use of the fetish is actually always possible, because, as Derrida says, "the construction of the fetish rests at once on the denial and on the affirmation, the assertion or the assumption of castration. This at-once . . . of the two contraries, of the two opposite operations, prohibits cutting through to a decision within the undecidable" (210). Here Derrida begins to discern an "economy of the undecidable" within Freud's description of fetishism, but he knows that Freud himself subscribes to an "economy of the decidable."

However, there would be no fetishism without the opening to undecidability: the fetish exists only on the condition that it oscillates (210–11, 227). Thus, as in his analysis of Hegel and fetishism, Derrida finds an oscillation between a decidable and an undecidable fetishism in Freud. The contrary positions between which the fetish oscillates can be understood dialectically (absence as the negation of presence), *but the oscillation itself cannot.* The oscillation of the fetish as its condition of possibility is what Derrida calls the "ligament" between contraries, a "double bond." This oscillating "double bond" is what gives the fetish its "power of excess in relation to opposition" (211).

Derrida does not attend to the most important subtlety of Freud's "subtle" case of fetishism. In passing, Freud says that his patient's use of the fetish to assign either men or women to the castrated and phallic positions "covered up the genitals entirely and concealed the distinction [*Unterschied*] between them" (1927, 156). The patient uses the fetish to disavow the reality of sexual difference. This was the linchpin of *Difference and Disavowal* (2000), the double oscillation in fetishism between intolerable difference and the fantasy of phallic monism, and then within the two positions of phallic monism. The latter, as Derrida says, appear decidable and opposable. But what Derrida might not explain here is that the *oscillation* between phallic and castrated is itself the registration and repudiation of the reality of sexual difference itself as oscillation. In other words, the *reality* that insists in the fantasy replacement for it is oscillation itself.

This is a crucial point. From within "decidable fetishism" one might still see the fetish as substitute for sexual difference as the "real thing." This would make sexual difference into an original presence, and would produce all essentialist views of it, purportedly grounded in ultimate biological reality. Freud probably intends just this sense when he speaks of his patient's fetish concealing actual perception of male and female genitals. However, Heidegger and Derrida teach that difference cannot be thought in terms of objective presence—and this would have to hold for sexual difference. In Derrida's terms, sexual difference would have to be undecidable. If so, then sexual difference would have to be "fetishistic" in the *general, undecidable* sense: it would have to be thought in terms of substitutability.

Here we have to reconsider Freud's own generalization of fetishism, of which Derrida seems unaware. Freud came to see the fetish as the model for all compromise formations. His point was that every defensive process is a repudiation of a registered reality. Once fetishism itself is a repudiation of registered difference, one has to ask about the nature of the reality of difference, which would have to be other than the reality of phallic absence and presence. On one hand, Freud did not specifically engage in a critique of presence; on the other, as Derrida has demonstrated, a thinking of *différance* is lodged within his most basic conceptions of unconscious processes. Therefore, wherever psychoanalysis comes up against the necessity of thinking the reality of difference, it must question presence if it is not to perpetuate the metaphysics it claims to go beyond. This is why fetishism as a repudiation of sexual difference must produce a thinking of sexual difference not confined to the actual presence of male and female genitals. Freud's generalization of fetishism would have to relate sexual difference to difference itself, that is, to the *différance* between strictly decidable and generally undecidable fetishism.

Derrida begins an analysis of sexual difference in these terms later in *Glas*. He is looking at Hegel's understanding of the Immaculate Conception as Absolute Knowledge. Derrida's very large point is that Hegel's "dialecticization" of the Immaculate Conception makes the absolute opposition of male and female, father and mother, the model of opposition itself. *Aufhebung* works to make sexual difference into opposition (1986, 223). (Nietzsche: metaphysics replaces difference with opposition.) Derrida says that once sexual difference becomes opposition in Absolute Knowledge, "conceptuality itself is homosexual [i.e. is structured by phallic presence and absence]. It begins to become such when the sexual differences efface themselves and determine themselves as the difference" (223). This is precisely what occurs in fetishism: sexual difference is replaced by phallic monism, and its apparent objectivity is grounded in *fantastic* absence and presence. And in *representation*: fantasy and opposition are representable, difference is not. This is why Derrida says that the myth of the Immaculate Conception is true:

> As soon as the difference is determined as opposition, no longer can the phantasm (a word to be determined) be avoided: to wit, a phantasm of infinite mastery of the two sides of the oppositional relation. The virgin mother does without the actual father. . . . The father . . . does without the woman. . . . All the oppositions that link themselves around the difference as opposition . . . have as cause and effect the immaculate maintenance of each of the terms, their independence, and consequently their absolute mastery. Absolute mastery that they see conferred on themselves phantasmatically. . . . For example, phantasmatic would be the effect of mastery produced by the determination of difference as opposition . . . , of sexual difference as sexual opposition in which each term would secure itself domination and absolute autonomy in the I[mmaculate] C[onception] . . . not only is this myth true, but it gives the measure of truth itself, the revelation of truth, the truth of truth. Then the (absolute) phantasm of the IC as (absolute) phantasm is (absolute) truth. Truth is the phantasm itself. The IC, sexual difference as opposition. (223–24)

The fantastic mastery of sexual opposition therefore controls the possible undecidability of sexual difference, or rather, as Derrida says, of sexual difference*s*. We do not yet know what this means. We do know that strict fetishism uses the decidable fantasies castrated-phallic to repudiate sexual difference. The clinical lesson of fetishistic transference (concreteness) is that the oscillation within strict fetishism is a result of the repudiated *registration* of *difference*, the trace of sexual difference.

Why, then, is Derrida speaking of sexual difference*s*? He clarifies what he means in an essay on Heidegger called "*Geschlecht*: sexual difference, ontological difference" (1983). His point of departure is Heidegger's alleged silence on the question of sexuality. (Derrida here does not attend to the "new interpretation of the sensuous" in volume 1 of *Nietzsche*. We will have to come back to this.) In *Being and Time* sexual difference does not belong to the existential structure of Dasein. But Derrida notices a direct reference to sexual difference in Heidegger's 1928 Marburg summer course on Leibniz. Revisiting the implications of the name "Da-sein," Heidegger emphasizes its "neutrality." Da-sein is more "neutral" than the name "Man." This neutrality is the entry into the question of being: Heidegger intends to neutralize everything that is not Da-sein's relation to itself as existing, as the being concerned with its being. In the Marburg course Heidegger's first example of this neutrality is sexual difference: Da-sein is *Geschlechtlos*, is neither of the two sexes, is neutral in relation to sexual difference (1983, 400).

Derrida asks why sexual difference is Heidegger's *first* example of Da-sein's neutrality. He says that "neutrality" refers to binarity: if Da-sein is neutral, if it is not "Man," then it is not "man" or "woman" either (401). But Derrida finds the space for a subtle question here. Heidegger's point that Da-sein is neither man nor woman alludes to sexual difference as it would be conceived in all the ontic disciplines he is attempting to neutralize: metaphysics, anthropology, biology, zoology, ethics. "Might one suspect that sexual difference cannot be reduced to an anthropological or ethical theme?" (401). Heidegger himself notes that the necessary negativity of words like "neutrality," or "asexual," should not blind us to an ontological "positivity," or even "power." He says that Da-sein's asexuality is not the indifference of empty nullity, but originary "positivity," the "power of being." Derrida comments:

> This specification leads to thinking that a-sexual neutrality does not desexualize—on the contrary; its *ontological* negativity is not deployed against *sexuality itself* (which it would liberate, rather), but against the marks of difference, more strictly against *sexual duality*. There would be *Geschlechtslosigkeit* [asexuality] only as concerns the "two"; asexuality would be determined as such only in the extent to which one immediately takes sexuality as binarity or sexual division. . . . If *Dasein* as such belongs to neither of the two sexes, this does not mean that the being it is is without sex. On the contrary, one can think here a . . . *pre-dual sexuality, which does not necessarily mean unitary, homogenous and undifferentiated*. . . . And on the basis of this sexuality more original than the dyad, one can attempt to think a "positivity" and a "power" . . . the positive and powerful source of all "sexuality." (402; emphasis added)

Derrida is careful here. He knows that Heidegger does not specifically associate "sexuality" with "power," and that he avoids any discussion of sexuality that would be foreign to the analytic of Da-sein. But again in 1928, in *The Essence of Reasons*, Heidegger returns to the question of Da-sein's asexuality, now in terms of its selfhood. Here Heidegger envisages another neutrality: Da-sein is neutral in relation to "being-I" and "being-you." He then intensifies: "and for the same reason even more so in relation to 'sexuality' [*Geschlechtlichkeit*]" (1983, 404). Derrida asks: "But if Heidegger insists . . . a suspicion continues to weigh on him: and if 'sexuality' already marked the most original *Selbstheit*? if it were an ontological structure of *ipseity*? if the *Da* of *Dasein* were already 'sexual'? and if sexual difference were already marked in the opening to the question of the meaning of being and to ontological difference?" (404).

What is Da-sein's selfhood? In *Being and Time* Heidegger distinguished between the self as the permanent subjectivity of infinite now-time and selfhood as the Da- of Da-sein in ecstatic time. This is Da-sein's being-in-the-world as Da-seins's being-outside-itself in the opening to each other of past, present, and future, Da-sein's *historicity* (1996, 305). To answer Derrida's question about sexual and ontological difference, then, one would have to think a nondual sexuality that is ecstatically temporal. There are hints in this direction in Heidegger's analysis of Nietzschean "rapture." It is an enhancement of corporeal force, like sexuality itself for Nietzsche. Heidegger says many times that we *are* as body. Nietzschean rapture becomes a way of thinking Da-sein's selfhood as body in relation to beings as a whole. Rapture is "neutral" in relation to the subject-object relation, or really "explodes" it (1979–1987, 1:123). Had Nietzsche been able to think through the issue of time, Heidegger might say, he would have been able to understand rapture as ecstatic selfhood. What Derrida is pushing toward, then, is an "ecstatic" sexuality, a "pre-dual sexuality, which does not necessarily mean unitary, homogenous and undifferentiated." What could this be?

To return to *Glas*, one can begin to think that a nondual sexual difference would be structured in terms of "general fetishism." Derrida writes: "one cannot cut through to a decision between the two contrary and recognized functions of the fetish, any more than between the thing itself and its supplement. Any more than between the sexes" (1986, 229). To paraphrase: for Derrida, the fetish has a decidable relation to castration, to sexual difference as opposition, *and* exists only as undecidable oscillation between the opposed positions castrated-phallic. To which we would have to add, as oscillation between sexual difference and sexual opposition, between nonpresent reality and representable fantasy. Hegel's dialectical interpretation of the Immaculate Conception thinks sexual difference as an opposition in which each term can be mastered. A nonmetaphysical thinking of sexual difference would have to view it as an oscillating structure, such that each term could serve as the "fetish"—i.e. the substitute—for "something" that itself cannot be thought as a center, a presence, an absence. In nondual sexual difference as ecstatic selfhood each term can substitute for the other: temporally, my "sexual self" is a relation to a differentiating double that "I am."

Freud's "primary phases" of the drives assert this possibility. Freud was able to explain why voyeurism can be substituted for exhibitionism, or sadism for masochism, by postulating a primary-intermediate, neither passive nor active, neither subjective nor objective, phases of voyeurism or masochism. The primary-intermediate phase is the always repeated source of the apparently discrete, periodic "eruptions" of voyeurism *or* exhibitionism, sadism *or* masochism. The repetition of the primary phase is the historicity, the possibility of the developmental history of the drives. The primary phase *is ecstatic selfhood, because in it* "I" am "you"—as in Heidegger's sense of Da-sein being neutral in relation to "I" and "you." Subject is object, passive is active—but there is always receptivity to the trace of this differentiating relation. Can one think sexual difference—male, female—in relation to this structure?

Here one must return to all of Freud's thinking about bisexuality. We know from the letters to Fliess that Freud early on enthusiastically embraced Fliess' notion of inherent bisexuality (1985, 292). At first, this was part of Freud's revolutionary effort to change what we think of as sexually normal. He had learned from the neuroses that sexuality extends over the entire body, does not begin at puberty, and is not inherently related to reproduction. His conclusion that the disposition to "perversion" is universal was an essential step in dismantling basic preconceptions about sexuality. But there was always a more subtle aspect to Freud's thinking about perversion—its relation to the historicization of sexuality. The theory of the neuroses itself was at first an attempt to demonstrate the role of memory in symptom formation. When memory also became a question of sexuality, there had to be a bridge between early repressions and the return of the repressed in adulthood. This bridge itself was the theory of infantile sexuality, in its perverse, autoerotic, fantasy-dominated aspects. The disposition to perversion is universal simply because we have all been children. The neurotic specifically suffers from the repression of perverse sexual impulses; but this is why neurotic conflicts are a question of memory, history, the past, childhood. Sexuality itself is historical. It has a long, complicated development before adolescence and the possibility of reproduction. Everyone has oral and anal, passive and active, voyeuristic-exhibitionistic, sadistic-masochistic, fetishistic, and incestuous wishes. When such wishes are repressed, they can exercise a deferred effect: they can return in adulthood, producing a symptom that is about the relation of past and present. And autoerotic infantile sexuality begins before the distinction between male and female has any psychological import. Infantile sexual fantasy is free to range anywhere. Unconsciously everyone has made both homosexual and heterosexual object choices, no matter what the apparent final outcome. We are inherently bisexual.

This inherent bisexuality has to have the same historical implications as the entire theory of infantile sexuality. It has to be related to the possibility of accounting for the historicity, the developmental mutability of sexuality. In the *Three Essays* (1905) Freud begins by discussing empirical variations of homosexual experience—from the accounts of those who have no conscious memories of anything but homosexual desire, to those who can move freely between homosexuality and heterosexuality, to those who have distinct periods of homosexuality and heterosexuality in their lives. In the discussion of the primary phases of the drive in "Instincts and Their Vicissitudes" (1915c) Freud gave an account of the historicity of sexual development, an explanation of how it is possible to have apparently discrete periods dominated by what appear to be sexual oppositions (active *or* passive, subjective *or* objective periods of erotic looking, erotic pain). The question then, would be whether bisexuality might function in the same way. If it did, then it could explain how Da-sein could be sexually neutral—neither "I" nor "you," neither male nor female, neither homosexual nor heterosexual—as the very possibility of its (ecstatic) sexual selfhood. This would be a predual, but nonhomogenous sexual difference.

There is a late discussion of bisexuality in *Analysis Terminable and Interminable* (1937) that begins to move in this direction. The context is significant. Freud is discussing the death drive as the tendency to self destruction manifest in such phenomena as masochism, neurotic guilt, and the negative therapeutic reaction (getting worse in treatment precisely when one begins to get better). He then says that to observe the operation of the death drive, one need not confine oneself to such phenomena: "Numerous facts of *normal* mental life call for an explanation of this kind, and the sharper our eye grows, the more copiously they strike us. The subject is too new and too important for me to treat it as a side issue" (1937, 243; emphasis added). Instead, Freud says, he will give an example.

In all periods of history, there have been people who can move between same-sex and opposite-sex object choice "without the one trend interfering with the other" (1937, 244). Psychoanalysis has shown that actually everyone is unconsciously bisexual—hence bisexuality as an example from "normal mental life." How to account for the discrepancy between "normal" bisexuality and the more typical experience of bisexuality as "irreconcilable conflict"? First, one must note what Freud does not say. He does not attribute this "irreconcilable conflict" to the castration complex, as one might have expected. Instead, to answer his question, Freud first says that conflict over bisexuality might be due to the fact that each individual has only a certain amount of libido; each side of the bisexual constitution would have to contend for its share. But no, he then says. If this were the case, why would there not be a simple division of libidinal supplies, instead of the typical conflict that homosexuality is a threat to heterosexuality? Rather, typical conflicts over bisexuality have nothing to do with the "quantity of libido," but illustrate an "independently emerging tendency to conflict . . . [which] can scarcely be attributed to anything but the intervention of an element of free aggressiveness." In other words, conflict over normal bisexuality is a manifestation of the death drive. Freud then makes his famous comparison of the life and death drives to Empedocles' *philia* (love) and *neikos* (strife), eternally at war such that there is a "never ceasing *alternation of periods*, in which the one or the other of the two fundamental forces gains the upper hand" (246; emphasis added).

The logic of this passage is that (normal) bisexuality belongs to the life drive, to Eros, which is inevitably in conflict with the death drive. Eros is the tension-raising "mischief maker" which the self directed aggression of the death drive attacks. As Eros, bisexuality would have to be binding-differentiating: it holds together and apart heterosexual and homosexual object choice, masculine and feminine identifications, maleness and femaleness. It can be conceived as sexual *différance* within the structure of general fetishism: bisexuality implies that homosexual and heterosexual object choice, masculine and feminine identifications can substitute for each other *over time*, such that there can even be discrete periods of heterosexuality and homosexuality in an individual's life. Even biologically, Freud had suggestively said in the *Three Essays*, each sex contains the "trace" of the other (1905, 141); he imagines bisexual "interstitial"—i.e. intermediate—"tissue" as a precondition for "specific sex-cells (spermatozoa and ovum)" (215). Thus, bisexuality is the tension of an oscillating structure, is the historicity of the history of apparently opposed sexual choices. But as such, particularly as differentiating tension, as Eros, it is the kind of disturbance that inevitably comes into conflict with the dedifferentiating force of the death drive. When it does so, the sexual *différance* of bisexuality becomes the apparent opposition of homosexuality and heterosexuality: homosexuality becomes a threat to heterosexuality.

The primary phases of the drives, in their transitional, intermediate way, are also the *différance* of active and passive, subjective and objective sexual aims. As such, they too are a function of Eros, and as such are a disturbance—the "volcano" that is the repeated source of the periodic eruptions of one side or the other of the sexual opposition. This is the repetition on the side of the "life drive" that always meets the repetition on the side of the "death drive." One might say that bisexuality is the primary phase of "object choice," except that as Heidegger says about Dasein, and as Freud says about the primary phase of voyeurism, it is neither "I" nor "you." It is autoaffective in a nonsubjective sense.

Sexual differences in Derrida's sense, then, are the interactions of active-passive, subjective-objective, bisexual, always repeated, always tension-raising, always binding possibilities of apparent sexual oppositions. From within Derrida's own logic one would have to speak more of sexual *différances* than of sexual differences. They explain the oscillation in which each "side" of the apparent opposition can substitute for the other, either periodically or in the present. And if sexual difference itself is unthinkable without bisexuality, with the reality that each sex is "intersitially" the *trace* of the other, then, like memory as "the opening to the effraction of the trace" ("Freud and the Scene of Writing" [1978]), sexual difference is threatened by its very possibility. As binding oscillation, sexual *différances* embody tension, disturbance. The dedifferentiating, unbinding, tension-reducing operation of the death drive then makes them into an ostensibly essential opposition. General substitutability, general fetishism, becomes decidable opposition, restricted fetishism. The fetish is both undecidable bisexual oscillation and oscillation between decidable fantasies of sexual opposition (phallic, castrated). But if restricted fetishism *substitutes* for general fetishism, then the basic metaphysics of fetishism—that there is a present thing for which the fetish substitutes—is upset: restricted fetishism as a *substitute* depends upon the *substitutability of general fetishism*. This substitutability, like the primary phases of the drives and "primary bisexuality," is repetitively before, during, and after two sexes, active and passive, subject and object. It has a kind of phantom existence.

Specters of Marx (1994) asks a question directly related to the idea of general fetishism: is there an absolute opposition between the thing itself and its simulacrum (31)? A ghost, a specter, is the simulacrum of living presence—not fully present, not fully alive, but not exactly absent, not completely dead. And a ghost is something that *returns*: in French a specter is a *revenant*, a "coming-back thing." Like difference as repetition, spectrality "begins by coming back" (32).

In scene 1 of *Hamlet*, when the ghost returns, Marcellus says, "Thou art a scholar; speak to it Horatio" (1.1.42). Derrida comments that the traditional scholar does not believe in phantoms, in what he calls "the virtual space of spectrality" (1994, 33). Rather, the traditional scholar believes in a decisive distinction between the real and the not real, the living and the nonliving, the present and the nonpresent. But to be able to address a specter—as Marcellus asks of Horatio—has to mean thinking beyond the opposition of presence and nonpresence, life and nonlife (34). Hamlet's later statement that "The time is out of joint" (1.5.188) leads Derrida to say that to think the specter *is* to think time itself as the "out of joint." The disjunction of time is the possibility of the other—the other of (traditional) presence: "To hold together in a speech which differs, *différant* not what it affirms, but *différant* in order to affirm, to hold together that which does not hold together, the disparate itself—all this can be thought, like the spectrality of the specter, only in a time of dislocated present, at the juncture of a radically dis-junctive time without assured conjunction" (1994, 41).

Freud, for Derrida, is always both "traditional scholar," all of whose concepts belong to the history of metaphysics, and the kind of scholar who can speak to ghosts in a time out of joint. When Freud, in his famous letter of September 21, 1897, wrote to Fliess that in the unconscious one cannot distinguish truth from fiction "cathected with affect" (1985, 264), he was beginning to elaborate a theory of "psychic reality" in which the traditional distinction between the real and the not real did not hold. Psychic reality would have to be uncanny, in Freud's later sense that uncanniness suspends the opposition of fiction and reality. And it would have to be uncanny in the sense that uncanniness suspends the opposition of the living and the nonliving: psychic reality is a function of a living-dead "machine," the psychic apparatus. In *The Interpretation of Dreams,* one of Freud's own dreams is about revenants: its manifest content is about the reappearance of the dead, who are made to disappear again by the dreamer's piercing gaze. The analysis of the dream illustrates the idea of transference itself as return of the ghosts of the past (1900, 421ff.).

Toward the end of *Being and Time* Heidegger had said that "'Time' is neither objectively present in the 'subject' nor in the 'object,' neither 'inside' nor 'outside,' and it is 'prior' to every subjectivity and objectivity, because it presents the condition of the very possibility of this 'prior.' Does it then have any 'being' at all? And if not, is it then a phantom or is it 'more in being' than any possible being?" (1996, 384–85). Heidegger's intent in this passage is clearly to say that time is not a phantom, but *is* "more in being" than an objectively present being. But Derrida would have us think that "ecstatic out-of-jointness" is itself spectral, that "phantom" is more than a metaphor for Heidegger. He jokes that instead of an ontology, we need a "hauntology" (1994, 31). Freud himself began to elaborate a hauntology with all his references to posthumous primary processes, virtuality, ghosts, and the nonsynchronous time of telepathy. And, of course, with the uncanny. When Heidegger himself returns to the uncanny in *On Time and Being* (1972) he examines opening as the fourth dimension of time, and the *Es gibt* (there is) of *Es gibt Sein* and *Es gibt Zeit*. He comments that the "It" of "It gives" "does not name the availability of something which is, but rather precisely something unavailable, what concerns us as something uncanny, the demonic" (40). The *Es gibt* is spectral occurrence.

Occurrence itself, then, cannot be thought within the simple opposition of real, living presence and its phantomatic simulacrum (1994, 119). (Recall Freud's questioning the status of the reality of a telepathic event in a dream.) Derrida is making a case for always including a revised thinking of unconscious processes in any conception of the "event": the *Es gibt* as spectral. One can potentially integrate Heidegger on the uncanniness of opening as the fourth dimension of time with Freud's nonsynchronous temporality of the unconscious. To do so, one would also have to integrate the "phantomaticity" of Da-sein with the virtual technology of the psychic apparatus. Derrida approaches this integration by noting a contradiction in Heidegger's dismissal of the phantomaticity of time. He writes: "there is no Dasein of the specter, but there is no Dasein without the uncanny, without the strange familiarity (*Unheimlichkeit*) of some specter" (165). For Freud too, there is no thinking of the unconscious without the uncanny. Whether it is a question of Da-sein or the unconscious, essential uncanniness means that life itself is "haunted." "The specter thinks, intensifies itself, condenses itself on the very interior of life, within the most living life. . . . Thus, to the extent that it lives, this life can have no pure identity with itself or assured interiority—all philosophies of life, of the real, living individual have to take this into account" (177). This is "the strangeness of care": the uncanniness of care in *Being and Time,* and the uncanniness of registration of the differentiating double (registration of the experience of satisfaction within primary narcissism), in Freud.

Horatio asks about the Ghost—"has this thing appeared again tonight?" (1.1.20). Derrida cites this question in relation to the "thing-like" intermediate state between life and death, and in relation to coming back, *revenance.* The paradoxical mother of primary narcissism, "the breast," is such a spectral coming-back-thing. Neither "I" nor "you," neither "I" nor "it," the breast returns with need, and as repetition opens a differentiating trace, *Bahnung.* And because the baby *is* the mother within primary narcissism, because, as Freud says, being the breast precedes having the breast (1941, 299), what we call selfhood has to begin as spectral thing. For Heidegger, Dasein's selfhood is temporal, ecstatic. For Freud, the ego itself is a product of identifications, which themselves are later versions of "being the breast." Derrida extends this way of thinking selfhood to say that the Ego, the living individual, is always "constituted by specters of which it becomes the host. . . . Ego = ghost. . . . 'I am' would mean 'I am haunted.' I am haunted by myself. . . . Wherever there is Ego, *es spukt*" (1994, 133).

In fact, says Derrida, "The idiom of this '*es spukt*' plays a singular role in . . . Freud's '*Das Unheimliche.*' Its translation always fails . . . to render the link between the impersonality . . . of an operation [*spuken*] without act, without real subject or object" (133). The *es spukt* is a way of thinking a phantomatic repetition: "The impersonal ghostly returning [*revenance*] of the '*es spukt*' produces an automatism of repetition" (173). Thus, the *Es*: the thinglike, automatic, impersonal repetition of opening as a function of the "It." Like the self giving of the *Es gibt*, *revenance* is the "impersonal" repetition of the transitional intermediate. *Es gibt* repetition of primary drive phases and bisexuality, which always accompany—without being present—objectively real sexuality. As repetitive and transitional, they are virtual sexuality. Where *Es gibt "Es," Es spukt.*

Freud himself uses the idiom *es spukt* in what Derrida calls an "unbelievable" paragraph of "The Uncanny" (1919). The paragraph says that the entire investigation should have begun with the *spuken*, because it is the strongest example of *Unheimlichkeit* (241). But, says Derrida, it is also where one is most afraid, because it is where the undecidability of *Heimlich-Unheimlich* is most intense (1994, 173). If *spuken* is the "strongest example" of the uncanny, is it the uncanny itself? Freud's choice not to begin where he says he should have begun then would also be a flight from spectrality, from the place of disruption of fundamental concepts. Thus, Derrida says, the typical "conjuring" of the specter, only to expel it once more. Heidegger too, dismissed the "phantomaticity" of being. For both Freud and Heidegger uncanniness is *primary*, makes their basic projects possible. But neither can remain in the out of joint time-space of disruptive spectrality of which both give glimpses.

Derrida thinks that the "paradoxical hunt" for the specter, in which that which is conjured must be excluded (the structure of Freud's dream of revenants), traverses "the whole history of philosophy. . . . As soon as there is some specter, hospitality and exclusion go together" (1994, 140–41). Just as the "living ego" for Freud can only *be* as haunted, so too the entire theory of the "living psyche" as transference producing, as *revenance*, attempts to exclude the spectrality which constitutes it. Both the "ego" and the "theory" have to protect themselves from what makes them possible. We are again on the terrain of Nietzsche's life against itself, and Heidegger's Da-sein in flight from itself. Derrida early on said that the unconscious as memory, as opening to the effraction of the trace, must protect itself from what makes it possible. He now calls this operation "autoimmune": "To protect its life, to constitute itself as unique living ego . . . it is necessarily led to welcome the other within (so many figures of death: différance of the technical apparatus . . .), it must therefore take the immune defenses apparently meant for the non-ego, the enemy, the opposite . . . and direct them at once *for itself and against itself*" (1994, 141;

original emphasis). Such autoimmune defense against the *différance* of the technical apparatus is the registration and repudiation of difference, the welcoming and expulsion of the spectral. It is the relation of general to restricted fetishism.

Restricted fetishism, as Derrida said, assumes the opposition of the thing and its substitute; Freud's analysis of fetishism opens onto the general form because of its inherently oscillating structure. Sexual *différances* and primary bisexuality are the registered oscillations, which then oscillate with their oscillating substitute: the apparently opposable positions phallic-castrated, active-passive, subject-object. General fetishism explains why the apparently opposed positions of restricted fetishism can actually substitute for each other: the oscillation of general fetishism inheres in the oppositional structure which substitutes for it.

As a *thing* the fetish is not quite dead, but not quite alive either. It is virtually alive, and thus must be thought "hauntologically." Integrating the oscillating structure of the fetish with its spectrality, Derrida asks in a note: "how to stabilize the sex of a fetish? Does it not pass from one sex to the other? Is it not this movement of passage, whatever may be its stases?" (1994, 19, n35). Even as oscillation between the phallic and castrated positions of phallic monism, such that—as in Freud's "subtle" example—either sex can be in either position, the fetish must be "bisexual." It occupies the intermediate time-space of nonbinary, but not homogenous and undifferentiated, sexual *différance*. This is the primary bisexuality always attacked by the dedifferentiating death drive—the *autoimmune response* to the spectral sexuality of the virtual apparatus.

Winnicott, the great psychoanalytic thinker of play and things, opposed the transitional object to the fetish. Because transitional phenomena derive from the neither subjective nor objective "third area" of experiencing, he says that their fate is neither to be lost nor mourned, but to expand into "cultural experience," in which illusion is maintained without conflating it with reality (1951, 233). This is the possibility of analytic interpretation, of a therapy which occurs in the overlap of two play spaces (1971, 38). The fetish, Winnicott thought, could not be given up, and was used to *control* reality through illusion (1951, 241). Such control closes off the play space of interpretation. Recall Derrida's analysis of the myth of the Immaculate Conception as true: it creates an illusion of control of sexual difference by making sexual opposition into Absolute Knowledge.

But the transitional "object" is also a fetish in Derrida's *general* sense, in that it holds open an intermediate space in which "mother," "me," and "thing" are substitutable. In a subtle analysis of "The Fetish and the Transitional Object" (1971), Phyllis Greenacre noticed that the transitional object is "Janus faced": it is both the first not-me possession and the link to the mother-me state. Similarly, she says, the fetish is "Janus faced" as a "conspicuously bisexual symbol [that] also serves as a bridge which would both deny and affirm the sexual differences" (321). ("Deny and affirm": these are exactly the terms used by Derrida to describe the oscillating structure of the fetish in *Glas*. This is the structure of disavowal.) The "Janus faced" doubleness of both is a way of thinking primary bisexuality in primary narcissism: the I-you, I-it, male-female, neutral time-space of oscillating structures.

Winnicott's understanding of transitional time-space explains interpretation as play. Greenacre's "Janus faced" structure of both the transitional object and the fetish addresses registration and repudiation of the intermediate. Freud would not bring such considerations to bear on a theory of interpretation. Once he focused on the repression of objectified mental contents, on wish fulfillments, fantasies, drives, he mistakenly assumed that interpretation itself could be objective. Ultimately this mistake is due to the "fetishistic," or concrete, assumption that perception equals reality. The defensive concreteness of fetishistic transferences, the intense anxiety over loss of control liberated when the analyst uses an active (Nietzsche), descriptive (Heidegger) *technique* to open transitional time-space, all demonstrate the registration and repudiation of the other *reality* lodged within entrenched objectivity. Nonobjective reality is experienced as "unreal," perverse, "weird," because of its uncanny, tension-raising, oscillating structure. The use of fantasies of opposition to insure mastery and control (Absolute Knowledge) is the autoimmune response to transitionality, to general fetishism. Even though Freud could not think about interpretation in this way, he did think that "normal" bisexuality encounters the self destruction of the death drive. The autoimmune response is directed against the *generally fetishistic*, "bisexual," play of transitional time-space, the time-space of interpretation.

"Hauntology" inevitably leads to a rethinking of interpretation. Referring to Marx's famous eleventh thesis on Feuerbach ("philosophers have only interpreted the world . . . ; the point is to change it"), Derrida says that spectral interpretation "transforms the very thing it interprets" (1994, 52). He calls this "performative interpretation." (By definition, however, it is not a performative in the strict sense of speech act theory—a statement that does not mean, but that creates in the act of stating, as in marriage vows, or christening a ship.) Certainly, psychoanalytic interpretation aims to transform what it interprets. The possibility of such transformation through interpretation is the internalization of the differential implicit to interpretation (Loewald, 1980), the connecting-separating possibility of transitional space (Winnicott, 1951). But neither Loewald nor Winnicott would think of transformative interpretation as disjunctive, out of joint, time.

Clinically, defense against differentiation, defense against interpretation, is always directed against the analyst's neutrality. This neutrality is what gives analysis its "impersonal" feel. Repetition of neutrality in each analytic session is the repetition of the uncanny opening of the *Es gibt* as the *Es spukt*. Like the mother of primary narcissism, in her *self-preservative, caring function*, the analyst is not simply a present person, but a spectral, virtual thing. Registration and repudiation of the other than present aspects of the setting—the neutral, differentiating stance—produces fetishistic transferences in the restricted sense: transference to the clock, to appointment times, to the objects in the room, as what is objectively present now. However, fetishism in the restricted sense is made possible by general fetishism, by transitional phenomena—but as the place of greatest uncanniness, greatest anxiety.

Entrenched fetishistic transferences to objective presence, in terms of early Heidegger, is Da-sein's flight from itself as disclosure (interpretation); in terms of late Heidegger it is the metaphysical concealment of the self-giving of opening. Such flight and concealment attack the pain of language as difference. Nietzsche thought that reactive postulation of identities is the narcotizing response to the pain-pleasure of active differentiation. This is the welcoming and exclusion, registration and repudiation of opening as "alarming time-space," opening as *Spuken*. The opening to unconscious processes is always at work when the analyst automatically maintains the neutral, interpretive stance. The time and space of analysis are a relation to the analyst and to oneself—or to the analyst *as* oneself, in the self-preservative, differentiating context of primary narcissism—as virtual, spectral thing, in time out of joint.

Binding, Sending, Chance

> Souls, fashioned of brown twilight, rise toward white ceilings. . . . they are unique to the Zone, they answer to the new Uncertainty.
>
> —Pynchon, *Gravity's Rainbow* (1973)

At the beginning of chapter 3 of *Beyond the Pleasure Principle* Freud quickly reviews the history of interpretation as a therapeutic measure. At first, he says, the analyst used interpretation to infer unconscious material, communicating it to the patient as quickly as possible. But this approach "did not solve the therapeutic problem" (1920, 18). The emphasis then shifted to analysis of the patient's resistances, which themselves are manifestations of the original defenses. But again a problem arose. Patients frequently "repeat the repressed material as a contemporary experience instead of . . . remembering it as something belonging to the past" (18). Freud calls such repetition "acting out." As a manifestation of the repetition compulsion it is a formidable obstacle to effective interpretation.

Freud's conception of the repetition compulsion seems to be the obverse of Nietzsche's conception of repetition: "eternal return of the same" is not a differentiating process for Freud. His discussion of acting out as a manifestation of the repetition compulsion in fact leads him to specify a condition of impossibility built into analysis as interpretation. When the patient acts out, the analyst's task is to help the patient to retain "some degree of aloofness, which will enable him . . . to recognize that what *appears to be reality* is in fact only a reflection of a forgotten past" (18; emphasis added). But, because transference *is* repetition, it can intersect with the repetition *compulsion*: some patients repeat past pain as a real "contemporary experience." Such people strangely repeat the same painful pattern over and over their lives and in analysis. There is then no "degree of aloofness" which permits interpretation of the transference as repetition of the past. Freud calls this form of repetition "demonic," precisely because it does produce a transference—the possibility of analysis—but is uninterpretable—the impossibility of analysis. This is actually the concrete, fetishistic, or desymbolizing transference—"You're a jerk, just like me." Freud does not consider that what he calls the "degree of aloofness" necessary for interpretation might concern something other than the patient's actual history, that it might concern space and time as historicity—the possibility of a relation between past and present. Historicity implies transitional, alarming, spectral opening. Thus, an autoimmune response—disavowal—is inevitably directed against it. But because transference *is* repetition, this process is built into transference itself: the condition of possibility of analysis contains its condition of impossibility.

Freud's thinking about repetition produces his postulation of a death drive. He modifies his previous definition of the drive as an internal stimulus, a tension-raising demand made by the body on the mind for a certain amount of work. Now, the emphasis is on tension reduction and repetition: the drive is an urge to return to a previous, less stimulated state. Freud famously speculates that this inherent urge to return to a less excited state is due to the emergence of life itself from inorganic, dead matter. However, he now also postulates a life drive as a differentiating, tension-raising principle. In its opposition to the life drive (Eros), the death drive then also embodies dedifferentiation. As Deleuze remarked, when Freud put repetition on the side of the death drive, the differentiating life drive was left without a principle of repetition, although difference itself can only be thought *as* repetition.[19]

From Derrida's perspective, because effects of difference are created by *différance*, life as difference could not simply be *opposed* to death. Death, then, cannot be thought *only* as a dedifferentiating force. (In *The Will to Power* Nietzsche noted that difference itself implies breaking down, decay, as well as life, tension [1968, §655].) Derrida, in *The Post Card* (1987), analyzes *Beyond the Pleasure Principle* in terms of the *différance* of life and death, which he calls "lifedeath" in "To Speculate—On 'Freud.'" He does not specifically address the limits of interpretation in relation to Freud's remarks on demonic repetition, but this will continue to be our focus.

Freud begins *Beyond . . .* with a restatement of principle: psychoanalysis assumes that unconscious processes are governed by the pleasure or tension reduction principle. Is this assumption correct? Are there data that contradict it? Is there a "beyond of the pleasure principle"? Derrida notices that even in Freud's initial review of the grounds for assuming the dominance of the pleasure principle there are complications. As always, Freud defines pleasure and unpleasure as decrease and increase of tension. But Freud carefully specifies that pleasure and unpleasure themselves are not directly proportional to increase and decrease of energy. He wonders whether pleasure and unpleasure themselves might be due to decrease or increase of energy "in a given period of time" (1920, 8).

Why the reference to periodicity in the initial review of the pleasure principle? There is no answer at this point. Freud then characteristically cites Fechner on pleasure and unpleasure. In 1873 Fechner had proposed a law defining pleasure as the approach to complete stability and unpleasure as the approach to complete instability. In the passage cited by Freud, Fechner also alluded to a "margin of aesthetic indifference" between the two limits. Derrida notes that Freud does nothing with this postulation of an intermediate zone between pleasure and unpleasure. But he is alert to the references to periodic time and to the "between" of pleasure and unpleasure right at the beginning of *Beyond . . .* , a question that will return at its very end.

The relation of the pleasure principle to the reality principle as delay (*différance*) is also restated in the first chapter of *Beyond*. If the reality principle allows the pleasure principle to reach its aims by more round-about paths, there is no absolute *opposition* between them. The pleasure principle, Derrida comments, uses the reality principle as its "delegate," its "representative," which also protects it from its own tendency to immediate, self-destructive, discharge. In submitting to the inhibition imposed by the reality principle, the pleasure principle "agrees" to its own modification; it fulfills its aims by deferring them. The delaying function of the reality principle is the pleasure principle's *modification of itself*. The pleasure principle *affects itself* with the principle of delay, with *différance*. The reality of the "reality principle," Derrida says, is an effect of this autoaffective *différance*. The pleasure principle, by "contracting with itself" when it submits to its other (the reality principle), is in a relation to otherness that is also itself. Heteroaffection is autoaffection: the "possibility of the totally-other (*than* the pleasure principle) is in advance inscribed within it, in the letter of engagement that it believes it sends to itself" (1987, 283).

Freud's description of how the pleasure principle defers its *self* through the reality principle illustrates how a differential, autoaffective structure lodges otherness within the self, the *autos*. Throughout "To Speculate" Derrida radicalizes the *autos* as this kind of "self sending"—the pleasure principle "sends itself" when it "contracts" with the reality principle as its *own* deferral. Derrida also finds such differential "self sending" in the way Freud writes about *himself* as he writes *Beyond. . . .* He notes the peculiar style of argumentation: each time Freud envisages the "step beyond" the pleasure principle, he restates the dominance of the pleasure principle. The pleasure principle returns. Reading the famous *fort/da* scene, Derrida notes that it too is autobiographical. Freud is writing about his own grandson, Ernst, throwing away and bringing back a spool. Derrida plays on "PP," for pleasure principle, in its French pronunciation as *pépé,* "grandpa." Freud, the grandfather of Ernst, who is playing at the sending and returning of his mother and himself in his game with the spool, is also the grandfather of psychoanalysis, who insistently seems to distance the mastery of the pleasure principle, only to make it return each time he envisages its beyond. There is a specular, mirroring, relation between what Ernst does with his spool and what his *pépé* does with the "PP." For Derrida, *Beyond . . .* is an *"auto*-biographical" text in that Freud is "speculating on himself," just as Ernst speculates on the return of what he sends away, and just as the pleasure principle speculates on its own return in its differential relation to the reality principle. The "self" here is difference as repetition; the *autos* is *revenance,* with all the implications of the word (returning, haunting, spectrality, transference). The "living self" constituted by differantial repetition is never entirely living—nor entirely itself.

Freud comes up against another question about the "self" in his discussion of demonic transference: how can the self choose pain over pleasure, how can it repetitively wound itself? Repetition of injury implies a beyond of the pleasure principle: it repeats a pain which promises no yield of pleasure. Its *automaticity,* its "perpetual recurrence," cannot be due to the repression of pleasurable wishes and fantasies. Rather, Freud centers on repetition of injuries to one's *self,* narcissistic wounds. The repetition of what is painful to *oneself,* Derrida comments, does not obey "the master, the name of the master being given to the subject constructed according to the economy of the PP" (1987, 341–42). If the pleasure principle achieves its aims, arrives at its destination, by submitting to the reality principle's deferring function, the repetition of a pain that never arrives at pleasure is a "pure" deferral of it. It is a "self sending" that threatens the return to self. Derrida calls such automatic repetition "the post in its 'pure' state, a kind of mailman without destination. Tele—without telos" (341).

Here we must pause and review the relations between the repetition of pain, "demonic repetition," and the uninterpretable "demonic transference." Derrida has understood repetition of pain as the challenge to the mastery of the pleasure principle. Demonic transference, however, insures mastery by *repudiating* the "degree of aloofness" necessary to see repetition as repetition. It closes the space of interpretation, precisely because of its potential tension and pain, in obedience to the pleasure principle. And it does so defensively, in order to hold on to a sense of subjective mastery that has *registered* the threat to mastery in the pain intrinsic to difference and interpretation. Heidegger's point that the self giving of opening "does not name the availability of something which is, but rather precisely something unavailable, what concerns us as something uncanny, the demonic" (1972, 40) is helpful here. The apparent mastery of demonic transference is a defensive version of the demonic repetition that threatens mastery: its constant repetition is a relation to the constant repetition of opening itself. The threat to mastery in opening can be considered the greatest potential narcissistic wound. But this threat to mastery inhabits the self: there is no possible self without Heidegger's autoaffection as *ek-stasis* and Derrida's self-sending. This is why the insistent, stubbornly repetitive objectivity of demonic transference *is* the return of what haunts it—*revenance*. Demonic repetition haunts the concept of transference itself: transference can be the possibility and impossibility of analysis.

Demonic repetition is "the post in its pure state," "tele- without telos." If the usual sense of sending is determined by the possibility of arrival at a destination, we have here a sending *not* determined by arrival at a destination. The defensive objectivity of demonic transference, which repetitively denies the possibility of repetition, is then a determinism haunted by nondeterminism. At the limit of transference interpretation one encounters the limit of determinism.

Freud envisages a beyond of the pleasure principle not only because of the repetition of narcissistic pain, but also because of the repetition of pain in the dreams of the severely traumatized. He says that traumatic dreams carry out a task "which must be accomplished before the dominance of the pleasure principle can even begin" (1920, 32). This task is the establishment, or reestablishment, of the signal anxiety that warns of an approaching danger, so that one can avoid unpleasure—the basic function of the pleasure principle. In Freud's view, one is traumatized not only because an experience has been painful, but because one was not prepared for it. In severe cases of trauma, the signal anxiety function has been preempted. Dreams that repeat the trauma remind the apparatus of what it should have been prepared for, and thus help to reinstate the mastery of the pleasure principle. Repetitively traumatic dreams "afford us a view of a function of the mental apparatus which, though it does not contradict the pleasure principle, is nevertheless independent of it and seems to be more primitive than the purpose of gaining pleasure and avoiding unpleasure" (32).

Freud calls this "before" of the pleasure principle the tendency to binding: were there not a tendency to binding prior to the pleasure principle, dreams could not repeat trauma in the service of reinstating it. In Freud's usual schema binding is a secondary process which comes *after* the unbinding of the primary process. Nonetheless, as Derrida writes, the entire analysis of the repetition of trauma in dreams means that the "psychic apparatus *also* attempts to bind its excitations 'in part' [*pace* Freud], without regard for the PP and before it. But still without being in opposition to it, without contradicting it" (1987, 350–51). The "before" of the pleasure principle as repetition also works with the *revenance*, the coming back, of the pleasure principle itself.

There are major implications to the idea that before the pleasure principle the psychic apparatus binds excitations "in part." The tendency to binding "collaborates with the PP without being of it. A median, *differing or indifferent* zone (and it is differing only by being indifferent to the oppositional or distinctive difference of the two borders), relates the primary process [unbinding] in its 'purity' . . . to the 'pure' secondary process [binding]" (1987, 351). This "indifferent zone" is the homologue of the "margin of aesthetic indifference" between pleasure and unpleasure noted by Fechner, as cited by Freud in chapter 1 of *Beyond*. . . . In fact, Derrida writes, this intermediate zone between pleasure and unpleasure is a kind of "belt" or "lace" that goes from one side to the other of the repetition that tends toward the mastery of the pleasure principle and the repetition of pain that disrupts this mastery. How to conceive the repetition of that which makes repetition work for and against mastery?

> Sometimes repetition, classically, repeats something that precedes it, repetition comes after . . . , repetition succeeds a first thing, an original, a primary, a prior, the repeated itself which in and of itself is supposed to be foreign to what is repetitive or repeating in repetition. . . . But sometimes, according to a logic that is other, and non-classical, repetition is "original," and induces . . . a general deconstruction: not only of the entire classical ontology of repetition . . . but also of the entire psychic construction, of everything . . . insuring the integrity of the organization . . . under the dominance of the PP. . . . Sometimes, consequently, repetition collaborates with the PP's mastery, and sometimes, older than the PP, and permitting itself to be repeated by the

PP, repetition haunts the PP, undermining it, threatening it, persecuting it by seeking an unbound pleasure which resembles . . . an unpleasure chosen for its very atrocity.

But there is no "sometimes . . . sometimes" . . . one repetition repeats the other. . . . It would take place . . . *in the zone* . . . two repetitions which are no more opposed to each other than they identically reproduce each other, and which, if they do repeat each other, are the repercussions of the constitutive duplicity of all repetition. (1987, 351–52)

The repetition of classical and nonclassical repetition "in the zone" is the repetition of the zone itself. As in the repetition of the primary phases of the drives, *repetition of the primary intermediate* is repetition of and as *différance*—hence the "constitutive duplicity of all repetition." This is what accounts for the *periodicity and substitutability* of apparently opposed drives (voyeurism/exhibitionism; sadism/masochism) and object choices (homosexual/heterosexual). But the zone between pleasure and unpleasure is tension, the binding *before* the pleasure principle. This is not the prior condition of classical repetition, the before of an objective presence that would be independent of repetition. It is rather the before of repetition as time, of time itself as the primary intermediate in Heidegger's sense (in *Kant and the Problem of Metaphysics* [1962]),[20] of time as the tension of differential (separate-connected) relation.

This nonclassical repetition of the intermediate zone between pleasure and unpleasure, of the tension of binding, is a function of the analytic setting. Repeated sessions with a neutral, interpretive stance, imply the repetition of the intermediate. Hence, the analyst is not simply an objective presence: the analyst can only be the analyst by maintaining the repetitive, differantial, frame. To be in the analytic setting is automatically to register the pain of opening, the ultimate narcissistic wound and threat to mastery. Because the repetitive tension of transitional space-time is not objectively present, the defensive response is repetitively to make the analyst into an "objectively real" presence, foreclosing the interpretation of repetition. But the "constitutive duplicity of repetition" is always at work: the repetition of demonic transference registers and repudiates demonic repetition itself.

Repetition is time. Derrida notices that Freud in *Beyond* . . . refers to a possible unconscious time in relation to trauma. To recapitulate: Freud criticizes his usual conception of the timelessness of the unconscious as too simple; it is only a negation of conscious time. Thinking of unconscious time as a disruptive force from within, he envisages conscious time as a "stimulus barrier," a protective device against unconscious time. Surprisingly, Derrida makes very little of unconscious, traumatic time. We have already discussed unconscious time as tension, pain, trauma, difference. Objective, conscious time—the Kantian time Freud begins to question here—is itself the protective shield which repudiates registered unconscious time. Or unconscious process in general, in its spatial-temporal opening to difference (*Bahnung*). The clock time of the fixed session is haunted by the spectral, out of joint time of interpretation. They are held together and apart, bound by tension.

Beyond . . . concludes with a discussion of binding and tension states. The latter are neither pleasure nor pain: they are the *before*, the prior condition, of the pleasure principle. For Nietzsche pleasurepain is the repetition of difference as relation; pleasure itself is a *rhythm* of small painful stimuli. Freud explains the pleasurepain of binding by noting that if the psychic apparatus did not bind drive excitations it could not function—as he has already said in relation to trauma. Binding not only sustains tension by inhibiting the tendency to automatic discharge (the primary process, the pleasure principle), it also replaces the primary process with the secondary process. Freud does not notice the evident paradox: a tendency to binding *precedes* the pleasure principle; binding *succeeds* the pleasure principle. Again we find the strange logic of the secondary (binding) preceding the primary. Derrida notes that binding now is unthinkable without its capacity to replace, to substitute, to represent. He writes: "To bind, therefore, is also *to detach,* to detach a representative, to send it on a mission, to liberate a missive in order to fulfill, at the destination, the destiny of what it represents. A *post* effect. . . . Postal: binding" (1987, 394).

But the "postal principle" is the possibility of nonarrival at a destination, an effect of nonmastery. Once binding as tension has to include the *sending* of a representative, nonarrival at a destination, nonmastery, is always possible. Freud has been examining the question of the mastery of the pleasure principle from the very first page of *Beyond*. . . . As in the discussion of repetition of trauma, Freud's point is that binding works to secure the dominance of the pleasure principle, but is not the pleasure principle itself. ("Binding is a preparatory act which introduces and assures the dominance of the pleasure principle" [1920, 62].) If so, then binding is in the position of a nonmastery that is the condition of mastery. Derrida writes: "There is no mastery which has not been prepared, introduced, and confirmed by *Bindung,* by the band or by the post" (1987, 395). Mastery itself then, presumes "postal technology," but in its nondeterministic sense. If mastery determines, is determinism, its reliance on postal technology makes it never entirely mastery—and this would have to hold for Freud's basic question about the mastery of the pleasure principle.

Concluding *Beyond . . .* with the discussion of binding as the tension of pleasurepain, Freud again raises the question of time as periodicity. "Again," because at the beginning of *Beyond . . . ,* Freud had wondered whether pleasure and unpleasure themselves might not be due to decrease or increase of energy "in a given period of time" (1920, 8). Now he asks whether feelings of tension, which can be either pleasurable or unpleasurable, permit a distinction between bound and unbound energic processes. Or does the "pleasure and unpleasure series indicate a change in the magnitude of the cathexis within a given unit of time"? (63) Derrida comments: "Inseparable from the phenomena of *binding* (and therefore of pleasure-unpleasure) as from the *quantities* (of cathexis), the so-called units of time cannot not also be *metrical and rhythmical* notions. Beyond opposition, *différance* and rhythm" (1987, 407–8). He then says that in several fragments of *The Will to Power* Nietzsche had already understood pleasure as a rhythm of small painful excitations (408).

Freud's discussion of binding and periodicity has already been related to Nietzsche on repetition and difference The paradox of the hungry baby is that need satisfaction, tension reduction, repetitively produces a tension-raising registration (the experience of satisfaction as *Bahnung*). Nietzsche, of course, would reject any linkage of hunger and *self* preservation to will to power and eternal return. But Heidegger's conception of care and time, and Derrida's conception of autoaffection as heteroaffection, both produce a thinking of the self as uncanny, temporal: *ekstasis, différance*. In these senses, and in the sense that Heidegger and Derrida both think temporality as a "prior intermediate," Nietzsche's rejection of *self* preservation can be modified. It becomes a question of pleasurepain, of repetition in or of the zone, and particularly of postal binding: nondeterministic self-sending.

Derrida notes here that Nietzsche appears to essentialize pain: the will to suffer as the will to power beyond self preservation. For Nietzsche, the "beyond of the pleasure principle" would be the affirmation of life as pain, the opposite of Freud's return to the inorganic. But postal binding undermines any opposition between pleasure and unpleasure. It is irreducibly "intervallic" (rhythmic), the "to be repeated" before of the pleasure principle. The essentialism of Nietzsche's affirmation of life as pain can be modified once it intersects with a conception of the *self* as auto-hetero-affection. In the time-space of demonic repetition, then, it is a question of pain against pain.[21] Freud knows that a patient may defensively repeat painful experience with the analyst as if it were objectively, uninterpretably present, but he does not know that the patient does so in order to repudiate the pleasurepain of interpretation as differantial relation.

When the "degree of aloofness" necessary for interpretation has collapsed, the patient not only clings to the objectively present, he or she also insists on rigid determinism. Hence, analytic neutrality, the interpretive stance itself, cannot presume mastery or determinism. When a patient's "because" is rigidly defensive, the analyst cannot intervene with a "counterbecause." Nietzsche's active interpretation and Heidegger's descriptive interpretation are not causal; both are theories of interpretation as relation. Noncausal interpretation as relation is "postal" in Derrida's sense: a sending without assured arrival at a destination. This again takes us back to "Structure, Sign, and Play," to Nietzschean interpretation as play, as affirmation of chance. Interpretation as the active-descriptive naming of a process dispenses with causality in order to modify rigidly defensive maintenance of it. But effective intervention into defensive maintenance of objectivity and determinism unleashes *Angst*-like anxiety about chaotic loss of control: there is an effect of chance in the neutral, interpretive stance.

Freud was willing to think chance only to a certain extent. Neutrality potentiates free association, but association is "free," nondetermined, only from the point of view of consciousness. The aim is to reveal unconscious determinism, the secret *mastery* of the pleasure principle. Thus, Freud can speak of the role of chance in the formation of symptoms, for example in the "Rat Man" case, without contradicting his conviction about unconscious determinism.

Rat Man suffered from an obsessional neurosis understood by Freud as defense against anal sadistic impulses directed against his father. Rat Man's conflict was exacerbated by an ambivalent reaction to the father's death, producing an identification with him. The father had not paid a gambling debt while in the army. On his own reserve maneuvers, the patient encountered a "cruel captain," whose stories of anal-sadistic rat tortures *by chance* intersected with his statement that the patient owed a small amount of money to Lieutenant A (1909, 210–11). The patient's major presenting symptom was an obsession about repaying this nonexistent debt. One could say that by chance the cruel captain had "interpreted" Rat Man's unconscious dynamics: that he was guilty about his anal sadistic wishes and had identified with his father's failure to pay a gambler's (*Spielratte*) debt. There is both determinism and chance here. Defense against anal sadistic impulses and identification with the dead father *determined* the patient's neurosis; by *chance* the same word, *Ratte*, has both anal and gambling resonances. By chance too, the cruel captain mistakenly identified the person to whom the money was owed. (This mistake will turn out to have major consequences.) The patient's inadvertent encounter with his unconscious dynamics could only intensify his defenses against them, as when "the return of the repressed" produces symptom formation. Hence his frenetic attempts to pay Lieutenant A. From Freud's point of view, once the anal sadistic impulses were expressed in the transference, he could use deterministic interpretation to resolve the very symptoms which the captain's chance remarks had exacerbated. This appears to be a cogent demonstration of unconscious determinism, of the mastery of the pleasure principle, and of interpretation which presumes both. Chance has a role in symptom formation as it intersects with determinism.

But Derrida has found in *Beyond* . . . a critical discussion of how the mastery of the pleasure principle is made possible by postal binding, which implies unconscious chance. Nietzsche advocated interpretation of unconscious differentials of force as play, as affirmation of chance, in order to think interpretation beyond metaphysical determinism. Derrida goes a step further. He demonstrates that chance would have to be implicit to interpretation, not only because postal binding precedes the pleasure principle, but because interpretation is a linguistic act. In an essay on psychoanalysis and literature called "My Chances" he begins with a discussion of chance and determinism in language itself:

> Language . . . is only one among those systems of *marks* that claim this curious tendency as their property: they *simultaneously* incline toward increasing the reserves of random indetermination *as well as* the capacity of coding and overcoding or, in other words, for control and self-regulation. Such compe-

tition between randomness and code disrupts the very systematicity of the system while it also, however, regulates the restless, unstable interplay of the system. (1984, 2)

This interplay of determinism and chance, of systematicity and disruption of systematicity, is another way of thinking the relation of the mastery of the pleasure principle (tension reduction) to binding (tension increase) as its prior condition. To return to the hungry baby: need simultaneously leads to the tension reduction of assuaging hunger and the tension increase of the differentiating, spectral, hetero-auto-affective trace of the mother of primary narcissism. Just as binding is the before of the pleasure principle, the trace of the mother of primary narcissism is the prior condition of the wish. If one focuses only on wishes, as Freud tends to do, tension reduction can seem to be the exclusive principle of "control and self-regulation." It then *determines* unconscious processes. However, because the tension increase of differential registration is irreducible, there is always potential disruption of "control and self-regulation," the narcissistic wound of the threat to mastery. Differential registration itself is not predictable: it is an occurrence that depends on an always mobile interplay of forces. As *Bahnung* it is an effect of chance, the unpredictable. It is an "event" as Derrida describes it: "The attempt to submit chance to thought implies in the first place an interest in the *experience* . . . of that which happens unexpectedly . . . unexpectability conditions the very structure of an event . . . an event worthy of this name cannot be foretold" (1984, 5–6).

This model describes the entire analytic situation. According to Freud, the patient maintains his or her compromise formations in obedience to the pleasure principle. In his earliest writings Freud emphasized that the pleasure principle works by replacing a painful experience with a pleasant one (wish fulfillment) *and/or* by repressing, defending against the painful experience. In his later writings, for example *Beyond . . .* , he rethinks this idea in terms of anxiety: because a pleasurable wish or fantasy is linked to anxiety, the pleasure principle insists upon elimination of the anxiety through defense. But Freud does not pursue the idea that reversal of defense can take place only because the mastery of the pleasure principle is not absolute. Loewald understood this idea quite well. He maintained that if there were not an unconscious force of tension increase, no interpretation of defense could ever be effective. This is why Loewald was so attentive to Freud's concept of Eros as both a sui generis drive to increase tension and as an expression of primary narcissism (1980, 74–75). However, Loewald did not attend to Freud's description of Eros as the "mischief maker" which opposes the regulation of tension decrease. This "mischief maker" is also responsible for chance differentiation. As a *drive*, as an unconscious force, Eros expresses irreducible randomness "in" the unconscious. Like language itself for Derrida, "the unconscious" would have to have the property of "increasing the reserves of random indetermination *as well as* the capacity . . . for control and self-regulation." To use language to intervene in defensive control, *to interpret*, is to rely on linguistic and unconscious openness to chance. Determinism cannot be modified by counterdeterminism——only by chance, by interpretation, as what Derrida calls "event." [22]

Free association had always assumed an interplay between determinism and chance. In this respect Derrida notes the frequent way in which chance is related to the idea of "fall." In German, he says, *Zufälligkeit* means "chance"; hence *Einfall*, the word usually rendered as "association," is "an idea that suddenly comes to mind in an apparently unforeseeable manner" (1984, 5). Freud's discussion of chance in symptom formation in the Rat Man case implies exactly this idea: it is as if the "cruel captain" uttered the *Einfallen* which the patient would have to let "befall" him in an analytic setting. However, one can find, as Derrida says, "a thousand declarations by Freud attesting a completely determinist conviction of the positivistic type prevalent in his day. . . . There is no chance in the unconscious" (24). Derrida argues that even if Freud "suspends all epistemological relations to the sciences or to the modern problems concerning chance"—for example, in physics and biology—he nonetheless wanders into this area with his conception of the drive, which is situated on the frontier of the mental and the physical (25). Frontier concepts maintain an intermediacy that is not completely deterministic. From this point of view, it is not by chance that Freud's paper on the destinies of the drives ("Instincts and Their Vicissitudes") should produce a self-sending that is itself intermediate, indeterminately active or passive, subjective or objective. Given that the self-sending of the primary, intermediate phase of scopophilia describes the relation of baby and mother in primary narcissism, it also describes the registration of difference not regulated by the pleasure principle—the possibility of effective interpretation.

This binding tension *marks* the unconscious. As Freud said in his brief discussion of originally unconscious thought, it is the tension-raising *impression* of a relation. Importantly, Freud had specified that such impressions are not linked to verbal language. Therefore, they cannot be spoken, will not emerge as associative *Einfallen*, unforeseen words, in analysis. But they are "language" in the sense that Derrida speaks here of "marks" whose randomness works with determinism. Because Freud in many ways thinks unconscious processes in terms of nonverbal, differentiating traces, Derrida can say that psychoanalysis is "a discourse that remains *open* [emphasis added] and that attempts at each instant to regulate itself—yet affirming its originality—according to the scientific and artistic treatment of randomness" (1984, 28).

For Heidegger such "opening" is the task of thinking, a task not possible for metaphysics or science. Such thinking is not causal, although it holds ground and cause together as perdurance. Psychoanalysis as a discipline has to be "open," because it depends upon an "open"—differentiable, "chance"—unconscious. But psychoanalysis has to account for the way in which its openness to nondeterministic processes can *appear* to be closed determinism. On both the theoretical and clinical levels this is the result of disavowal of difference. And on both levels this amounts to privileging verbal expression and determinism over the chance effects of "mark" or "trace." As a linguistic act, interpretation must be thought as mark, especially if it is to modify defensive determinism.

The modification of unconscious process as chance mark is another way to understand interpretation which modifies what it interprets—"spectral interpretation." Spectrality itself implies Freud's "psychic reality," the virtuality which Derrida called the "*différance* of the technical apparatus." Psychic reality itself is suspended between the fictive and the real. Clinically, defensive determinism is often accompanied by rejection of the "fictitious" or "as if" quality of psychic reality, particularly as expressed in the transference. Interpretation of defensive determinism involves interpretation of defenses against fictiveness, against the uncanniness of psychic reality. This means that there is a link between "fictive reality" and chance, the conditions of possibility of transformative interpretation.

When Freud speaks of psychic *reality*, and at the end of his life of the registration and repudiation of *reality*, he in general does not see that both imply the reality of difference. "Difference" in general is an effect of *différance*—hence its link to play or chance as undecidably "fictive-real." But hence too its link to what Derrida has called life-death, the suspension between the alive and the mechanical. Interpretation as mark or trace, as chance opening of fictive play, has to have a relation to the problematic of life-death. This relation is expressed in the concept Derrida calls "ex-appropriation."

"Ex-appropriation" is the movement in which the attempt to grasp the "proper" disappropriates itself. In his analysis of the death drive, Derrida notes a critical correspondence between Heidegger and Freud on the idea that the aim of life is one's *own* death, the authentic, *proper* death. For Freud, each organism wants to die in its *own* way. For Heidegger, the "'authenticity' of *Dasein* 'resolutely' assuming its Being-toward-death in the original (non-'vulgar') temporality of its 'care,' was also a certain quality of the relation to the proper: *Eigentlichkeit* assumed" (1979–1987, 358). This is Da-sein's "*ownmost* non-relational possibility not to be bypassed." For both Heidegger and Freud, Derrida says, the relation of death to life functions as "the law of the proper . . . it is indeed a question of an *economy* of death, of a law of the proper (*oikos* [one's house], *oikonomia*) which . . . indefatigably seeks the proper event, its own" (1984, 359). In other words, death as the proper event is arrival at *the* destination.

But just as there is a kink in arrival at a destination, so there is a kink in the search for the proper event. Recall the relation of the pleasure principle and the reality principle. The pleasure principle *affects itself* with its other, the reality principle, through delay, *différance*. Reality, Derrida had said interpreting Freud, is then an effect of this autoaffection. Similarly, Freud understands life as the detour, the delay, on the route to one's proper death. Like reality, "life" is bound to autoaffective *différance*. This is why Derrida asserts that everything Freud says about time in this context has to be "related to the auto-affective structure of time . . . such as it is described in Heidegger's *Kantbuch.*"[23] (This is a question we have followed throughout.) But to think autoaffection *as différance* produces the kink:

> measures of prolongation or abbreviation [longer or shorter detours toward death] have no "objective" signification, *they do not belong to objective time* [emphasis added]. They have value only as concerns the oneself (*soi-meme*) which apostrophizes and calls (to) itself as an other in auto-affection. Before all else one must auto-affect oneself with one's proper death (and the self does not exist before all else, before this movement of auto-affection), make certain that death is the auto-affection of life or life the auto-affection of death. . . . It auto-delegates itself and arrives only by itself differing/deferring

itself in (its) totally-other, in a totally-other which should no longer be its own. . . . In the guarding of the proper, beyond the opposition of life/death, its privilege is also its vulnerability, one can even say its essential impropriety, the exappropriation (*Enteignis*) which constitutes it. (1987, 359)

This is another glimpse into nonobjective time, the time of delay always there in the drive *toward* the proper, i.e. the delay, the *différance* of the proper. *This is the temporality of interpretation as chance mark*, the time of the "degree of aloofness" necessary to experience the unanticipated, to play with reality as fiction. Life-death can mean *either* one's ownmost, the proper, *or* the out of joint time of the spectral (living-dead) apparatus, whose fictive reality "exappropriates" the self. In the area of disavowal of difference, interpretation must have this ex-appropriative effect if it is to make fictive play possible.

Because the disavowal of difference is defense against tension-raising aspects of Eros, one can see it as an expression of the death drive: it de-differentiates. It seems to work for the mastery of the pleasure principle, for tension reduction. But it does so in order to prevent the opening of the exappropriative time-space of the fictive and the spectral, the division within the self that makes the self possible. (Recall the clinical example in Chapter 2 in which the patient seemed to "lose her self" as interpretation of her "attention deficit disorder" became possible. In the next session, the patient was increasingly preoccupied with objective clock time.) Neutrality then is exappropriative. It is based on the interplay of objective time and reality with the nonobjective time of autoaffective delay. All the non-present aspects of the analytic setting are designed to effect chance exappropriation. These nonpresent aspects are essential to the preservation of a "self" whose very condition of possibility is exappropriative, beginning with the registration of the experience of satisfaction. The patients who resist interpretation paradoxically treat what is helpful as a threat. But there is no paradox: what is helpful, what they need, is also differentiating, an intrinsic threat to the patient's conscious sense of what is his or her ownmost, what is most proper, what protects one from uncanniness and loss of control—all of which are implicit to the relation to the mother of primary narcissism. Hence, the strange reality of interpretive *care*. The flight from such care is manifest in the pull toward tension reduction, toward self-destruction, the defensive mastery of the pleasure principle.

Representation, Fantasy, Language, Names

> Names by themselves may be empty, but the *act of naming* . . .
> —Pynchon, *Gravity's Rainbow* (1973)

> I wired to my opticians in Vienna to send me another pair by the next post.
> Freud, *Notes upon a Case of Obsessional Neurosis* (1909)

Difference and divisibility as effects of *différance* are the relation to what is other than presence, what is not presentable or re-presentable. Representation is a critical issue for Heidegger: technology as the end of metaphysics is the planetary triumph of calculative-representational thinking. Difference is the unthought of metaphysics, because difference as active process cannot be representational (1969, 62). "Since metaphysics thinks of beings as such as a whole, it represents beings in respect of what differs in the difference, and without heeding the difference as difference" (70). In the modern era, for Heidegger, representation (*Vorstellung*) is central to the determination of beings as objects placed before (*Vor-stellen*) subjects. Truth becomes the subject's adequate representation of the object.

In an essay on representation called "Envoi," an extension of his thinking about nondeterministic "sending," Derrida writes that Heidegger would have to see Freud as part of the modern metaphysics of subjectivity, because representation has "such an organizing role in the obscure problematics of the drive and of repression. . . . [T]he notions of fantasy and of fetish maintain a strict relation with a logic of representation" (1980, 122). But Derrida is also quite attentive to problems in the critique of representation. He says that a deconstruction of representation would be in vain if it led to any "rehabilitation of immediacy, of originary simplicity, of presence without repetition or delegation, or if it induced a critique of calculable objectivity, of science, of technology, of political representation. The worst regressions can let themselves be governed by an anti-representational stance" (1980, 122–23).

In other words, just as one must think the interplay of ground and cause, chance and determinism, so too one must integrate the necessary deconstruction of representation with the necessity of representation. Take the essential psychoanalytic concept of fantasy. For Heidegger, as Derrida summarizes, the "re-" of "representation" translates the "*Vor-*" of the German *Vorstellung* (representation), because in the modern era the subject makes the object stand *before* him, makes the object available to him through re-presentation. In psychoanalysis, psychic representations of objects are the essence of fantasy, beginning with the hallucinated breast, which the "baby" sees before it—the origin of wish fulfillment. According to Heidegger, *phantasma*, in its original Greek sense, did not mean representative reproduction of an object in the imagination; in the modern sense, however, this is exactly what it means (1980, 126). Heidegger's point is that representational "imagination" has to think beings as objective in a world taken as an image conceived by a mind (126). This means that representation, objectivity, and fantasy are conjoined, that truth as the subject's adequate representation of objects cannot be divorced from fantasy. Hence, truth as unconcealment [*aletheia*] is incompatible with the assumption that *reality* is objective presence. Clinically, we already know this from "concreteness" (fetishistic or "demonic" transference), in which fantasy is conflated with reality to produce entrenched objectivity. As Derrida has said, fantasy and fetish have a strict relation to a logic of representation. The analysis of the Immaculate Conception in *Glas* is analogous to Heidegger's demonstration that fantasy and objectivity are conjoined: truth as fantasy determines difference as opposition and insures the *mastery* of each term of the opposition.

How then can one deconstruct representation while understanding its necessity? Derrida's answer is like his understanding of the "proper": the idea of "one's own" implies autoaffective *differance*, spacing or division. Heidegger's unconcealment, coming-into-presence (*Anwesenheit*)—which is not presentation, or representation—is itself the site of a division, the ontico-ontological difference. After *Being and Time* and *Kant and the Problem of Metaphysics* Heidegger concentrates less on *Daseinsanalyse* and more on rethinking the history of metaphysics. This history is still "symptomatic": it thinks the different eras of the forgetting of being as forms of the *sending*, the *Gechick*, of being. Sending itself is for Derrida divided between arrival and nonarrival at a destination, between unification and division, between propriation and exappropriation. Analyzing Heidegger's idea that the history of metaphysics implies that *there is* sending of being, Derrida says:

> For the era of representation to have its meaning and its unity as era, it has to belong to the reassembling of a more originary and more powerful sending (*envoi*). And if there were not the assembling of this *envoi*, the *Gechick* of being . . . , no interpretation of the era of representation could co-ordinate it

with the unity of a history of metaphysics. Doubtless . . . the assembling of
the *envoi* and of destinality, the *Gechick*, does not have the form of a *telos*, . . .
of the *envoi's* arrival at a destination. But at very least there is (*gibt es*) an *envoi*.
. . . [But] it is only by banking on the indivisible reassembly of the *envoi* that
Heidegger's reading can detach eras, including the most powerful, the longest,
the most dangerous of all—the era of representation in modern times. (1980,
135–36)

Derrida's gesture here is akin to the one we have already seen in his analysis of Freud on chance and determinism. In Freud's overall thinking, there
is chance, but not in the unconscious—even if close reading shows that
the theory of the unconscious has to be open to chance. Similarly, for
Heidegger, despite his deconstructions of causality and determinism, the
possibility of a history of the eras of metaphysics implies a reassembling, a
unification, of the sending of divided being itself. Heidegger might coun-
terargue that he is describing something like the "they-self" on the level
of the history of the forgetting of being: the historical mutations of how
the ontico-ontological difference is sent, but forgotten, because oblivion
belongs to the difference. But Derrida's point is that wherever there is
sending (*Geschick, envoi*), chance and division are always operative, even
if they appear not to be. This compromises the demarcation of eras.

  In this context Derrida returns to the linked questions of the drive,
representation, and sending, of *Triebeschicksale*, the destinies of the drives.
Drive is a concept on the frontier of the psychic and the somatic. It is representative, in the sense of delegation. Repression itself is carried out on
representatives, delegates (1980, 137). Delegation itself, however, is what
Derrida has called "postal binding": the before of the pleasure principle
as a structure of replacement, as in the replacement of the (so-called) primary process with the secondary process. Freud's entire theory of drives
always implies sending, *Schicken*, precisely because drives themselves are
always subject to replacement and representation, have varied *Schicksale*.
Thus, the drive's very "existence" is divided between representation and
sending. What then, asks Derrida, "does to legate or to delegate mean, if
this motion cannot be derived, interpreted, or compared on the basis of
anything else?" (138).

  There is the same kink in representation as in the "proper." There can
be no delegation, representation, or sending without a division. If sending is irreducible, so too is divisibility. It makes representation possible,
but is not representative. Heidegger's history of the various *Schicksale* of

being itself depends upon a "preontological" divisibility, which would make the *Schicken* of being possible. Such sending is "reassembled only in dividing itself, in differing/deferring itself. . . . This divisibility of the *envoi* is in no way negative, is not a lack, is completely other than the subject" (1980, 141). In other words, sending itself implies *différance*. Because the *différance* of sending is the condition of possibility of representation, once *there is* (*gibt es*) sending there is always representation. One can deconstruct representation, while maintaining its necessity. The Freudian drive itself, which is always a question of the *Schicken*, oscillates between divisibility and representation—between chance and determinism. From a revised Heideggerian or Freudian perspective, one can then envisage a disavowal of divisibility and chance in which determinism becomes defensive, and the space of representation is collapsed.

In "Freud and the Scene of Writing" Derrida said that "every symbolic synthesis . . . includes within itself spacing as difference (1978, 219). This is why defense against differentiation produces nonsymbolic, nonrepresentational, transferences. But such defenses are directed against the possibility of representation, not against representations themselves. Therefore, as Derrida has just said, they are not directed against anything that can be construed as a lack. They have the nonsubjective automaticity of "demonic repetition" or transference, of Heidegger's uncanny self-giving of opening. They appear uninterpretable if one assumes that interpretation itself bears on representations. Automatic defense against the possibility of interpretation is so rigidly deterministic because it attempts to control the chance implicit to the division within representation. But such defenses *are* interpretable, if interpretation itself is understood as trace or mark, as "random" and "fictive" (the scare quotes here indicating the relation to determinism and reality.)

Traces or marks also have the property Derrida calls "insignificance" (1984, 15). To illustrate what this means, he uses the example of the proper name. In and of itself a name has no significance and refers to no one specifically (e.g. *Pierre*). Certainly a proper name can come to have a meaning and reference (e.g. *pierre*, stone), and this can bring about a falling together, a "symptom" in the etymological sense. But such "symptoms" imply the chance concatenation of nonmeaning and meaning. Such chance concatenations imply yet another property of marks or traces. A mark, to be a mark, must be identifiable, recognized as the same in different contexts (e.g. *Pierre, pierre*). What makes a mark identifiable is its

difference from other marks. To use an identifiable mark in different contexts is to repeat it: "insignificance in marking" is an effect of repetition
and difference. When describing this property of marks Derrida often
prefers the word "iteration" to "repetition," because of its derivation from
the Sanskrit *itara*, "other," *autre*. Iteration itself speaks of repetition as
otherness:

> The ideal iterability that forms the structure of all marks is that which un-
> doubtedly allows them to be released from any context, to be freed from all
> determined bonds to [their] origin, meaning, or referent, to emigrate in order
> to play elsewhere, in whole or in part, another role . . . by means of this es-
> sential insignificance the ideality or ideal identity of each mark (which is only
> a differential function without an ontological basis) can continue to divide
> itself and to give rise to the proliferation of other ideal identities. This iter-
> ability is thus that which allows a mark to be used more than once. It is more
> than one. It multiplies and divides itself internally. This imprints a capacity
> for diversion within its very movement. . . . There is no assured destination
> precisely because of the mark and the proper name: in other words, because
> of this insignificance. (1984, 16; translation slightly modified)

Nietzschean interpretation gives a *name* to a *process*. To name, to desig-
nate, is in Heidegger's early sense to describe something *as* something (the
as-structure of interpretation); in his later sense, it is to heed difference *as*
difference. All imply a process of marking, or re-marking. To re-mark defense against chance, against the automatic process of division that makes
representation possible, is "to submit chance to thought," which requires
"an interest in the *experience* . . . of that which happens unexpectedly"
(1984, 5–6). But that which happens unexpectedly is potentially traumatic, precisely because it differentiates, divides, disrupts. As the model
for modification of "the unconscious," the *experience* of satisfaction itself
implies a differentiating trace, *Bahnung*—which is why one can say that it
is linked to the *possibility of the proper name as ex-appropriative*. Interpretation of defense against differentiation *names* the differentiating function
of the analytic relation in order to *mark*, *re-mark*, or *open* the collapsed
(spectral, uncanny) space of representation. To name, or to mark in this
way, is to use interpretation to modify that which it interprets. But it is
not to bring repressed fantasies—representations—into consciousness.

What happens if the analyst has no conception of this active, descriptive, marking function of interpretation? When interpretation assumes

representation and causality? Here there is more to say about Freud's Rat Man case. The patient initially told Freud that he had read a few pages of *The Psychopathology of Everyday Life*. He "had come across the explanation of some curious verbal associations which had so much reminded him of some of his own 'efforts of thought' in connection with his ideas that he had decided to put himself in my hands" (1909, 159). Although Rat Man claimed he was seeking relief from his tormenting obsessional symptoms, Freud tells us that he really wanted a doctor to write a letter attesting to the medical necessity of permitting him to pay his "debt" to Lieutenant A. The patient in fact told Freud an incredible story of constantly changing trains on his return from maneuvers, in a frantic attempt to locate the lieutenant. But the debt was a *symptom*, due to chance falling together of the cruel captain's story about rat torture and his mistaken idea that the patient owed money to Lieutenant A. Freud's own name for the patient illustrates his idea that chance can play a role in symptom formation, as long as it is finally understood in terms of unconscious determinism. Derrida could remind us that the name, the iterable mark, puts chance, exappropriation, and divisible sending at the heart of the symptom. Does this idea have any clinical relevance to the case?

The patient's wish to have Freud write a letter that would permit him to pay his symptomatic debt is a "concretization" of his symptom, a fetish. It is a compulsive attempt to have something that is an effect of chance arrive at a destination, a collapse of the space of representation. Freud presents the case as an eventual interpretive triumph: the patient's unconscious conflicts are expressed transferentially, interpreted, and his symptoms relieved. There seems to be no reason to question the presumption of representation. But the patient initially defends against representation itself: his obsessive thoughts about the debt to Lieutenant A are not for him a symptom, but a concrete reality. Did this defense simply fade away as he engaged in the analytic process? Or was it replaced with the determinism implicit to Freud's interpretive stance? When the patient says that Freud's "explanation of some curious verbal associations . . . reminded him of some of his own 'efforts of thought' in connection with his ideas," there is a strong hint that the patient found his own "determinism" mirrored in Freud's interpretive stance.

In *The Psychopathology of Everyday Life* (1901) Freud presents one of his strongest cases about why there is no chance in the unconscious (a discussion analyzed by Derrida in "My Chances" [1984]). Could it be that Rat Man and Freud shared the defense against submitting "chance to thought," against the experience of the unexpected? And that this process was never *named*, because it is not representational? Once Freud interpretively determined the source of the patient's imaginary debt, his concrete insistence on paying it is presumably gone. Curiously, though, we learn that in fact the patient *did* have a small debt—the COD for his new glasses. This COD had been paid by the young mistress of the post office where the glasses had arrived while the patient was on maneuvers. Was his concrete demand that Freud write a letter allowing him to pay Lieutenant A a registration and repudiation, a disavowal, of his debt to the postmistress? Freud makes it clear that he quickly realized that Rat Man had to "have known that he owed the amount of the charges due upon the packet *to no one but the official at the post office.*" Another officer had told Rat Man that the postmistress "had been of the opinion that she could trust the unknown lieutenant and had said that in the meantime she would pay the charges herself . . . he had *suppressed to himself, just as in telling the story he had suppressed to me, the . . . existence of the trusting young lady at the post office*" (1909, 172–73; emphasis added). Moreover, the patient told Freud that upon his arrival in Vienna he spoke to a friend about his tormenting need to pay the "debt" to Lieutenant A. The friend also quickly realized that the money was owed to the postmistress, so that the next "morning they had gone together to the post office, to dispatch the 3.80 *kronen* to the post office [Z—] at which the packet containing the pince-nez had arrived" (172). Most likely the friend naively assumed that once the real debt was paid, the imaginary one would vanish. Freud could justifiably say that the friend had no conception of the symbolic nature of the debt, of the need to *interpret* its unconscious determinants.

But neither the friend nor Freud is interested in the question of why Rat Man so insistently disavows the real debt, *even once it is paid*, why he "suppressed to himself, just as in telling the story he had suppressed to me the . . . existence of the trusting young lady at the post office." Could she have marked him in a way he could not tolerate? Was it a chance experience of satisfaction whose reality was disavowed because of its relation to postal binding? The postmistress, after all, had obligingly paid for his glasses, a supplementary, mechanical device he *needed*, just as he needed postal technology to have them sent to him, and just as he used it to repay the "trusting young lady." This is not to say that Freud's analysis of the patient's symptomatic rat fantasies was incorrect, but rather to wonder whether it was incomplete. Were he and the patient all too relieved to focus on the representational determinism implicit to naming the father, and defended against the "marking insigificance" implicit to this naming itself? Freud would say that the obsession with the debt to Lieutenant A was a reedition of the causal psychodynamics already established in the patient's childhood. However, there was also disavowal of an *event*: the chance of the postmistress's kind gesture, her "technological care." When *everything* is owed to the father, the *trace* of the "postal mother" is registered and repudiated. Freud does not seem at all interested in Rat Man's insistent disavowal of his paid debt to the postmistress, perhaps because he cannot interpret it causally and representationally. Can interpretation modify what it interprets if the time and space of this disavowal are not reopened? If interpretation is brought to bear only on representable fantasy?

Archives and Analysis

Mark or trace implies inscription on a surface. Heidegger's being-in-the-world as neither subjective nor objective itself implied "being-on" to describe surface interactions of care. In "Freud and the Scene of Writing," the interacting surfaces of the *Wunderblock* described the being-in-the-world of the psychic apparatus. Care—as in the postmistress's kind gesture—is registration of the differentiating trace of primary narcissism, the repetitive process carried out by the unconscious as spectral apparatus. This is the possibility of marking interpretation.

Heidegger thought that the unconscious as container for repressed representations, regulated by classical mechanics, "could never arrive at the structure of care" (2001, 172). But he could not conceive a nondeterministic "surface apparatus" structured by care. Care as difference and repetition describes a self and self-preservation as exappropriative life-death: life as intrinsically technological, the psychic apparatus registering the differential traces of primary narcissism. The spectral reality of such registrations is uncanny and uncontrollable, threatening to usurp the mastery sought in opposition, presence, and tension reduction. But spectral reality is also "autoimmune." When registration of differentiating process creates traumatic tension, the "unconscious" splits itself: an interaction of surfaces becomes the opposition of an internal subject and an external objective reality. The result is the picture of an unconscious whose "kernel," to use Freud's expression, is wish fulfillment: representable fantasy governed by the tension reduction principle. Did Rat Man repudiate the reality that was "right on the surface"—the unexpected event of the postmistress's care—as an autoimmune response to "spectral self-preservation"? Did Freud not want to consider that in order to use interpretation to modify what it interprets ("spectral interpretation"), he would have to think about *the analyst as the postmistress*, about interpretation as unexpected, marking care, as *Bahnung*?

Freud's intermittent thoughts about unconscious, *primary* "binding," of articulating-connecting inscription, do potentially open onto the possibility of marking care. An example is the momentary insight into *originally* unconscious thought as trace—the *"impression of a relation."* *Archive Fever (Mal d'archive)* (1995), subtitled "A Freudian Impression," expands Derrida's thinking of trace, binding, self-preservation—and violence. He shows that the unconscious as memory, as surface open to the force of the *impress of relation* (the "effraction of the trace"), *and* as (postal) binding is always given over to its own destruction.

Derrida starts with an apparently trivial passage of *Civilization and Its Discontents,* in which Freud apologizes. He is publishing a book that mainly restates the obvious, so he is wasting his own paper and ink, the printer's work and materials. His only justification is to restate what is new in psychoanalysis: aggression as a modification of the basic theory of the drives (1930, 117). Freud here assimilates "aggression" to everything he had said in *Beyond . . .* about a death drive and a destructive drive. In *Beyond . . .* he had been more careful: the death drive was a drive toward *self* destruction (and thus the entire question of the drive toward one's own, proper death). Aggression against another person was a deflection, a projection "outward," of dangerous self destructiveness. Life protects itself, delays rushing to its end, through hatred of one's neighbor.

In "Instincts and Their Vicissitudes" (1915c) Freud had already said that the "object" is created by projection, the placing "outside" whatever is frustrating and threatening. Hence his idea that "hate as a relation to objects is older than love" (139). The subsequent logic of the death drive is that hatred of the object is a necessary defense: my wish to murder you protects me from ultimate tension reduction, the drive toward my own death. (Nietzsche would understand Freud's death drive as an expression of the ascetic ideal: pleasure as avoidance of pain, the death drive as an aptly named Nirvana principle.) The "discontent" (*Unbehagen*) of civilization is that it is made possible by inhibiting murderous wishes, which in turn protect against self destruction. But once such wishes are inhibited, destructiveness is again directed against oneself, in the form of guilt. This is why Freud links the superego to the death drive in *The Ego and the Id* (1923, 53). (The Nietzschean resonance is clear: the superego as the tormenting bad conscience of the ascetic ideal.) In *Beyond . . .* , Freud had also said that the death drive works in silence. If so, Derrida comments, the death drive as self destruction

> never leaves any archives of its own. It destroys in advance its own archive. . . . It works *to destroy the archive: on the condition of effacing* but also *with a view to effacing* its own "proper" traces—which consequently cannot properly be called "proper" . . . the death drive is above all *anarchivic*. . . . It will always have been archive-destroying by silent vocation. (1995, 10)

Everything in *Archive Fever* follows from this point. But there is a knot here.

Derrida's initial point is that Freud's apology for *wasting* the "material substrate" of paper, ink, and printing as he speaks of the *aggressive* drive is an echo of "archive fever," the "diabolical death, . . . aggression, or destruction drive: a drive of pure loss" (1995, 9). The death drive is assimilated to aggression and destruction, "as if these three words were . . . synonyms" (10). Construing the death drive as a drive of pure loss, of pure destruction, Derrida *also* says that it is not a "principle," like the pleasure and reality principles. Rather, it is the threat to "every principality" (12). Derrida seems to forget the essential difficulty from *Beyond . . .* : "the pleasure principle seems actually to serve the death instincts" (Freud, 1920, 63). Mastery is insured by tension reduction. This was why Derrida could juxtapose the death drive to being-toward-death as the "drive of the proper," the reappropriative drive (*The Post Card*). Mastery and the "proper" presume certain metaphysical oppositions: subject and object, inside and outside, pleasure and pain, *life and death*. The death drive in its *opposition* to life, conservation, differentiation, serves such mastery, which is why it can be seen as dedifferentiating.

We know from Derrida himself that the mastery of tension reduction has a "prior condition": binding as pleasurepain, as repetition, as *lifedeath*. Freud tends to put differentiation on the "side" of the life drive and repetition on the "side" of the death drive, leaving them isolated from each other. But just as unconscious trace is always a question of difference and repetition, so too it is always a question of lifedeath, the spectral as *rev-*

enance. The "death drive" can be seen as an *independent* force of destruction, serving the pleasure principle, only by splitting it from the life drive, from Eros. Because Eros itself is both tension raising and differentiating—binding—it must always be thought in relation to tension reduction and dedifferentiation. It is simultaneously "self-preservative" *and* "self-destructive." When Freud says that the object is created by projection, making hatred older than love, he as usual forgets "registration of the experience of satisfaction," "originally unconscious thought," the impress of the *relation* to the "object," as the "prior" condition of such projection (and of the wish). Because Eros is primary narcissism, it is, as Heidegger says about Dasein, neutral in relation to "I" and "you." As Freud himself finally says, initially the baby *is* the breast. To translate: unconsciously "I" *am* "the memory of you," I register your trace, I am haunted by you, I "exist" spectrally, this is pleasurepain, the trauma of binding as self preservation, the strangeness of care. Hence, I create an opposition between "me" and "you," pleasure and pain, life and death, which permits me to believe that *my* aggression against *you* is *not* derived from my attempted destruction of the differentiating trace that preserves me.

Freud says that the death drive deflected outward becomes aggression, which must be inhibited if there is to be civilization. To do so he has to assume the opposition of self and object created by hatred. Thus, he not only founds civilization on the inhibition of aggression, but also on the metaphysical opposition of "I" and "you," on the disavowal of primary narcissism. In the largest sense this is the psychoanalytic equivalent of the forgetting of being *as* the ontotheological exclusion of the trace. This disavowal creates the illusion that I can attempt to destroy you without destroying myself. It repudiates the self-preservation/self-destruction of Eros, making it appear that the problem is solely the inhibition of the wish to murder the object. The discontent of civilization is then the autoimmune response to the possibility of the object, the tension-raising registration of the experience of satisfaction. This tension is a "bond" from which I seek release. I attempt to *master* "you," and believe that I do so to preserve myself, when I am actually destroying myself. What is more blindly self destructive than the mastery of every "master race"? No accident that Derrida raises the question of "radical evil" in this context.

He calls the drive to conserve the "archive drive" (1995, 19). Such a need to archive, he reminds us, implies the material substrate as *supplement*: If memory in and of itself were not finite, if it did not *need* the memory-aid in order to be memory, there would be no memory. Hence, because memory *is* archive it must also be thought in terms of destruction of the archive, "a forgetfulness which does not limit itself to repression" (19). The "radical finitude" of the archive, of supplementarity, always encounters "archive fever" (*mal d'archive*), the *in-finite* threat which "sweeps away the logic of finitude . . . enlisting the in-finite, archive fever verges on radical evil" (19–20). Derrida finds this infinite threat in the death-aggression-destruction drive; he notes that Freud in *Civilization* . . . confesses his own resistance to the idea of "an instinct of destruction" (1930, 120). But again, Freud and Derrida seem to concur here that there is an *independent* destructive drive that infinitely threatens a drive to conserve and the finitude of its necessary supplements. However, if difference, in Nietzsche's terms, is both life *and* decay, if, in Derrida's terms, difference is trace, and if, in Heidegger's terms, *oblivion* belongs to the difference, then the finitude of the archive and the infinite threat of its destruction are a function of lifedeath. Of spectral care. Of registration-repudiation of difference as the way in which a living machine becomes the *opposition* of life and machine, life and death, life drive and death drive. The finitude of the *differentiating* supplement *is* the threat of its infinite destruction.

Thus, when Derrida says that the death drive threatens every principle (1995, 12), he not only forgets that as tension reduction the death drive *is* the pleasure principle, he also seems unaware of Freud's scattered remarks about the life drive as differentiating tension increase, the "mischief making" threat to the pleasure principle. In the posthumous *Outline of Psychoanalysis* Freud makes his clearest statement on this topic. Again reviewing the relation between the life and death drives, he explicitly says that the life drive does *not* obey the tension reduction principle. To assume that it did would be to "presuppose that living substance was once a unity which had been torn apart and was now striving towards re-union" (1940a, 149). In other words, once there is a "life drive" which is not regulated by the principle of tension reduction, life itself cannot be conceived as an original unity. The origin of life is difference and tension.[24] But once the origin of life is difference, as Derrida would say, life is trace before it is presence, and is threatened by its condition of possibility. This is another version of Nietzsche's life against itself, of Heidegger's Dasein in flight from itself. Because "life" is difference as trace, memory contains archive fever, the archive as destruction of the archive, technology against itself, autoimmune.

Derrida is always highly sensitive to Freud's technological images. Inscription, registration, hieroglyphics, apparatus, microscope and telescope (*The Interpretation of Dreams*), telephone, telepathy, automaton, *Wunderblock*, are, as Derrida says, always more than metaphors, since they are a meditation on the technology of tele-transport that makes something like meta-phor or trans-ference possible. Freud had to take his metaphors from the technology available to him. How well did such metaphors capture not only the content and structure of the unconscious, but also its functioning, its *processing*? Derrida wonders if one can

> ask whether, *concerning the essentials, and beyond the extrinsic details*, the structure of the psychic apparatus . . . , which Freud sought to describe with the "mystic pad," resists the evolution of archival techno-science or not. Is the psychic apparatus *better represented* or is it *affected differently* by all the technical mechanisms for achivization and for reproduction, for prostheses of so-called live memory . . . which already are, and will increasingly be, more refined, complicated, powerful than the "mystic pad" (microcomputing, electronization, computerization, etc.)? . . . if the upheavals in progress affected the very structures of the psychic apparatus, for example in their spatial architecture and in their economy of speed, in their *processing* [emphasis added] of spacing and of temporalization, it would be a question no longer of simple continuous progress in representation, in the *representative* value of the model, but rather of an entirely different logic. (15)

These questions and implications, Derrida says, concern "the future of psychoanalysis in its relation to the future of science" (14). Freud had a complicated relation to this question. In "Telepathy" he compared the unconscious to such discoveries as radioactivity and relativity, but in order to confirm *postivistic, deterministic* science, à la Einstein.[25] Derrida was well aware of the contradiction here: if something like telepathy is an effect of the disjunctive time of unconscious "postal" technology (sending), then psychoanalysis has to be open to all the scientific advances in the thinking of randomness (nonarrival at a destination). Disjunctive unconscious time can formulaically be described as "differantial auto-affection," for which "measures of prolongation or abbreviation have no 'objective' signification" (1987, 359). Because there is no measurable time without this nonmeasurable time (or even because conscious objective time is the "stimulus barrier" against unconscious nonobjective time), the psychic apparatus is a "clock" that functions according to both. This means that we must think of the *registration of difference itself* as an archival technology, whose "*processing* of spacing and of temporalization" implies a simultaneous immediacy and delay that no clock can measure.

Here the concept of the unconscious as *surface for inscription* is critical. Very little is more clinically astonishing than the way in which a chance, seemingly superficial, remark by the analyst can have an "instantaneous" differentiating effect on a "concrete" patient, who then defers its effect as if it were trauma. A patient who seems to be in an unaltered state of consciousness *immediately* claims not to have heard, blanks out, gets dizzy, or even falls asleep. It is as if a switch had been flipped. The uncanniness and loss of control implicit to the setting as an *unconscious surface open to registration of difference* has been unpredictably let loose. Does any currently existing archival technology account for such instantaneous and unpredictable registration of differentiating time space, *and* for its repudiation, the destruction of its own archive?

And can any currently existing archival technology account for what Derrida calls the archive of the future? Recall the essential role of the future, but as being-toward-death, for Heidegger. Derrida, in what he calls a "science fiction"—a term that must be taken beyond its ordinary sense, because of the essential role of fiction in the sciences of the random—says that

> the technical structure of the *archiving* archive also determines the structure of the *archivable* content in its very coming into existence and in its relationship to the future. The archivization produces as much as it records the event. . . . It conditions not only the form or the structure that prints, but the printed content of the printing: the *pressure* of the *printing*, the *impression*, before the division between the printed and the printer. (17–18; original emphases)

Printing before the division between the printed and the printer describes "inscriptions within primary narcissism": unconscious as "being-in-the-world," as receptive surface of differentiation, as opening. Opening in this sense is opening as the possibility of a future and of interpretation. For Heidegger, the "self giving of opening," the fourth dimension of time as the *relation* of the three ecstasies, is uncanny. In Derrida's terms it would be the *process of revenance*, the spectral return of virtual time-space. The unconscious as archive has always been a "virtual apparatus" producing "virtual events," starting with the *hallucination* of the breast as the *origin* of the virtual reality of dreams. But this "origin" is not original. The hallucination of the breast is the virtual as *representative of the nonrepre-sentational*—"spectral" registration and repudiation, an-archivic printing before the division between the printed and the printer (inscription in primary narcissism). The force, the pressure, of the *impression* that Freud called "originally unconscious thought" is itself registered and repudiated in the virtual reality of the wish, the use of the hallucination to reduce tension. Without unconscious binding, without openness to "printing before the division between the printer and the printed," would interpretation of fantasy, of the re-presentatives of the drives, i.e. of virtuality, be an opening to the future?

Heidegger spoke of the *binding* nature of opening as tension. Derrida calls the *binding* nature of opening the *promise*, the promise of the *return* of disjunctive opening—*revenance*, autoaffective *différance*. Derrida claims that he is "never far from Freud" when he speaks of the promise of the future as a "spectral messianicity" that is not messianic (1995, 36) In other words, Freud's theory of the unconscious, and particularly the inevitability of transference, is always the expectation of the *return* of the virtual, the spectral. (Recall Freud's dream about revenants, about transference.) Analysis itself is the "promise" of *revenance*, the promise of a repetition poised on the tip of the opening and closure of the time-space of interpretation. On the tip of representation (the virtual) as the chance process of sending and as deterministic content. When Derrida speaks of the necessity of thinking the unconscious as the "archive of the virtual" and the promise of the future, he is extending all of Freud's thinking about a memory device that "records" nonobjective reality, "destroys" this archive by transforming it into apparently purely representational *fantasy*, and in turn represses such fantasies—all of which *returns as transference*. Hence the necessary intersection of psychoanalysis with the "*archive of the virtual*. . . . The moment has come to accept a great stirring in our conceptual archive, and in it to cross a 'logic of the unconscious' with a way of thinking of the virtual which is no longer limited by the traditional philosophical opposition between act and power" (66–67). Or limited by the traditional philosophical understanding of reality as objective presence. Either one is inimical to the unconscious as memory and as psychic reality. To the unconscious as memory which produces "fictions cathected with affect" whose *reality* is inherently uncanny. This is why "each time the word *unheimlich* appears in Freud's text . . . one can localize an uncontrollable undecidability . . . and the same is true, in just as significant a way, of Heidegger" (46).

The archive of the virtual as the inscription of the trace of the other on an unconscious surface is the *bond* to the other. Derrida conceives this bond not only as "promise," but as "justice": "if it is just to remember the future and the injunction to remember, namely the archontic injunction to guard and gather the archive, it is no less just to remember the others, the other others and the others in oneself" (77). The memory of the others in oneself pertains to every possible identification, whether of an individual, a group, or a nation (the exappropriative nature of the proper name). On this question of the singular individual as the trace of the other Derrida proposes to cross "psychoanalysis with deconstruction, a certain 'psychoanalysis' and a certain 'deconstruction.'" From a psychoanalytic-deconstructive point of view, a just recall of the other is impossible without the force and violence of the *impression,* archive fever:

> the injustice of this justice can concentrate its violence in the very constitution of the *One* and of the Unique . . . the difference of the One in the form of uniqueness. . . . The gathering into itself of the One is never without violence, nor is the self-affirmation of the Unique, the law of the archontic . . . which orders the archive. Consignation is never without that excessive pressure (impression, repression, suppression) of which repression (*Verdrangung* or *Urverdrangung*) and suppression (*Unterdruckung*) are at least figures. (1995, 77–78)

The "press" common to "impress" and "repress" is both justice and violence: the force of the trace of the other which *must be defended against.* Repression, or even primal repression (*Urverdrangung*), one might translate, is a "figure" of registration and repudiation of difference, another way of thinking "archive fever."

Constitution of the One, preservation of the self as trace of the other, then must entail the autoimmune response, Freud's "splitting of the ego in the *process* of defense." As Derrida puts it, expanding the intersection of deconstruction and psychoanalysis:

> *L'Un se garde de l'autre.* The One guards against/keeps some of the other. It protects *itself* from the other, but in the movement of this jealous violence, it comprises in itself, thus guarding it, the self-otherness or self-difference (the difference from within oneself) which makes it One. The "One differing, deferring from itself." The One as the Other. At once, at the same time, but

in a same time that is out of joint, the One forgets to remember itself to itself, it *keeps and erases the archive* [emphasis added: registers and repudiates trace as *différance*] of this injustice that it is. Of the violence that it does. *L'Un se fait violence*. It becomes what it is, the very violence—that it does to itself. Self-determination as violence. *L'Un se garde de l'autre pour se faire violence* (*because* it makes itself violence [i.e. in order to do violence to itself; my insertion] and *so as* to make itself violence). (1995, 78).

This is the archive fever of *Bahnung*, opening to the effraction of the trace. Before the division between the printer and the printed, "One" (I, the baby) *is* the "Other" (you, mother). "I" preserve myself (*je me garde*) as the impress of "you"—constitution of the self in the middle voice, as autoaffective *Bahnung*. But the force of this self-preservative impress calls for protection against it (*se garder de l'autre*). In protecting myself against "it," against "you" who preserve me, I become me, and you become you, as "units" (*l'Un*). I become me through destroying—repudiating—the trace of you. The time and space of this entire process are not objectively measurable. They are the time and space of intervallic division: "existential" *space* (being-in as being-outside) and *time* (*ek-stasis*, autoaffection) rethought as inscription of *différance*. In preserving myself as the trace of you, I preserve myself by doing violence to myself (lifedeath), and I become this violence to protect myself against you. Lifedeath in primary narcissism becomes creation of the object outside of me, the object I must try to destroy as if I were not destroying myself: *je me fais violence*. The *Unbehagen* of civilization as *mal d'archive*.

Because all of this is differential, intervallic, rhythmic, because it expresses the finitude of need as supplementarity (I must be an "archive" if I am to preserve myself as the memory of you), it is *necessarily* repetition, repetition of autoaffective *différance*:

Now it is necessary that this repeat itself. It is Necessity itself, *Ananke* [Freud's term]. The One, as self-repetition [as iterable mark, as name, which Derrida elsewhere calls "signature"], can only repeat and recall this instituting violence. It can only affirm itself and engage itself in this repetition. This is even what ties in depth the injunction of memory with the anticipation of the future to come [*l'a-venir*]. . . . It orders to promise, but it orders repetition, and first of all self-repetition. . . . If repetition is thus inscribed at the heart of the future to come [*l'a-venir*], one must also import there, *in the same stroke* [*du même coup*], the death drive, the very thing, whatever its name, which *carries*

the law in its tradition . . . what carries the law and *who* carries the table, the
subjectile, the substrate, and the subject of the law. (79)

This passage is not only an expansion of Derrida's thinking of the unconscious trace as self preservative *and* violent. It is also an elliptical sum-
mary of his debate with Yerushalmi (1991) about Freud's *Moses and Monotheism* (1934), a debate that occupies much of *Archive Fever*. Yerushalmi
objected strenuously to Freud's analysis of the story of Moses. For Freud,
the "material truth" of Exodus is that a group of Semitic slaves was led
from Egypt by a prince who still believed in Ikhnaton's suppressed monotheistic sun god. This Egyptian prince was the first Moses. At Sinai, the
group of distraught former slaves rebelled against their demanding leader
and killed him, reverting to Egyptian polytheism. They then wandered
for centuries, finally merging with the Canaanites led by Moses II, who
believed in a volcanic god, Yahweh. But these Semites carried with them
the repressed memory of the murder of Moses I and of his monotheism.
This repressed memory returned, producing the amalgamation of Yahweh
with a monotheistic god, along with all the ethical prescriptions and pro-
hibitions on image making Moses I had failed to impose. For Freud, the
Jewish tradition of monotheism, with its millennial emphasis on law and
abstraction, depends upon the unconscious transmission of the memory of
a murder. As in *Totem and Taboo* (1913) and *Civilization and Its Discontents*
(1930), advances in humanity come at the expense of violence, or violent
wishes. Yerushalmi compellingly challenged this analysis. His main weap-
ons were biblical scholarship and criticism of Freud's reliance on Lamarck-
ian mechanisms of inheritance (to explain the transmission over centuries
of the unconscious memory of the alleged murder of Moses I).

Doing violence to the detailed debate on both sides, I will state only
what is necessary to understand the passage about the inevitable violence
against that which carries the law. First, Derrida reminds Yerushalmi that
his own biblical evidence supports Freud's interpretation. Numbers 14:10
speaks of the "Jews" threatening to stone Moses and Aaron, stopped only
by a Cloud, the glory of the Lord (1995, 65). Derrida is most interested in
the passage in Numbers as the expression of the *wish* to murder Moses.
In psychic reality the wish to murder, the fantasy of murder, can have
enormous consequences. The unconscious can produce such fantasies and
can store them: it is the archive of the virtual, an idea Yerushalmi seems to
ignore. Second, the tradition of the law depends upon its inscription on a

substrate—the tables carried down by Moses. "Substrate" itself is in Greek *hupokeimenon*, the under-lying, which is for Heidegger the origin of the idea of the sub-ject, which in the modern era under-lies all representations of objects. Hence Derrida pulls together the table, the substrate, and the subject of the law, all *subject to archive fever*: the inevitable attempt to destroy the surface of inscription or its representative (Moses).

The inscription and the representative subject of the law are "substrate": the *necessary* supplement of the *necessary* other. Supplementarity is the finitude of need, the finitude of difference, infinitely threatened by destruction. *Need and difference* as repetition implies that the violence of inscription (before the division between the printer and printed) itself is always repeated. The coimplication of subject and substrate, need and violence, is lifedeath. Derrida, then, is again somewhat one-sided when he speaks of the violence of forgetting as the "death drive." It is rather the unconscious as repetition of need and open to the effraction of the trace. Necessity, *Ananke*, as "trace before presence."

Speaking of the necessary destruction of the necessary substrate, of the "press" of which "impression" and "repression" are figures, Derrida called the "an-archive" "super-repression" (1995, 79). "Super-repression" is actually the general structure of disavowal of difference as the possibility of any defense, the general structure of registration-repudiation of "reality," "need," "necessity" (archive fever). Freud, at the end of his life, intuited registration and repudiation of reality as the process of which neurotic repression and psychotic denial were figures. But he did not see that as an extension of the structure of fetishism, this had to mean a rethinking of reality as difference. And of the bond of difference to need in terms of both "care" and memory: trace in/of primary narcissism. By means of "superrepression," disavowal of the traces of primary narcissism, I become subject, you become object, and I believe that I can master and control you. This is the transformation of the supplementarity of general fetishism—I can become me because you and I *are* each other—into the concreteness of restricted fetishism. In the latter, wish fulfillment and fantasy conflated with *reality* are used to control and master virtual space-time. This is the *necessary* attempt to destroy *necessary* opening, the possibility of interpretation. In the autoimmune response need is played against need, just as (signal) anxiety played against (internalization) anxiety, pain against pain, destruction against destruction. Freud's theory of sexuality itself *always* speaks of drive against drive. Autoimmune disavowal or splitting are built into all unconscious processes—e.g. need, anxiety, pain, aggression, sexuality, drive—as a consequence of the division within identity, identity as the preservative-violent trace of the other.

Toward the end of *Archive Fever* Derrida again speaks of the "primary impression" as "the instant of pure autoaffection, . . . the indistinction of the active and the passive, of [the] touching and the touched" (98). Or the seeing and the seen, as in Freud's "primary scopophilia." The primary, intermediate phases of the drives already explained the possibility of drive against drive intrinsic to the historicity, the "archivability" of the drive. (The primary intermediate phase which virtually accompanies the history of the drive also makes it possible for the active form to replace the passive, and vice versa.) And in Freud's own description the primary intermediate drive is *volcanic*—periodically eruptive. It is *the to-be-repeated opening of the historicity of the drive, of the unconscious as the archive of drive.* In speaking of primary scopophilia as the "volcanic" registration of the experience of satisfaction, we not only have another example of archive fever, but of archive fever as lifedeath, as the trace of the spectral ("mother").

Archive Fever ends with another "ghost and volcano" story, another psychoanalysis of the archive: Freud's *Dreams and Delusions in Jensen's "Gradiva"* (1907). Jensen's novella is about an *arche*-ologist (the kind of archivist who digs up the archaic, the original), Norbert Hanold. Hanold becomes obsessed with the particular footprint of a young woman in a Roman bas-relief—hence "Gradiva." As his obsession gains in intensity, he becomes convinced that she died in the explosion of Vesuvius. In a delusional state he travels to Pompeii to find the traces of Gradiva's footstep. And in the ruins of Pompeii, at midday, the hour of ghosts for the ancients, he encounters her. In Jensen's novella, of course, there is no "real ghost": the young woman who appears to be a ghost is actually Zoe Bertgang, a childhood companion of Hanold's who is in love with him, but aware of his "insanity." In Freud's reading, it is all important that Zoe cures Hanold, that she has intuitively grasped the repression of erotic feelings responsible for his delusions. But Derrida is interested in Hanold's search for the *imprint* of Gradiva's unique step:

> Hanold has come to search for . . . traces. . . . He dreams of bringing back to life . . . , of reliving the other. Of reliving the singular pressure or impression which Gradiva's step, the step itself . . . must have left in the ashes. He dreams

this irreplaceable place, the very ash, where the singular imprint, like a signature, barely distinguishes itself from the impression. And this is the condition of singularity [the One] . . . the condition for the uniqueness of the printer-printed, of the impression and the imprint, of the pressure and its trace in the unique *instant* where they are not yet distinguished the one from the other. . . . The trace no longer distinguishes itself from its substrate. (1995, 98–99)

Hanold's quest for what Freud calls "'traces' in the literal sense" (1995, 65) is the quest for a "reliving" which can only be an encounter with the spectral. It is the repetition of the singular instant of the impress, whose preservation in the ashen substrate is a condition of volcanic explosion.

But Freud, as Derrida says, wants "to explain the haunting of the archeologist with a logic of repression" (1995, 97). Freud had frequently compared the work of the analyst to the work of the archeologist. Derrida cites the famous early passage in which Freud said that analysts and archeologists seek to dig up relics of the past, relics that often have apparently indecipherable inscriptions on them. The archeologist-analyst can translate the inscriptions into the language of the present, so that "stones speak" (93–94). But Derrida here does not attend to another metaphoric complication. Freud *also* often used the explosion of Vesuvius, and consequent buried preservation of Pompeii, as a metaphor for repression: repression preserves the past intact, a past whose excavation is also the possibility of its destruction (1909, 176). The logic of this comparison is not only that "stones speak," but that repression accounts for the timelessness of the unconscious: what is buried effectively enough is not worn away by the passage of time. Hence archeological relics and neurotic symptoms only crumble once they are excavated. But the atemporal preservation and temporal destruction of such relics depends upon their status as "things," "objects." Psychoanalytic archeology unearths stone-like representations. Even if they are wishes and fantasies (i.e. virtual), because they have been re-presented, they have the properties of objective reality. They deteriorate in objective time.

But the *literal* tracing Hanold wants to relive is the differentiating, autoaffective *instant* of the printer-printed, the substrate-impression. This is the active-passive touching-touched—or seeing-seen—*instant of volcanic preservation*. Which produces the dreams and delusions, whose Oedipal representations register and repudiate the *literal trace* of the spectral. Derrida had said that the thinking of telepathy has to free itself from the

"Oedipal code" that coexists with traditional assumptions about reality, time, and space. This Oedipal code can function as an archeological "key" precisely because it is representational in the conventional sense. But (Oedipal) fantasy, or even the ur-fantasy of the hallucinated breast, is re-presentation, is virtuality as the possibility of objectivity: the Oedipal, *desired*, mother *and* the *wish* fulfilling breast are the *trace* of the *needed* mother of primary narcissism. "Mother" here is a figure for processes in primary narcissism, which always imply the *unique instant of repetition of opening*, *Bahnung*, the eruption of primary-intermediate drives. For archeological interpretation to *excavate* objects or representations preserved *after* the eruption, it must dig into the surface. But psychoanalytic interpretation is *virtual excavation of the virtual archive*. What is it to dig into a virtual surface? To mark it virtually, in the instantaneously delayed time-space of autoaffective *différance*. This is archive fever as the preservative trauma of volcanic *revenance*—the strange care of *analytic* time and space. Does not Zoe (life) cure Hanold as *ghost* (*revenance*), i.e. transferentially, the very promise of *analysis as a practice of spectral, binding interpretation*?

In *Zollikon Seminars* Heidegger had contrasted "analysis of the existentiality of existence" with Freud's sense of "analysis." Again, the word derives from the Greek *analuein*, with all its connotations of "untying," "unknotting," "dismantling," and "liberating." Psychoanalysis, he said, breaks symptoms down into their composite elements, a kind of chemical analysis, while *Daseinsanalyse* is the articulation of the unity of a *composite* structure. This is why Heidegger said that his conception of analysis is derived from Kant: the tracing back of the *possibility* of objects of experience to an *a priori synthesis*. Heidegger's point was that the Freudian concept of analysis presumes that interpretation can "liberate" simply by "dismantling" (2001, 113–15). Interpretation of *possibility*, whether in the existential or Kantian senses, is synthetic, although in different ways. But once one is dealing with defense against the *possibility* of interpretation, something like "analysis" in Heidegger's sense has to be taken into account. As synthetic, such analysis is *binding*. Defense against the possibility of "binding interpretation" is, in Freudian terms, *resistance* to it. This raises the very large question of *resistance to binding as resistance to analysis itself*.

Derrida takes up this question in *Resistances—Of Psychoanalysis* (1996). His topic is Freud on the *unanalyzable* "navel of the dream." The "navel" *resists analysis in and of itself*. Freud alludes to it in chapter 2 of *The In-*

terpretation of Dreams, where he *first* demonstrates that dreams are *interpretable* as wish fulfillments. The demonstration is made on a dream of
his own, the all-too-famous "dream of Irma's injection." By Freud's own
account, the "secret of dreams" was revealed to him through this moment
of self-analysis in July 1895. We know from his correspondence that this
was before he even had the idea of writing a book on dreams, and before
his more systematic self-analysis (undertaken after his father's death in
October 1896). We also know how difficult the writing of the dream-
book was, how doubtful Freud remained about his ability to complete
it (1985, 362). By the time Freud wrote the last chapter in the summer of
1899, his theory of wish fulfillment itself had grown more elaborate than
it was when he first analyzed the Irma dream. Moreover, the last chapter
is also a reworking of the *Project,* including its idea that registration of the
experience of satisfaction is the prior condition of the wish. All the more
significant that the last chapter contains another reference to the uninterpretable "navel."

Each time, at the beginning and at the end, Derrida is interested in
why Freud should speak of that which resists analysis as a "navel." On the
whole, Freud's project, as Derrida puts it, is to make the dream "*homogenous to the order of the analyzable. It comes under psychoanalytic reason. Psychoanalytic reason as hermeneutic reason*" (1996, 4; original emphasis). Analytic reason will obey the principle of reason, which prescribes that one
"render reason," restore reason, even where it appears missing, because
everything *has* its reason, including the apparently unreasonable (dreams,
neurosis). Certainly there is resistance to reason, to interpretation, to
analysis. This is a situation Freud recounts in his associations to the Irma
dream: Irma is a patient who *resists* his analysis, his "solution." "Solution"
itself is derived from the Latin *solutio,* which combines the "disengaging"
sense of *analuein* with the sense of having rendered what is due (reason,
for example), and hence of being ab*solved,* freed (of debt, for example). It
is also the derivation of the German *Lösung,* "solution" not only as "untying" ("loosening"), but also as "chemical solution," in which elements are
"dis-*solved*" (1996, 3, 7; recall Heidegger on Freudian "chemical analysis").
Freud even compares Irma in the dream to a more "amenable" patient,
whose symptoms could be more easily *resolved,* because she would not
have *resisted his solution* in the same way. Derrida comments:

At no moment does Freud have even an inkling that a resistance might be . . . something other than a resistance to his solution, to his analysis . . . that a resistance might be something other than a resistance full of meaning to an analysis full of meaning . . . resistance belongs, along with what it resists, to the order of sense, of a sense whose secret is only the hidden secret, the dissimulated meaning, the veiled truth: to be interpreted, analyzed, made explicit, explained. (1996, 10)

Psychoanalysts ever since have operated with the same assumption. Hence, they have tended either to continue to insist on meaning itself when a patient resists interpretation per se, or to give up. And yet Freud himself, as he analyzes his own dream, with all its references to resistance to interpretation, theorizes that which seems *uninterpretable in and of itself*. Right after discussing Irma's resistance to his "solution," he says in a footnote that every dream has at least one place that is unanalyzable, *gleichsam einen Nabel*, like a navel. Derrida picks up on the relation of the uninterpretable, which does not belong to the order of reason, to a navel, an umbilicus, with all its resonances of birth, cut, and knot:

Such a proposition . . . no longer concerns . . . a reserve of meaning that still awaits us; it concerns rather . . . an absolute unknown that is originarily, congenitally bound or tied (but also in itself unbound because ab-solute) to the essence and to the birth of the dream, attached to the place from which it departs and of which it keeps the birthmark: the umbilicus, the omphalic place is the place of a *tie*, a knot-scar that keeps the memory of a cut and even of a severed thread at birth. . . . What forever exceeds the analysis of the dream is indeed a knot that cannot be untied, a thread that, even if it is cut, like an umbilical cord, nevertheless remains forever knotted, *right on the body* [emphasis added], at the place of the navel. The scar is a knot against which analysis can do nothing. (1996, 10–11)

In other words, the *possibility of dreams as interpretable, in the sense of "hermeneutic reason," is marked by uninterpretability*. The stakes here are enormous. Freud's largest intent in writing *The Interpretation of Dreams* was to demonstrate that universal dreaming obeys the same laws as apparently exceptional neurotic symptom formation. Since these are the laws of the unconscious, the theory of dreams itself can yield a universal theory of mind. The *interpretability* of dreams justifies a *scientific interpretive therapy*. But if the "birthplace" of dreams is marked by uninterpretability, then so are the laws of the unconscious and the interpretive technique of psychoanalysis. Clinically, this has always been the case: psychoanalysts have always encountered patients who appear to be analyzable, and yet who resist interpretation as they conceive it. (Karl Abraham, a first-generation Freudian, described this "syndrome" in 1919.) This is the phenomenon Freud was to describe in *Beyond . . .* as the missing "degree of aloofness" which makes (transference) interpretation effective. It is the phenomenon of the fetishistic or concrete patient. Could Irma have been such a patient? One will never know. But if she were, it would be inevitable that in thinking about her, about wish fulfillment, about dreams, and about interpretation, Freud would have to stumble across not only the uninterpretable, but the *uninterpretable as the condition of possibility which marks the origin of the interpretable.*

Deutung—intepretation—as "umbilical *analuein*" is then a question of "a knot, threads to be untied, and *untied where there has been a cut*" (1996, 12). Derrida adds a parenthetical remark here, which is anything but parenthetical in relation to how the resistance to interpretation affects the entire theory and practice of analysis: "(It is thus always a matter for us of thinking how the cut can tie a knot or, inversely, how the link can be interruption itself. And of thinking 'resistance' starting from the necessity of what does anything but *play* with [this] paradox)" (12). Cut as tie, link as interruption: this is difference as articulation-connection. It produces archive fever, the trauma of Eros, the strangeness of care—all of which are the conditions of possibility and impossibility of interpretation. The resistance to interpretation per se is *there*, in Heidegger's sense of the *Da-* as opening, and in Derrida's sense of the unconscious as "opening to the effraction of the trace." And this (im)possibility is *there* in the neutral analytic setting, the repetitive, timed analytic frame. As the promise of transference as repetition, of interpretation of transference at the heart of analysis of resistance, the frame *itself* is also the promise of the impossibility of interpretation, of (demonic) transference as the resistance to analysis at the heart of transference.

We began with Derrida's affirmation of Nietzsche's conception of active, differentiating interpretation as play. When he says here that the resistance of the *uninterpretable at the origin of interpretation* does "anything but play" with this paradox, perhaps he is right in one sense, wrong in another. Right, in the sense that as demonic, as destruction of difference, resistance to interpretation is the deadly serious *Unbehagen* of civilization. Wrong, in the sense that to interpret the conditions of possibility and impossibility of interpretation is to be in the space of irreducible paradox.

It is a kind of playing with fire, the fire of archive fever, the necessary destruction of interpretation as *resistance to* the uncanniness and chance, the loss of mastery and control, built into interpretation. This is a Nietz-schean-Derridean extension of Winnicott's conception of analysis as play. The promise of analysis *plays* with this risk, *is* this risk.

This is why Derrida says that there are two Freuds. One is an *Aufklärer* who believes in inevitable progress in understanding according to the principle of reason. The other believes in the "absolute limit to this progress" (1996, 13). Derrida cites the second passage on the navel of the dream, which gives a better sense of this limit. He inserts important German phrases in the citation of this passage, to which I will add other emphases and insertions:

> There is often a passage [a place, *eine Stelle*] in even the most thoroughly interpreted dream which has to be [*man muss*] left obscure [*muss man oft eine Stelle im Dunkel lassen*]; this is because we become aware during the work of interpretation that at that point there is a tangle [*Knauel*, like a ball of yarn] of dream-thoughts which cannot be unravelled [*der sich nicht entwirren will*] and which moreover adds nothing to our knowledge of the *content* [*Trauminhalt*; my insertion] of the dream. This is the dream's navel [*der Nabel des Traums*], the spot where it reaches *down into the unknown* [*an der Unerkannten aufsitz*; my insertion]. The dream-thoughts to which we are led by interpretation cannot, from the nature of things, have any definite endings [*mussen bleiben ohne Abschluss*]; they are bound to branch out in every direction into the intricate network [*in die netzartige Verstrickung*] of our world of thought. It is at some point where this meshwork [*Geflecht*] is particularly close that the dream-wish grows *up* [*erhebt sich*; my insertion], like a mushroom out of its mycelium [1900, 525]. (1996, 14).

An important question of translation must be noted immediately. Weber (1982) pointed out that where the *Standard Edition* says that the "dream's navel . . . *reaches down* into the unknown," Freud actually wrote *an der Unerkannten aufsitz*, literally meaning "sits upon the unknown," in the way one sits upon a horse.[26] Derrida is emphasizing that the navel *must* be left "obscure." If it is "seated" on the unknown, there is *necessary* non-interpretation at the heart of the interpretable. This necessity is a *place* of knotting, of a "tangle," which "challenges analysis as a methodical operation of unknotting and technique of untying" (1996, 15). Hence, at the birthplace of the *wish* there is a "meshwork," like the spot in the mycelium out of which the mushroom grows.

Derrida does not attend to a technical complication in dream theory that Freud relies upon in this passage. This is one of the changes in the theory from the moment of the analysis of the Irma dream to the completion of the dream book four years later. In 1895 Freud had not distinguished between dream *thoughts* and the dream *wish* in the way he does here. The distinction is simple. The dream thoughts are elements from the dreamer's current conscious or preconscious life. They are expressed in disguised form as fulfilled wishes in the dream's manifest content. For example, in Freud's analysis of the Irma dream, the wish fulfilled is actually what he calls here the dream thought: I (Freud) wish not to be responsible for my patient's continued suffering. My dream portrays this wish as fulfilled by blaming the patient: if she is still suffering, it is her fault, she has not accepted my solution. (There are other dream thoughts connected to this one.) Freud's theory is that such ordinary, if troubling, thoughts are *disguised* in the manifest dream content because they are associatively connected to repressed, infantile wishes. Such wishes are always unconsciously active; in the somewhat lowered state of censorship during sleep, they seek admission to consciousness. But censorship—defense—is not completely inactive during sleep. Rather, such wishes are permitted connection to current thoughts, which themselves are then distorted by the dream work, in order to permit disguised discharge of aroused infantile wishes, which could disturb sleep.

These details are important because Freud is describing the "navel of the dream" as a "tangle" of dream *thoughts*. This is why he says that the "dream thoughts to which we are led by interpretation cannot . . . have any definite endings; they are bound to branch out in every direction into the intricate network of our world of thought." In "The Aetiology of Hysteria" he had similarly said that neurotic symptoms were not symbols of single memories, but of chains of memories, which intersect at "nodal points" (1896, 198–99). He compared such nodal points to the tangle of intersecting branches of genealogical trees. The logic of the navel of the dream, or of the nodal points of symptoms, is that there is greatest density of connection of past to present, of infantile wish or memory to current thoughts, at the point where the repressed past is *secretly* governing the associations of present thoughts. In this reading, the navel "sits upon" the unknown (*auf der Unerkannten aufsitz*), but rises *up* (*erhebt sich*) to the surface—like a mushroom emerging from its mycelium—for the same reason: the unknown *wish* rises to the surface at the point of greatest associative density. If the analysis of the Irma dream, including its reference to the navel, concerns dream *thoughts*, the second reference to the navel more specifically emphasizes the relation between dream thoughts and wishes. What Derrida calls the "unanalyzable synthesis" of the navel as meshwork, the *Geflecht*, is in this sense *not* in conflict with the ultimate interpretability of the dream wish. When Freud speaks of the umbilical spot at which the "tangle" sits upon the unknown, he means the *apparently unknown* of repressed wishes. The "unknown" is ultimately knowable.

But this "Enlightenment" reading gives short shrift to unknowability, to "knotting" (binding), to the complicated relations of "surface" and "depth," and to Freud's statement that the navel adds "nothing to our knowledge of the content of the dream (*Trauminhalt*)." Why should Freud even call the entangled mass of conscious and preconscious associations to the interpretable past "unanalyzable," "uninterpretable," unbudgeably *resistant*? Why is there "unknowability," and why in relation to a "navel"—with all the inevitable resonances of birth, tie, cut? Both the *Project* and chapter 7B of *The Interpretation of Dreams* tell us that the archive of the experience of satisfaction gives birth to the dream wish per se. Like a navel, such inscription is a "knot" that "keeps the memory of a cut" on a *surface*, but a surface *which as memory is unconscious.* This place of entangled articulation-connection has no *content*, because it is a process in primary narcissism, before *words*, before subject and object. Freud will call it "originally unconscious *thought*" in 1911. He will momentarily understand originally unconscious thought as the possibility of thought itself. Unlike primary process, thought does not tend toward immediate discharge: thought as tension-raising *binding*, the "impression of a relation" before words, is the possibility of tension sustaining "secondary" process thinking in words. When one "disavows" this logic of unconscious binding, one does not encounter the paradox of the "secondary" before the "primary," of *impression of relation before wish*. (Or, to combine Freud, Heidegger, and Derrida, of registration of care as tension-raising bond: the condition of possibility of the wish.) One then can operate with the logic of repression, of wishes as buried interpretable unconscious content, which secretly govern conscious associations at their most entangled points of intersection. But originally unconscious thought is an unconscious *process which cannot be buried.* It is a surface for inscription that is the possibility of both the unconscious wish and conscious-preconscious "associations"—*words connected to and different from these wishes*. It is the possibility of *differentiated relation* itself. Interpretable dream wishes are always "seated upon" the "unknowability" of differentiated relation, which itself is the irreducible "binding" or knot of "unconscious" and "world."

Derrida points out that the word Freud uses for "meshwork," *Geflecht*, is also a word used by Heidegger to describe a kind of irreducible binding. Heidegger also thought that Kant recoiled from the transcendental imagi-nation as the "*unknown* root" of the aesthetic and the logic. The transcen-dental imagination becomes the possibility of the a priori synthesis itself, because it is autoaffective time as *relation*. But for Heidegger, Kant had to "repudiate" this "abyss of metaphysics," which was a threat to Enlight-enment thinking, to foundational conceptions of time and truth. Does Freud unwittingly come up against what would have to be an uninterpre-table "unknown root"—the condition of possibility of dreams which "sits upon the *unknown*"—in his "registration and repudiation" of trace itself as the birthplace of the dream? If so, then "the navel" would have to be, as Derrida puts it, "radically heterogeneous, in its very secret, to signifiable sense . . . one may . . . wonder whether what discourages the analyst, pro-visionally or definitively, is homogenous or not with the space of analytic work, the work of interpretation" (1996, 16). Like Kant in Heidegger's reading, Freud for Derrida is here at the place from which he would have to recoil, the "abyss" of analysis according to the principle of reason.

Derrida makes another important point about Freud's use of the word "analysis" in this context. On one hand, a theory of the unconscious which claims to escape metaphysics, would seem to presume "*another concept of analysis* . . . a concept different from the one that has held sway in the history of philosophy, logic, science" (19; original emphasis). On the other,

> Freud had no choice, if he wished to make himself understood, but to inherit from tradition . . . the *two motifs* that are constitutive for every concept of analysis . . . [i.e.] the *archeological* or *anagogical* motif, which is marked in the movement of *ana* (recurrent return toward the principal, the most originary, the simplest . . .); and, *on the other hand*, a motif . . . marked in the *lysis* (breaking down, untying, unknotting, deliverance, solution . . .). Keeping as legacy the two motifs . . . —which is [the legacy] of science no less than of philosophy—Freud was neither able nor willing to inaugurate a *new concept of analysis*. (19–20; original emphases)

The implication is that *resistance to analysis* is resistance to everything the tradition of science and philosophy presumes about truth, objectivity, reality, opposition, time, and space. This is why Heidegger can both derive his concept of analysis from Kant, and then show why Kant himself had to pull back from the results of his analysis—demonstrating where a new concept of analysis is necessary. The impasse of clinical work has always been that resistance to interpretation has been understood from within the assumption that *analysis is reason itself, while the patient makes the same claim in order to resist analysis.* The "necessary degree of aloofness" is assumed to be the foothold in conventional assumptions about truth, objectivity, reality, opposition, time, and space. Its "lack" is presumed to be unreason by the analyst and reason by the patient. However, the resistance to interpretation can be repeated in analysis itself, in an interminably repetitious *resistance to analysis in analysis.* Would it not be at precisely this point that another concept of analysis, not thinkable by the tradition of science and philosophy, not confined to the "archeological" and "lytic" motifs, is necessary? A concept of analysis that takes into account the *resistance to the possibility of another concept of analysis implicit in defensive objectivity?* Would this not have to be "synthetic" in Heidegger's sense—the interpretation of the possibility of interpretation as a "composite structure," a differentiating, *active description* of resistance to *relation,* to *binding?*

Freud catalogued five forms of resistance in *Inhibition, Symptom, and Anxiety* (1926). Three, he said, are from the ego: transference itself, secondary gains, repression. One is from the superego: the need for punishment, producing the negative therapeutic reaction. And one is from the id: the repetition compulsion, which maintains resistances even where the ego's repressions have been modified, necessitating repetitive "working through." Derrida here, as in *Archive Fever,* assimilates the repetition compulsion to the death drive. In this sense, the resistance of the id, as the source of the greatest resistance, as the "hyperbolic paradigm of the series" of resistances, is what Derrida calls a "nonresistance." The death drive itself—as regressive (*ana-*) and unbinding (*lysis*)—is "*of an analytic structure or vocation*" (1996, 23–24; original emphasis). This is true, if *analysis* is confined to its two traditional motifs. But this is why the "death drive itself," as an "independent" force, is so problematic, and can be accommodated to a dedifferentiating drive of the proper. Derrida says that to understand the death drive as the "nonresistant resistance" is "very close to the navel of the dream, to the place where the desire for death and desire *tout court* call for and speak the analysis they prohibit" (24). But again, this is to confine analysis *to* analysis of desire, of wish as both regressive (*ana-*, return) and unbinding (*lysis*, discharge). The "resistance of the id" as *repetition* would have to partake of all the characteristics of the id, *das Es*: unbinding (death) and binding (life), tension decrease and tension increase, memory, trace. All these characteristics concern difference as repetition. Thus, one would have to add to Freud's understanding of the resistance of the id the possibility of the "id against itself," the autoimmune response to the "mischief making" drive to tension increase, to repetition *as need and as archive*: the navel of dream as knotted memory of a cut. This explains the paradox of repetition of resistance to analysis in analysis: there can be instantaneous delay of the *need* for analysis, for interpretation as opening, for strange care. This is the immeasurably fast and slow registration and repudiation of difference, the ecstatic, autoaffective time of *différance* which haunts measurable time, the time of *analytic* space.

Derrida analyzes resistance to the *analytic*—i.e. traditionally philosophical or psychoanalytic—concept of analysis in terms of a necessary "double *bind*." The double bind is binding itself: every resistance "supposes a tension, above all, an internal tension. Since a purely internal tension is impossible, it is a matter of an absolute inherence of the other or the outside at the heart of the internal and auto-affective tension" (1996, 26). Autoaffective tension as heteroaffection is the structural "pain" of primary narcissism as trace. As Derrida puts it, again describing what he called in *Archive Fever* the intersection of a certain psychoanalysis with a certain deconstruction:

> At the heart of the present, at the origin of presence, the trace, writing, or the mark is a movement of referral to the other, to otherness, a reference as *différance* that would resemble an *a priori* synthesis if it were of the order of judgment and if it were thetic [i.e. if it could give rise to the positing of a thesis]. But in a pre-thetic and prejudicative order, the trace is indeed an *irreducible binding* (*Verbindung* [emphasis added]). Because of this originary composition, it *resists* a chemical type of analysis [as Heidegger said about Freud]. But this binding . . . does not proceed either from an activity . . . or from a passivity. (1996, 27–28)

A binding which does not proceed from activity or passivity is *driven* by repetitive eruption of the primary intermediate. This binding *différance* produces the necessary *analytic* double bind.

A double bind is *synthetic* and oscillating. As one opens (unties) one of its ends, one closes (ties) the other. Clinically, this is the *process* of resistance to analysis in analysis: every opening produces a closure; the closure is the trace of the possibility of opening. To conceptualize this resistance to analysis inherent to analysis, Derrida, like Heidegger when he refers to Kant, thinks *analysis as articulation of an a priori synthesis.* But Derrida specifies that he is conceptualizing such synthesis as *différance*, as the trace of what is other than presence or absence, which cannot belong to the order of reason (the thetic or judicative). Close to what Heidegger calls the "self giving of opening" unthinkable by metaphysics or science, it "remains the ultimate *unknown* [emphasis added] for the analysis that it nevertheless puts in motion" (1996, 29). This is the navel as knot, "formed without closing *there* [*Da-*; my insertion] . . . in the *re-* of a repetition that, without repeating or representing anything that would be before it in space or time . . . will have come to inscribe . . . like a wedge" (30).

Repetition that does not repeat or represent anything present before it is nonclassical repetition, repetition as/of difference. *This* repetition compulsion, automatic repetition of the interval, is repetition as lifedeath Thus, for Derrida, "there is nothing fortuitous about the fact that the most decisive and difficult stakes between . . . 'psychoanalysis' and 'deconstruction' should have taken a relatively organized form around the question of the repetition compulsion" (1996, 32). The repetition compulsion as nonclassical repetition of lifedeath (difference) accounts for binding, differentiating relation, as the condition of possibility of "unbinding" (*ana-lysis*). To account for the resistance to analysis in this sense, Freud, for example, would have had to account for the id's repetitive double bind, its necessary defense against Eros, the differentially binding, tension-raising, "mischief maker." The clinical manifestation of this constitutive double bind is the resistance to, the repudiation of, registered difference. This is yet another way of thinking how the *repetition of resistance to analysis* concerns the very possibility of analysis.

Deconstruction, like the analysis of resistance to analysis, is a thinking of difference *bound to* the (im)possibility of analysis: If . . . there were . . . a sole *thesis* of "Deconstruction," it would pose divisibility: differance as divisibility. Paradoxically, this amounts to raising the analytical stakes for a thinking *that is very careful to take account of what always rejects analysis* [emphasis added: the explanation of why the clinical problem of resistance to analysis is at the point of intersection of deconstruction and psychoanalysis]. The paradox is merely apparent: it is because there is no indivisible element or simple origin that analysis is interminable. Divisibility, dissociability, and thus the impossibility of arresting an analysis . . . would be perhaps . . . the truth without truth of deconstruction. (1996, 33–34)

And of the psychoanalysis that meets deconstruction as the thinking of the repetition compulsion, of archive fever, of registration and repudiation of difference. This then is also the truth without truth—that is, the necessity of what will never yield to a *truth* of interpretation as subjective, objective, or representational—of why one can, or even *must*, resist analysis in analysis. It is the "truth without truth" of the repeated, timed, neutral, interpretive analytic setting. The bond to, the promise of, transference as repetition, *revenance* of the virtual, spectral trace of the necessary other as the possibility of interpretation.

Notes

1. However, Freud does modify this view in "The Economic Problem of Masochism" (1925b).

2. There is also a singular reference to a nonsynchronous unconscious temporality in the second paper on telepathy (Freud, 1922a), which will be discussed in Chapter 3.

3. This connection was first pointed out by Derrida (1987, 408) and will be discussed again in Chapter 3.

4. "Apparently" because Freud assumes that drives themselves come from the body as an interior space. However, the libidinal–self-preservative *drive* operating within an organization of primary narcissism is responsible for the registration of the trace of the object. Thus it is not only an internal force. Neither would unconscious time be strictly internal.

5. Deleuze (1983) had pointed out that despite many discrepancies, Kant and Nietzsche are both thinkers of synthesis. We will return to this issue at the conclusion of Chapter 3, in relation to Derrida's understanding of "analysis" in relation to the a priori synthesis.

6. In Chapter 2, we will discuss a patient who was convinced, against all objective evidence, that she had attention *deficit* disorder.

7. In her rigorous analysis of Freud's metapsychology, Schmidt-Hellerau speaks of the "phenomenological differentiability of the unconscious" (2001, 158), a differentiability that can never be grasped perceptually (113).

8. Because life and death are intertwined, or bound, in this way, one cannot simply ascribe dedifferentiation to death and differentiation to life, as will be discussed below, p. 31.

9. Heidegger, in volume 4 of *Nietzsche,* nonetheless will argue that despite this conception, Nietzsche actually does "start" with an isolated individual, because will to power produces its own version of subjectivity (1979–1987, 136–38).

10. In *Zollikon Seminars* (2001) Heidegger takes Sullivan as an example of object relations theories and says: "When they assert that a human being is determined as a being . . . in a relationship to other humans, the American Harry Stack Sullivan and his similarly oriented colleagues make an essential assertion about the human being, the foundations of which are not even questioned. . . . Relationship to . . . , the being-in-relation-to . . . characterizes the unfolding essence of the human being" (153) Further on: "The existential relationship cannot be objectified. Its basic essence is one's being concerned and letting oneself be concerned . . . a being responsive on grounds of the clearedness of the relationship" (185).

11. On the entire question of "helplessness," time, finitude, and technology, the essential reference is Stiegler (1998).

12. In "Perspectives on Memory," Loewald makes the point that in terms of primary narcissism, perception *is* memory (1980, 154–55).

13. Dimen (2002) also has developed a theory of sexual difference in terms of transitional space, which includes consideration of pleasurable *tension*.

14. One current exception is the work of Christopher Bollas (1987), who speaks of what he calls the nonrepresentational "unthought known." The unthought known for Bollas comprises the "ways of being," the "rules of behavior" unconsciously laid down before a subject-object structure. Bollas does not think of time and difference in relation to the unthought known.

15. Thus in *Moses and Monotheism* (1934) Freud will explain the inheritance of repressed—i.e. unconscious—traumatic memories over generations by recalling that the id, as the seat of the drives, is the part of the mind closest to the body, and thus inheritable.

16. Russell (2003) has also investigated the relation between the play of *différance* and Winnicott's conception of play.

17. This is why we earlier emphasized the notion of surface, "being-on," in relation to Heidegger's being-in. See Chapter 2, p. 85.

18. Stiegler's great theme is the technicity of time.

19. However, Eros as binding has an implicit relation to need, periodicity, and repetition. See above, Chapter 1, p. 25.

20. In the discussion of repetition and the *Es gibt* above (p. 93), there was already reference to repetition of identity, classical repetition, and repetition of difference, a nonclassical, "demonic" repetition. In "Freud and the Scene of Writing" (1978) Derrida emphasized that *Bahnung* implies an irreducible principle of repetition and then tension of differential forces; see above, pp. 103–4.

21. Above (Chapter 2, p. 88–89), we discussed pain against pain in relation to Heidegger's notion of the "stress" intrinsic to the preservation of life.

22. Theodor Reik was perhaps the premier theoretician of interpretation as "event," as what he calls "surprise," a theme that dominates his *Listening with*

the Third Ear (1948). However, his clinical emphasis on surprise did not lead to any questioning of basic Freudian theory. Lacan too, in "Direction of the Treatment and the Principles of Its Power" (1977), said that effective interpretation had nothing to do with the analyst's "fancy of understanding," but rather with the unexpected naming of signifiers of desire. But as Derrida has demonstrated in several places, this did not lead Lacan to question Freudian determinism: for Lacan, it is in the nature of the "letter," the signifier of desire, "always to arrive at its destination." See "Le facteur de la verité" in *The Post Card* (1987) and "My Chances" (1984).

23. Derrida also says that one would have to relate what Freud says about time here to Husserl's *Lectures on Internal Time Consciousness*. Although this is not my topic here, I can refer the interested reader to Stiegler on this question.

24. In relation to Nietzsche and Deleuze on difference and repetition, we already cited the idea that Eros is differentiating without being a return to a state of lowered tension (p. xi, pp. 21–27). At that point Derrida's conception of difference in terms of trace and binding had not yet been introduced.

25. However, there is a fascinating glimpse into another possibility in Freud's correspondence with Marie Bonaparte. She had been to visit Niels Bohr in Copenhagen and wrote to Freud about his conception of nondeterministic processes on the subatomic level. Freud's response seems clearly to indicate his grasp of the implications: "It is here that the breakdown of today's *Weltanschauung* is actually taking place" (Bass, 1997, 253). On the coimplications of Bohr's and Derrida's thinking, the essential reference is Plotnitsky (1993).

26. Weber (1982) renders *aufsitzen* as "straddles." The French translation cited by Derrida avoids the issue altogether, giving the phrase as *communique avec l'inconnu*, "communicates with the unknown."

References

Abraham, Karl. 1919 [1927]. A special form of resistance to the psychoanalytic method. In *Selected Papers on Psychoanalysis.* London: Maresfield.

———. 1924/1927. A short history of the development of the libido. In *Selected Papers on Psychoanalysis.* London: Maresfield.

Assoun, Paul-Laurent. 1980. *Freud et Nietzsche.* Paris: Presses Universitaires de France.

Bass, Alan. 1997. The status of an analogy: Psychoanalysis and physics. *American Imago* 54:235–56.

———. 2000. *Difference and Disavowal: The Trauma of Eros.* Stanford, CA: Stanford University Press.

Bion, Wilfred. 1967. *Second Thoughts.* London: Heinemann.

Bollas, Christopher. 1987. *The Shadow of the Object.* New York: Columbia University Press.

Deleuze, Gilles. 1983. *Nietzsche and Philosophy.* Trans. H. Tomlinson. New York: Columbia University Press.

———. 1994. *Difference and Repetition.* Trans. P. Patton. New York: Columbia University Press.

Derrida, Jacques. 1966/1978. Freud and the scene of writing. In *Writing and Difference.* Trans. A. Bass. Chicago: University of Chicago Press.

———. 1968/1982. *Différance.* In *Margins—Of Philosophy.* Trans. A. Bass. Chicago: University of Chicago Press.

———. 1973. *Voice and Phenomena.* Trans. D. Allison. Evanston, IL: Northwestern University Press.

———. 1976. *Of Grammatology.* Trans. G. Spivak. Baltimore, MD: Johns Hopkins University Press.

———. 1980 [1987]. Envoi. In *Psyche: Inventions de l'autre.* Paris: Galilee.

———. 1981 [1987]. Télépathie. In *Psyche: Inventions de l'autre.* Paris: Galilee.

————. 1983 [1987]. Gechlecht: Différence sexuelle, différence ontologique. In *Psyche: Inventions de l'autre.* Paris: Galilee.

————. 1984. My chances. Trans. I. Harvey and A. Ronell. In *Taking Chances: Derrida, Psychoanalysis, and Literature.* Baltimore, MD: Johns Hopkins University Press.

————. 1986. *Glas.* Trans. J. Leavey and R. Rand. Lincoln: University of Nebraska Press.

————. 1987. *The Post Card: From Socrates to Freud and Beyond.* Trans. A. Bass. Chicago: University of Chicago Press.

————. 1994. *Specters of Marx.* Trans. P. Kamuf. New York: Routledge.

————. 1995. *Archive Fever: A Freudian Impression.* Trans. E. Prenowitz. Chicago: University of Chicago Press.

————. 1996. *Resistances—Of Psychoanalysis.* Trans. P. Kamuf. Stanford, CA: Stanford University Press.

Dimen, Muriel. 2002. Deconstructing difference: Gender, splitting, and transitional space. In *Gender in Psychoanalytic Space,* ed. M. Dimen and V. Goldner. New York: Other Press.

Feldman, Michael. 1997. Projective identification: The analyst's involvement. *International Journal of Psychoanalysis* 78:227–41.

Freud, Sigmund. 1895. *Project for a Scientific Psychology: Standard Edition of the Complete Psychological Works of Sigmund Freud.* Ed. J. Strachey. Vol. 1. London: Hogarth Press.

————. 1896. The aetiology of hysteria. *Standard Edition,* 3.

————. 1900. *Interpretation of Dreams. Standard Edition,* 4–5.

————. 1901. *The Psychopathology of Everyday Life. Standard Edition,* 6.

————. 1905. *Three Essays on the Theory of Sexuality. Standard Edition,* 7.

————. 1907. *Delusions and Dreams in Jensen's "Gradiva." Standard Edition,* 9.

————. 1909. *Notes upon a Case of Obsessional Neurosis. Standard Edition,* 10.

————. 1910. "On the antithetical meaning of primal words." *Standard Edition,* 11.

————. 1911. Formulations on the two principles of mental functioning. *Standard Edition,* 12.

————. 1912. Recommendations to physicians practicing psychoanalysis. *Standard Edition,* 12.

————. 1913. *Totem and Taboo. Standard Edition,* 13.

————. 1914. On narcissism. *Standard Edition,* 14.

————. 1915a. Remembering, repeating, and working through. *Standard Edition,* 14.

————. 1915b. The unconscious. *Standard Edition,* 14.

————. 1915c. Instincts and their vicissitudes. *Standard Edition,* 14.

————. 1919. The uncanny. *Standard Edition,* 17.

————. 1920. *Beyond the Pleasure Principle. Standard Edition*, 18.

————. 1921a. *Group Psychology and the Analysis of the Ego. Standard Edition*, 18.

————. 1921b. Psychoanalysis and telepathy. *Standard Edition*, 18.

————. 1922a. Dreams and telepathy. *Standard Edition*, 18.

————. 1922b. Some neurotic mechanisms in homosexuality, jealousy, and paranoia. *Standard Edition*, 18.

————. 1923. *The Ego and the Id. Standard Edition*, 19.

————. 1924a. Neurosis and psychosis. *Standard Edition*, 19.

————. 1924b. The loss of reality in neurosis and psychosis. *Standard Edition*, 19.

————. 1925a. *An Autobiographical Study. Standard Edition*, 20.

————. 1925b. The economic problem of masochism. *Standard Edition*, 19.

————. 1925c. A note on the mystic writing pad. *Standard Edition*, 19.

————. 1926. *Inhibition, Symptom and Anxiety. Standard Edition*, 20.

————. 1927. Fetishism. *Standard Edition*, 21.

————. 1930. *Civilization and Its Discontents. Standard Edition*, 21.

————. 1933. The question of a *Weltanschauung*. In *New Introductory Lectures. Standard Edition*, 22.

————. 1934. *Moses and Monotheism. Standard Edition*, 23.

————. 1937. *Analysis Terminable and Interminable. Standard Edition*, 23.

————. 1940a. *An Outline of Psychoanalysis. Standard Edition*, 23.

————. 1940b. The splitting of the ego in the process of defense. *Standard Edition*, 23.

————. 1941. Findings, ideas, problems. *Standard Edition*, 23.

————. 1985. *The Complete Letters of Sigmund Freud to Wilhelm Fliess.* Trans. and ed. J. Masson. Cambridge, MA: Harvard University Press.

Frosch, Allen. 1995. The preconceptual organization of emotion. *Journal of the American Psychoanalytic Association* 43:423–47.

Greenacre, Phyllis. 1971. The fetish and the transitional object. In *Emotional Growth,* Vol. 1. New York: International Universities Press.

Heidegger, Martin. 1962. *Kant and the Problem of Metaphysics.* Trans. J. Churchill. Bloomington: Indiana University Press.

————. 1969. *Identity and Difference.* Trans. J. Stambaugh. New York: Harper and Row.

————. 1971. Language. In *Poetry, Language, Thought.* Trans. A. Hofstadter. New York: Harper and Row.

————. 1972. Time and being. In *On Time and Being.* Trans. J. Stambaugh. New York: Harper and Row.

————. 1972. The end of philosophy and the task of thinking. In *On Time and Being.*

————. 1979–1987. *Nietzsche*. Vols. 1–4. Ed. D. F. Krell. New York: Harper and Row.

————. 1996. *Being and Time*. Trans. J. Stambaugh. Albany: SUNY Press.

————. 2001. *Zollikon Seminars*. Ed. M. Boss. Evanston, IL: Northwestern University Press.

Klein, Melanie. 1946. Notes on some schizoid mechanisms. In *The Selected Melanie Klein*. Ed. J. Mitchell. New York: Free Press.

Lacan, Jacques. 1977. Direction of the treatment and the principles of its power. In *Ecrits: A Selection*. Trans. A. Sheridan. New York: W. W. Norton.

Laplanche, Jean. 1999. *Essays on Otherness*. Trans. J. Fletcher. New York: Routledge.

Loewald, Hans. 1980. *Papers on Psychoanalysis*. New Haven, CT: Yale University Press.

Nietzsche, Friedrich. 1956. *The Birth of Tragedy*. Trans. F. Golfing. Garden City, NY: Doubleday.

————. 1967. *On the Genealogy of Morals and Ecce Homo*. Trans. W. Kaufmann. New York: Vintage.

————. 1968. *The Will to Power*. Ed. W. Kaufmann. New York: Vintage.

————. 1974. *The Gay Science*. Trans. W. Kaufmann. New York: Vintage.

————. 1990. *Twilight of the Idols*. Trans. R. Hollingdale. London: Penguin.

————. 1995. *Human, All Too Human*. Trans. I. G. Handwerk. Stanford, CA: Stanford University Press.

Nunberg, Herman, and Federn, Ernst. 1962–1967. *Minutes of the Vienna Psychoanalytic Society*. Vols. 1 and 2. New York: International Universities Press.

Plotnitsky, Arkady. 1993. *In the Shadow of Hegel*. Gainesville: University Press of Florida.

Pynchon, Thomas. 1973. *Gravity's Rainbow*. New York: Penguin Books.

Reik, Theodor. 1948. *Listening with the Third Ear*. New York: Farrar, Strauss.

Ricoeur, Paul. 1970. *Freud and Philosophy: An Essay in Interpretation*. Trans. D. Savage. New Haven, CT: Yale University Press.

Russell, Jared. 2003. Differance and psychic space. *American Imago* 60:501–28.

Schmidt-Hellerau, Cordelia. 2001. *Life Drive and Death Drive, Libido and Lethe*. New York: Other Press.

Shakespeare, William. 1600 [1957]. *Hamlet*. Baltimore, MD: Penguin Books.

Stiegler, Bernard. 1998. *Technics and Time I: The Fault of Epimetheus*. Trans. R. Beardsworth and G. Collins. Stanford, CA: Stanford University Press.

Weber, Samuel. 1982. *The Legend of Freud*. Minneapolis: University of Minnesota Press.

Winnicott, Donald. 1951 [1975]. Transitional object and transitional phenomena. In *Through Pediatrics to Psychoanalysis*. New York: Basic Books.

————. 1954 [1975]. The depressive position in normal emotional development.
In *Through Pediatrics to Psychoanalysis.* New York: Basic Books.
————. 1971. *Playing and Reality.* New York: Routledge.
Yerushalmi, Yosef. 1991. *Freud's Moses: Judaism Terminable and Interminable.*
New Haven, CT: Yale University Press.

MERIDIAN

Crossing Aesthetics

Aris Fioretos, *The Gray Book*

Deborah Esch, *In the Event: Reading Journalism, Reading Theory*

Winfried Menninghaus, *In Praise of Nonsense: Kant and Bluebeard*

Giorgio Agamben, *The Man Without Content*

Giorgio Agamben, *The End of the Poem: Studies in Poetics*

Theodor W. Adorno, *Sound Figures*

Louis Marin, *Sublime Poussin*

Philippe Lacoue-Labarthe, *Poetry as Experience*

Ernst Bloch, *Literary Essays*

Jacques Derrida, *Resistances of Psychoanalysis*

Marc Froment-Meurice, *That Is to Say: Heidegger's Poetics*

Francis Ponge, *Soap*

Philippe Lacoue-Labarthe, *Typography: Mimesis, Philosophy, Politics*

Giorgio Agamben, *Homo Sacer: Sovereign Power and Bare Life*

Emmanuel Levinas, *Of God Who Comes To Mind*

Bernard Stiegler, *Technics and Time, 1: The Fault of Epimetheus*

Werner Hamacher, *pleroma—Reading in Hegel*

Serge Leclaire, *Psychoanalyzing: On the Order of the Unconscious and the Practice of the Letter*

Serge Leclaire, *A Child Is Being Killed: On Primary Narcissism and the Death Drive*

Sigmund Freud, *Writings on Art and Literature*

Cornelius Castoriadis, *World in Fragments: Writings on Politics, Society, Psychoanalysis, and the Imagination*

Thomas Keenan, *Fables of Responsibility: Aberrations and Predicaments in Ethics and Politics*

Emmanuel Levinas, *Proper Names*

DATE DUE
